Whither has the Mon

Jianfeng Yin · Jianwei Wu · Zengwu Wang

Whither has the Money Gone

Fund Flow and Mechanism Under a Grand Asset Management Framework

SSAP

Springer

Jianfeng Yin
The Institute of Finance and Banking
Chinese Academy of Social Sciences
Beijing, China

Zengwu Wang
The Institute of Finance and Banking
Chinese Academy of Social Sciences
Beijing, China

Jianwei Wu
China Zheshang Bank
Beijing, China

Published with financial support of the Innovation Program of the Chinese Academy of Social Sciences

ISBN 978-981-16-4930-1 ISBN 978-981-16-4931-8 (eBook)
https://doi.org/10.1007/978-981-16-4931-8

Jointly published with Social Sciences Academic Press
The print edition is not for sale in China (Mainland). Customers from China (Mainland) please order the print book from: Social Sciences Academic Press.

Translation from the *Chinese* language edition: *钱去哪了: 大资管框架下的资金流向和机制* by Jianfeng Yin, et al.,© Social Science Academic Press 2017. Published by Social Science Academic Press. All Rights Reserved.

This Springer imprint is published by the registered company Springer Nature Singapore Pte Ltd.
The registered company address is: 152 Beach Road, #21-01/04 Gateway East, Singapore 189721, Singapore

Foreword

"Where's money: capital flows and mechanisms under the framework of the Great Assets Management" is the result of a joint research collaboration between the National Finance and Development Laboratory and China Zheshang Bank Co., Ltd. This report analyzes capital flows of various types of financial organizations and put forward constructive opinions. The report guides us to think deeply: Where has the money of financial institutions gone? Has it moved around within the financial sector, pushing up asset prices too fast, or has it gone to the real sectors to drive economic development?

The Party Central Committee and the State Council attach great importance to the work of financial services to the real economy. General Secretary Xi Jinping pointed out that a strong country relies on the real economy. We need to improve financial services, and clear the channels for the financial sector to enter into the real economy, especially small- and medium-sized enterprises and small and micro enterprises, and guide social funds to invest more in the real economy. Premier Li Keqiang also pointed out that financial and real economy is closely linked and is in mutual symbiotic relationships. The primary task of finance is to support the development of the real economy and to allow more financial "live water" to flow to the real economy. Finance and the real economy are inseparable; they all rise and fall together. The real economy is the foundation of financial development. Promoting the development of the real economy is fundamental to establish financial industry. Serving the real economy is an essential requirement for finance. If we break away from the real economy and engage in extracorporeal circulation, the real economy will become "water without source," and sooner or later, the financial industry will become "a tree without roots."

Since the 21st century, China's financial industry has continued to grow with the country's reform and development, and the financial format has been continuously enriched, gradually forming a relatively complete financial system including banks, trusts, securities, insurance, funds, and futures. With the advancement of financial globalization and the application of big data, cloud computing and financial technology, the financial industry is developing and changing with each passing day, and financial innovations are emerging in an endless stream. However, innovations are also mixed, many of them are "Pseudo-innovations" which actually prompt distracting financial resources from real economy to fictitious one. Financial innovation should adhere to the rule of "three favorable." The first is to improve the capability to serve the real economy, rather than avoiding supervision through so-called innovation, that is to say, financial innovation should be based on the real economy, otherwise, innovation can only be something fake.

With the completion of China's initial stage of industrialization and the gradual rise of the service industry, the scope of the real economy that financial services are committed to is also expanding. This includes not only tangible material production but also intangible service production. The primary industry, secondary industry, and tertiary industry are all real economy. Therefore, there is wide space for finance to serve entity economy and finance does not need to be "self-entertained." For example, financial institutions would coordinate the national strategy and major projects such as the "Belt and Road Initiative" and collaborative development of Beijing, Tianjin and Hebei, and assist in economic and social key fields such as advanced manufacturing, green finance, agriculture, rural areas and farmers, small and micro enterprises, and affordable housing projects. It also support domestic enterprises "going out," and cooperation of international production capacity. All above are examples of how finance could support the real economy.

In the process of supply-side structural reform with the focus on "cutting overcapacity, reducing excess inventory, deleveraging, lowering costs, and strengthening areas of weakness," financial institutions serving the real economy need to play a role in helping companies "deleverage," "reduce cost," and "strengthen areas of weakness." China Zheshang Bank is committed to serving the real economy. In recent years, China Zheshang Bank has taken the initiative to adapt to the new normal of economy, actively implemented various national financial and industrial policies, vigorously promoted supply-side structural reforms through financial services, and developed its ability to provide financial services as well as the scale, quality and efficiency at the same time. In the course of practice, it gradually explored the business development model that meets the needs of its own customers and summed up experiences of some characteristic transformations. The first is in liquidity service, focusing on the two core requirements of "lowering financing costs and improving service efficiency" of enterprises, we helped companies activate their assets and solve the difficulties in fund liquidity management. We set up Yongjin bill pools, asset pools, and export pools as well as a series of liquidity service products such as ultra-short-term loan and supremeness loan et cetera, the pooled and onlineized financing business management helps companies to deleverage, reduce costs, and improve efficiency. Second, in the field of small and micro financial services, in response to small enterprises' request for "short, small, frequent, and urgent" capital, through innovative product design, we actively take measures to help small and micro enterprises to deleverage and reduce costs, such as three-year-loans, ten-year-loans, "pay back through the loan and convertible at maturity" and so on. The products not only meet the medium to long term financing needs for up to 10 years, but also support the company in borrowing and paying back at all times and recurring usage of fund. We calculated the interest on their actual amount of borrowings on a daily basis to reduce interest expenses. Thirdly, in terms of retail business, we designed a number of scenario-based packages for working class with the payroll card as the key product, which can meet multiple needs such as customer cash flow, free money channel transfer and high-return financial management products et cetera. Our wealth pool, financial market pool and other platforms have solved the pain points that previously commercial banks could not have both "high-yield" and "liquidity," helping companies increase their wage income for employees without increasing their financial costs, and helping their employees achieve one-stop service of wealth management, financing, increasing credibility, and transfer of managed wealth.

At the same time, China Zheshang Bank actively practices the concept of whole-asset management and strengthens cooperation with banks and non-banking financial institutions to serve the real economy and realizes the integration and intensive management of financial markets such as credit markets, money markets, capital markets, and foreign exchange markets, promoting the diversified development of credit assets, trading assets, interbank assets, and investment assets. Through integrated operations and business linkages, we provide customers with a full range of financial solutions, and continue to strengthen market-oriented and customer experience guided product and business model innovation. For example, through cooperation with private equity institutions, fund companies and other institutions, we explored the creation of a new financial services to bridge investments and loans, provided companies with full chain, comprehensive investment and financing services and multi-currency, multi-market direct financing consultant services to help them participate in direct financing and optimize and reshape their balance sheets.

China's financial industry is undergoing an unprecedented storm of supervision. In recent months, regulatory documents have been issued in an intensive manner from "One bank and three commissions," which fully demonstrates the determination of various regulatory agencies to push finance back to its origin. This regulatory storm has important implications for altering excessive expansion in the financial industry and preventing financial risks from escalating. This report collects a large amount of public data, based on surveys, statistics, calculations, and other methods, detailed analysis was done for financial sources, trends and related business models of different financial formats, and put forward a lot of constructive comments and prospects, it bears certain inspirational and reference values to the financial regulatory authorities and financial institutions.

During the "Thirteenth Five-Year Plan" period, the operating environment of financial institutions faced a series of major changes such as interest rate marketization, RMB internationalization, multi-tiered financial market development, intensified cross-border competition, lower industry barriers, fiscal system reform, and reform of regulatory ideas. We are experiencing the pain and hardship when the reforms have entered into deep water areas. However, the direction of the Central Committee for reform is clear, and the determination is firm. We are full of confidence in the future development of the financial industry.

Victory only comes from hard work and only deep self-determination can set the course. How to continue to effectively support the development of the real economy while achieving its own transformation and upgrading is a subject that all financial institutions need to seriously think about and explore.

Beijing, China

Xiaochun Liu
President of China Zheshang Bank Co., Ltd.

Preface

Three Questions About Money

In China, it is said that every time a visitor encounters the security of the residential community, two profound "philosophical" questions have to be answered: "Where are you from? and Where are you going?" If "you" is replaced with "money," then these two issues are actually also causing the financial community to scratch their heads. After the global crisis, "shadow banking" became a hot topic at home and abroad, and the financial community was arguing over its historical origins and categories. In 2013, in regard to China's bank-led financial structure, the author proposed a new concept—"the bank's shadow".[1] Regardless of "shadow banking" or "shadow of the bank," it is nothing more than to answer the question of residential security, only the object is "money": Where does the money come from? Where to go?

The financial community feels that "money" is tacky, so they all like to use the name "currency". However, in the 2013 report, the author has pointed out that currency is the bank's liability and only corresponds to the credit creation activities of the bank's assets, and cannot reflect the financial capabilities of the entire financial sector including non-bank financial institutions (Total Financial Capacity). To this end, the author organized a team at the time and constructed a macro-financial indicator: "total credit amount." In the asset side of the financial sector, this indicator covers debt financing instruments created by the financial sector for the entire non-financial sector including government, businesses, and residents (similar to the "Debt Outstanding by Sector" in the Fed's U.S. capital flow chart); In the debtor side of the financial sector, this index corresponds to the currency, the bank's liabilities, and also corresponds to various contractual or quasi-contractual financial instruments issued by banks and non-banking financial institutions to finance their asset operations.

[1] Jianfeng Yin , Zengwu Wang , "Shadow of Shadow Banks and Banks: Development and Evaluation of China's Financial Product Market (2010–2012)", Social Sciences Academic Press, 2013.

The bank's financial management, trust plans, insurance reserves, mutual funds, and so on discussed in this book are all contractual or quasi-contractual[2] financial instruments, and the corresponding "funds" are various forms of debt financing instruments—credit. Here, we use the total credit amount indicator to discuss where "money" has been from and gone in recent years. At the same time, we also want to add a question that community security will not ask but standard economics must answer: Where should "money" go?

Whither Has Gone the Money?

The Scale and Direction of Money Flow

First of all, we can see (see Table 1) that the broad sense of money M2 can no longer reflect the full scale of China's "money": In 2009, the total credit amount was only 88% of M2, and by 2016, the total credit amount was equivalent to 1.2 times of M2. In other words, 20% of "money" is not within the scope of M2 statistics. If further consideration is given to the financial sector liabilities discussed later, the information that M2 has omitted will be even greater. Therefore, we have seen a major shift in the monetary policy that was originally targeted at M2 in recent years, although the government's report always refers to M2. As for where the "money" goes, the distribution of the credit totals provides a clear answer. In 2016, of the total credit volume of nearly 182 trillion yuan, the government sector was 36.8 trillion yuan, accounting for about 20% of the total, an increase of 5 percentage points from 2009. Among them, the proportion of central government fell from 11% in 2009 to 7% in 2016, while the proportion of local governments rose from 4 to 14% in the same period; non-financial enterprises accounted for 110.8 trillion yuan, fell from 71% in 2009 to 61% in 2016; the resident sector was 34.3 trillion yuan, accounting for an increase from 15% in 2009 to 19% in 2016. The change in the distribution of credit aggregates clearly shows that although enterprises are still the place where the bulk of the "money" went, the "money" has flowed more to the local government and the resident sector after the crisis.

The change in the distribution of the credit totals reveals an interesting phenomenon. Consistent with the expansionary fiscal policy for dealing with the crisis, other countries have increased their liabilities by the central government. However, in China, compared with other sectors, the central government is actually moving "backwards". At the same time, the corporate sector that created wealth and promoted economic growth also adopted a relatively cautious debt strategy after the crisis. On the contrary, local governments and resident sectors have become the main force to increase debt and offset the cyclical economic downturn.

[2] Call it "quasi-contractual" products because the legal relationship of many wealth management products in China is unclear, and the issue of rigid payment has not been resolved.

Table 1 China's broad money M2, total credit and distribution unit: 100 million yuan

Project Year	M2	Credit total	Credit total/M2	Government	Among it: Central government	Among it: Local government	Non-financial enterprise	Resident
2009	610225	535275	88%	82967	58892	24074	378133	81819
2010	725852	670793	92%	101754	65303	36451	462807	112586
2011	851591	805548	95%	114608	68575	46034	554867	136073
2012	974149	976513	100%	137034	72369	64665	678084	161395
2013	1106525	1161915	105%	174148	87688	86459	788939	198870
2014	1228375	1338475	109%	209953	96714	113239	895556	232547
2015	1392300	1561506	112%	275972	107683	168289	1012467	274708
2016	1517730	1819243	120%	368395	120869	247526	1108172	342676

Source National Finance and Development Laboratory
Note "Non-financial enterprises" do not include local platform loans and city investment bonds. These two parts of the debt are classified as "local governments"

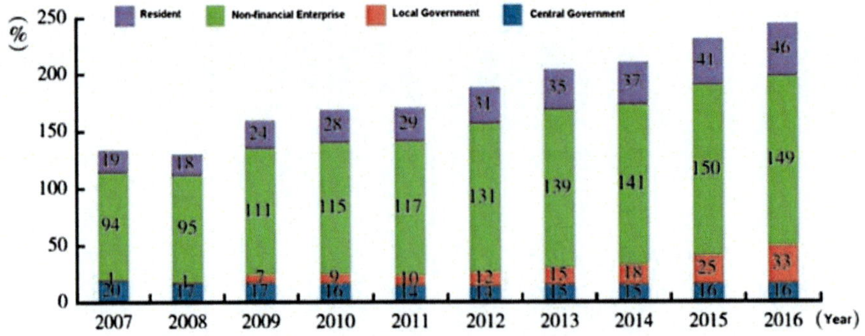

Fig. 1 Non-financial sector leverage Ratio. *Source* National finance and development laboratory

Flow of "Money" and Leverage of Non-financial Corporations

The "money" characterized by the total amount of credit is essentially the liability of the non-financial sector. Therefore, the change in the flow of "money" determines the distribution of leverage ratio (debt/GDP). In 2016, the overall leverage ratio (credit amount/GDP) of the non-financial sector continued to increase, but the growth rate slowed down (see Fig. 1). In 2016, the overall leverage ratio was approximately 244%, which represented an increase of 12% compared with 2015, and 2015 was 21% higher than that of 2014. Consistent with changes in the above-mentioned total credits, the slowdown in the growth rate of leverage is mainly due to the progress of deleveraging by non-financial companies. At the same time, the central government's leverage rate remains unchanged, and the leverage ratio of local government and the resident sector are increased by 8 and 5 percentage points respectively compared with 2015.

In 2016, the leverage ratio of non-financial companies (excluding local platform loans and urban investment bonds) was 149%, which was a drop of 1 percentage point from 2015. In fact, after the "four trillion yuan" in 2009, except for a short-term rebound between 2011 and 2012, the non-financial company's debt growth rate generally showed a declining trend. This feature is similar to the situation in the United States after the crisis, indicating that after deducting local platforms and city investment companies, the balance sheet of non-financial corporate sectors in China is not as bad as many people think. For example, looking at the "microscopic leverage ratio" of industrial enterprises, that is, the asset-liability ratio of industrial enterprises, we can see (see Fig. 2) that after the global crisis, industrial enterprises generally showed a trend of deleveraging. Among them, private enterprises performed more clearly. The asset-liability ratio of joint-stock companies indicates a typical (rational) pro-cyclical behavior: increase leverage before the crisis in 2008 and deleverage after the crisis. Even in the case of state-owned industrial enterprises, although they have rapidly increased their leverage to respond to the crisis after 2009,

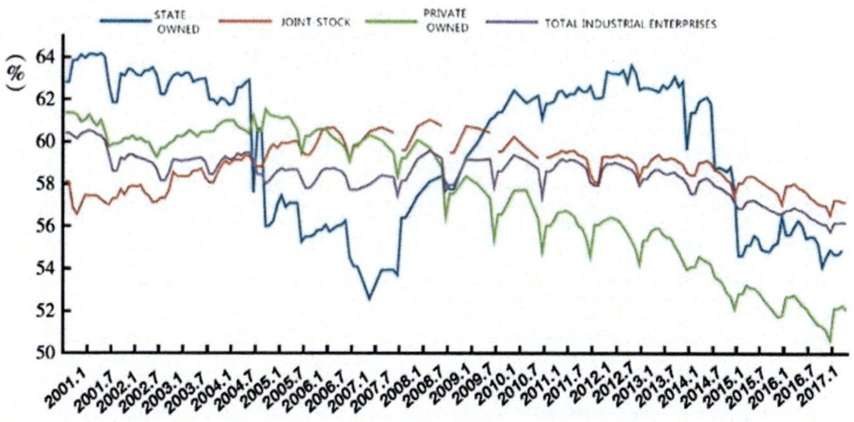

Fig. 2 Asset-liability ratios of industrial enterprises. *Source* CEIC

After 2013 they are also deleveraging. At present, the asset-liability ratio of state-owned industrial enterprises is close to the lowest level in 2007.

Therefore, after cleaning up the local platform companies and urban investment companies, the problem of non-financial companies deleveraging is not so pressing as the current public opinion says, especially after further diluting the part of financial enterprise debt involving infrastructure and real estate. On the contrary, non-financial companies need to increase leverage as the economy rebounds. From the data for the first quarter of 2017, it is exactly the same: In the first quarter, non-financial corporate debt growth reached 11.6%, which was higher than 9.4% in the fourth quarter of 2016. However, according to the structure of debt financing tools, the rebound in non-financial corporate debt financing mainly relies on the credit supply of non-bank financial institutions, and loan growth rate and bond growth rate are all lower than even the level of the previous quarter. From this perspective, if the current financial deleveraging is too rapid, it will not only increase the market interest rate, but also reduce the credit availability of non-financial companies.

The Flow of "Money" and the Leverage of Local Governments and Residents

Local government is the sector with the fastest increase in leverage in 2016 and its risk is closely observed. The local government's fiscal revenue has always been lower than the fiscal expenditure at same level, and the local fiscal deficit is compensated by the central government's transfer payments, and the other is the local land transfer income from local fund. In recent years, the proportion of land transfer fees to local fiscal revenue has remained stable at about 40%, which has become the main disposable financial resource of many local governments, especially those in the

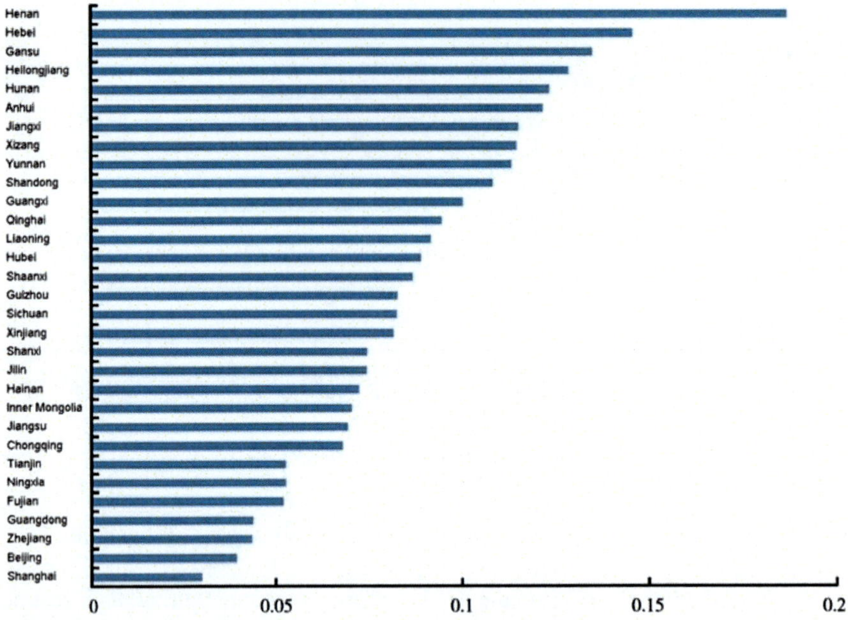

Fig. 3 Housing Price Increase for 2009–2016/2015 Foreign Resident Population. *Source* CEIC

central and western regions. Therefore, the local real estate situation is crucial to the solvency of the local government.

With regard to China's real estate market, it is too naive to discuss the bubble again. The current point is to prevent regional risk events. From the perspective of "the house is for people to live in", the population is the basis for determining whether or not regional house prices can "stuck". Therefore, we can compare local housing prices with local population indicators. It can be seen that the ratio of housing price increase to the population registered in other places (see Fig. 3) is higher in provinces in the Midwest and Northeast China, while the housing prices of eastern regions of Shanghai, Beijing, Zhejiang, and Guangdong are much higher than Midwest; their indicators are among the lowest. This situation shows that the rise in housing prices in the eastern region reflects, to a considerable extent, the tendency of the population to accumulate locally, while the real estate market in the central and western regions still depends mainly on regional factors. Further observations using the ratio of house price increases and population increases have basically the same conclusions, except that the ratios of the three provinces of Heilongjiang, Guangxi and Jilin are negative because of negative population growth.

The resident sector is also a sector of fast-rising leverage, and its risk cannot be ignored either. In 2016, a significant change in the resident sector was that new residents' debt exceeded new savings, and the resident sector became a net funded sector. This phenomenon also happened in 2007 when China's real estate market was at the historical peak. One indicator for judging risk in the resident sector is the ratio

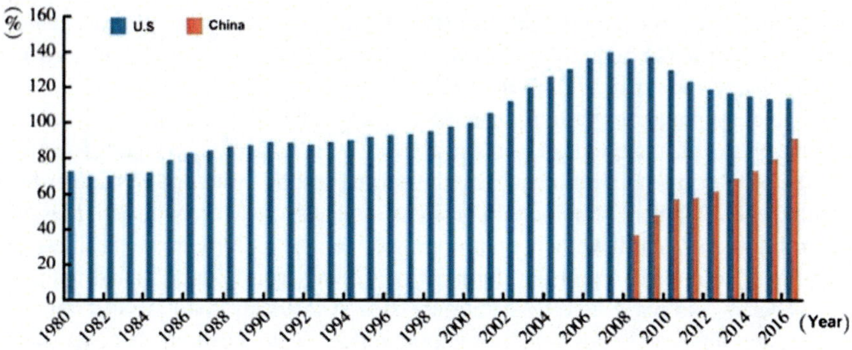

Fig. 4 Residents' Liabilities/Remuneration. *Source* CEIC

of the resident's debt to the labor's remuneration (see Fig. 4). In 2016, this indicator has reached 90% in China, which is roughly equivalent to the level of the United States in 1994, it seems that the problem is not significant yet. However, the U.S. resident sector has a large amount of income from asset, while the Chinese resident sector's income from asset is insignificant. Looking further at the inter-departmental distribution of national income, the disposable income of the resident sector in China only accounts for 60% of the country's disposable income and is less than 70% of that of the United States. Regarding the income distribution gap between individuals, the Gini coefficient in China is as high as 0.46, which has already exceeded the international warning line of 0.4. From the perspective of the distribution of stock assets, the 1.2 million high-net-worth people in the country can invest nearly 30% of the total investable assets. All of these indicators of income and asset distribution have only one meaning: liabilities accumulate to middle and low income families, and assets accumulate to middle- and high-income households. Therefore, just as with the judgment of local government risk, the risk for the resident sector needs to be analyzed by sub-regions and sub-families, and cannot rely on the average total indicators.

Where Does "Money" Come From?

The Distribution of Source "Money"

"Money" in terms of credit totals corresponds to the liabilities of the non-financial sector on the one hand and to the assets of the financial sector on the other. Therefore, the source of money is bound to be closely related to the structural changes in the financial sector. The author once pointed out that,[3] a major change in our financial system since 2009 is the rise of non-bank financial institutions and non-financial

[3] Jianfeng Yin: "The Rise of the Non-Bank Financial Sector", China Finance, May 2017.

bond markets. Accordingly this change shall have a similarly significant impact on the source structure of "money." However, after the veil was revealed, we discovered that "money" was mainly from the banks.

Table 2 summarizes various channels for bank credit creation. It can be seen that on the one hand, as a traditional banking business the scale of bank credit is declining in the proportion of credit created by the entire banking system; on the other hand, with the development of non-credit business of banks, credit creation activities other than traditional one have become the growth engine of bank assets business. For example, despite the rapid development of China's non-financial bond market in these years, the main holding institution of non-financial bonds is still banks. In 2016, non-financial bonds held by banks amounted to 26.8 trillion yuan, accounting for over 60% of the non-financial bond stocks. In addition, credit creation activities conducted by banks through out-of-balance-sheet businesses (such as bank-trust-government cooperation and entrusted loans) have also developed rapidly. Therefore, on the whole, in the total credit in non-financial sector, bank credit is still as high as nearly 88% although the share of banks has declined.

Although "money" is mainly from banks, the share of non-bank financial institutions does indeed increase. From the credit creation activities of non-banking financial institutions, the non-financial bonds held by them are the most important, but their share in total non-bank financial institutions' credits is declining. The increase in share is mainly the creation of trust loans, trusts and insurance. By 2016, the ratio of non-bank financial institutions' credit has risen to 11% in the total non-financial sector credits (see Table 3).

The Source of "Money" and the Leverage of the Financial Sector

With the decline of traditional bank credit, the rise of non-traditional banking services and non-banking financial institutions, the sources of "money" have become increasingly diversified. This has also led to an increase in mutual debts within the financial sector and continued rising leverage. Similar to the changes in the leverage ratio of the non-financial sector, the leverage ratio of China's financial sector (financial sector debt without deposits/GDP) continues to rise but the growth rate has slowed down (see Fig. 5). In 2016, the leverage ratio of China's financial sector was 97%, an increase of 9 percentage points from 2015, and 2015 was 11% higher than that of 2014. Compared with the United States, the leverage ratio of China's financial sector is roughly equivalent to its 2002 level. However, considering the relative changes in the financial sector between the United States and China, China has surpassed the United States for two consecutive years in 2015 and 2016.

Observing the mutual debts within the financial sector, the liabilities of non-bank financial institutions to banks ("claims on other financial companies" in Fig. 6) have become the largest item since the first quarter of 2015, and have also risen the most

Table 2 Bank credits and composition unit: 100 million yuan

Project Year	Bank credit	Non-financial debt held by bank	Inter-bank business	Bank-trust-government cooperation	Entrusted loans	Bank credit total	Bank credit/Total credit
2009	420260	65628	15221	6449	3202	510759	95.42%
2010	502871	82831	33872	16605	3813	639993	95.41%
2011	581893	96238	37594	19246	18008	752979	93.48%
2012	672875	111422	57886	25319	25712	893214	91.49%
2013	766327	129586	71629	31460	40992	1039993	89.52%
2014	867868	147944	83319	42810	56033	1197974	89.51%
2015	984875	200056	92068	54214	65580	1396793	89.45%
2016	1110976	267983	76048	60928	79189	1595123	87.79%

Source National Finance and Development Laboratory
Note "Non-financial debt held by banks" includes the portion of the bank that is held through wealth management products

Table 3 Credits and structure of non-bank financial institutions unit: 100 million yuan

Project Year	Bond held by non-bank financial institutions	Entrusted loans	Trust	Insurance	Credit total of non-bank financial institutions	Non-bank credit/Credit total
2009	19887	2135	717	985	23723	4.43%
2010	22451	2542	3033	1946	29972	4.47%
2011	28320	12005	7262	3882	51470	6.39%
2012	39582	17142	16675	7806	81204	8.32%
2013	45943	27328	33911	10560	117742	10.13%
2014	54027	37356	29310	12999	133691	9.99%
2015	76303	43720	18023	16034	154079	9.87%
2016	108605	52792	23995	19269	204661	11.26%

Source National Finance and Development Laboratory
Note "bonds held by non-bank financial institutions" have deducted the bonds held by wealth management products; "trust" does not include Bank-Trust-Government cooperation

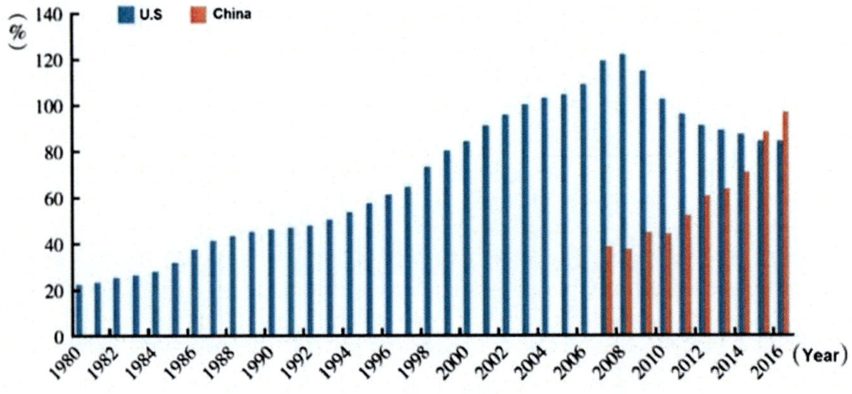

Fig. 5 Financial sector leverage. *Source* CEIC, National finance and development laboratory

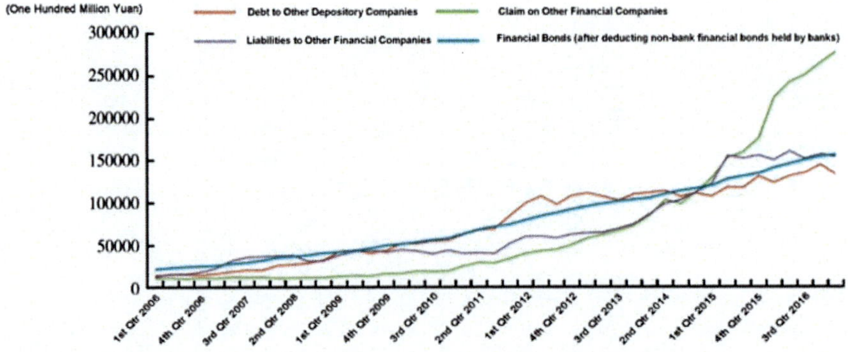

Fig. 6 Financial sector liabilities. *Source* National finance and development laboratory

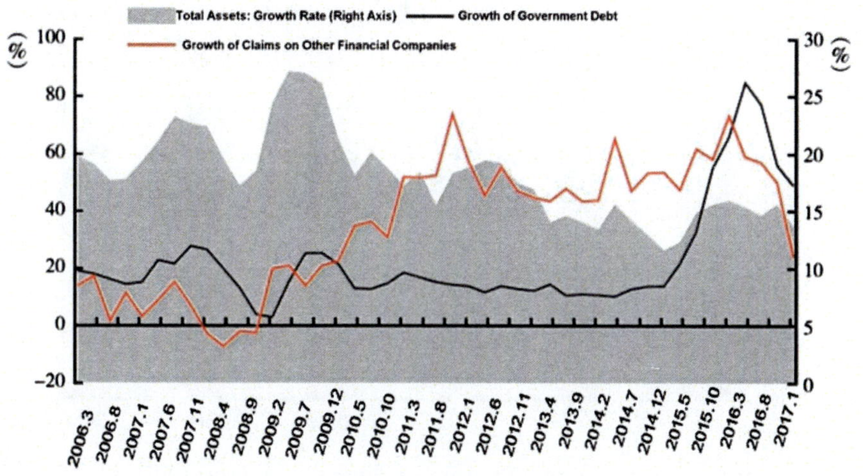

Fig. 7 Growth rate of bank assets and major subjects. *Source* CEIC

quickly—this further explained that many of the "money" of non-bank financial institutions are still the "money" of banks. In the fourth quarter of 2016, the "claims on other financial companies" reached 26.5 trillion yuan, accounting for 36.7% of the total liabilities of the financial sector, an increase of nearly 10 trillion yuan from the fourth quarter of 2015. In the first quarter of 2017, the "claims on other financial companies" further rose to 27.8 trillion yuan, and the proportion of liabilities in the financial sector reached 38.5%.

For banks, "claims on other financial companies" has become the main item of asset expansion in recent years (see Fig. 7). After "4 trillion yuan" in 2009, the growth rate has increased from 20 to 60% in 2011 and remained relatively stable until the third quarter of 2016. By the first quarter of 2017, the "claims on other financial companies" had already approached 28 trillion yuan, accounting for about 11% of the total assets of the banking sector. In addition, another item of concern in the banking sector's assets is "claims on government", which has accelerated since the implementation of local government debt swaps in the first quarter of 2015. In the first quarter of 2017, the scale of "claims on government" reached 17.5 trillion yuan, an increase of about 10 trillion yuan from the first quarter of 2015. This part of increase is basically local governments' bonds.

The Source of "Money" and the Mismatch of Financial Resources

Although the sources of "money" are diversified, the flow of "money" still prefers real estate, including those directly related to it, such as real estate business loans, personal mortgage loans and some indirectly related infrastructure projects. It can be

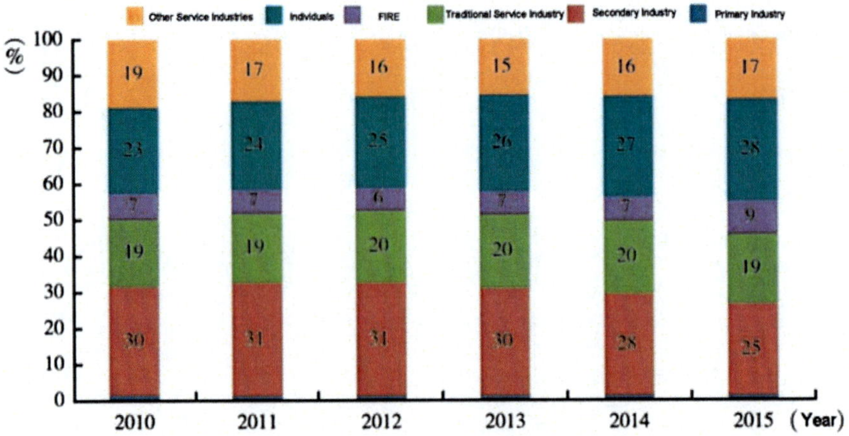

Fig. 8 Industry structures of domestic and foreign currency loans. *Source* CEIC

seen that once the non-banking financial institution obtains financing including bank funds, a considerable part of the fund enters the local governments' infrastructure projects and real estate. Taking the fund trust as an example, among of the 17 trillion yuan at the end of 2016, the invested portion in local basic industries was 2.7 trillion yuan, accounting for 16%; and the investment in real estate was 1.4 trillion yuan, accounting for 8%; Excluding financing related to local governments and real estate in projects of investing in industrial and commercial enterprises and bond purchases, at least 24% of capital trusts are invested in local government infrastructure and real estate projects. As for the use of funds by other non-bank financial institutions, such as insurance claim investment plans, it is almost entirely flow to this area. According to a rough estimate, at least 30% of the 25 trillion yuan that non-bank financial institutions provide to real entities, that is about 8 trillion yuan, are related to local government infrastructure and real estate projects.

Besides non-bank financial institutions that prefer investing in infrastructure and real estate, traditional bank credit is also the case. According to the industrial structure of domestic and foreign currency credits (see Fig. 8), if we combine personal loans (mostly mortgage loans), FIRE (financial real estate), and traditional service industries (which are mostly related to infrastructure), in 2015 56% if loans are directly and indirectly related to real estate. Calculating the situation in 2016 at the rate of 50%, about 60 trillion yuan in current bank credit is related to infrastructure and real estate. This part of the credit plus local government bonds held by banks (about 10 trillion yuan), city investment bonds (about 1.2 trillion yuan), and funds indirectly invested by banks through non-bank financial institutions to local infrastructure and real estate (about 80,000 yuan) Billion), the total exposure is nearly 80 trillion yuan, accounting for 40% of the bank's assets.

In short, bank credit, non-bank financial institution funds, and the rapidly developing bond market in recent years have all become, to a considerable extent, the channel of financial resources to infrastructure and real estate. The recent financial

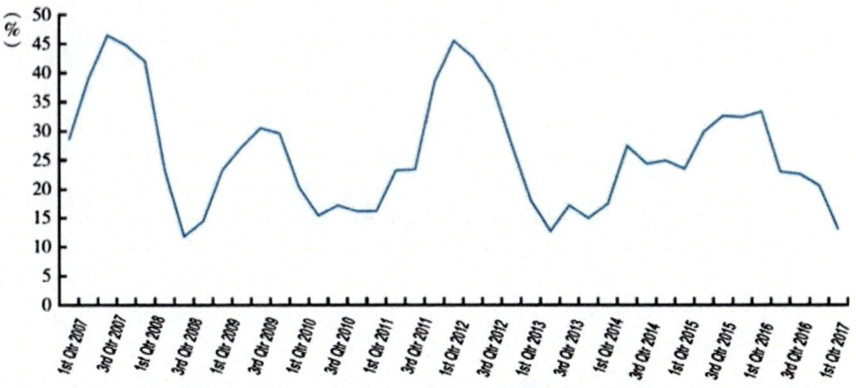

Fig. 9 Financial sector debt growth rate. *Source* National finance and development laboratory

deleveraging process helps reverse the pattern of resource mismatch. With the rapid decline in the growth rate of financial interbank liabilities, the growth rate of financial liabilities in the 1st quarter of 2017 (see Fig. 9) has dropped to the lowest level in the past decade (just above the 2008 level). However, even so, the growth rate is still about 13%. If the annual GDP growth rate remains at around 6.9%, and considering that financial deleveraging speed cannot be too fast, it is expected that China's financial leverage rate will continue to increase in 2017.

Where Should Money go?

Case Study in the United States

The experience of the United States before the subprime mortgage crisis has many similarities to China since 2009. Therefore, it is instructive to look at the changes in the United States' "money" after the crisis. After the rupture of the information technology bubble in the United States in 2000, the investment returns in the real sector declined and there was lack of investment opportunities. However, financial innovation has become very active, besides, monetary and financial management authorities have acquiesced to this to a certain extent, the source of "money" was increasingly diversified and the scale constantly increasing. But in the end it all went to real estate. After the crisis, the United States has undergone profound changes in the direction and source of "money." In terms of leverage changes, it shifts between departments—not just simply deleverage.

Looking at the leverage structure of the non-financial sector in the United States (see Fig. 10), it can be seen that the family sector and the state government have been deleveraging so far since the crisis: the former's leverage rate dropped from 98% in 2007 to 79% in 2016; The latter dropped from 20 to 17%. Comparatively speaking,

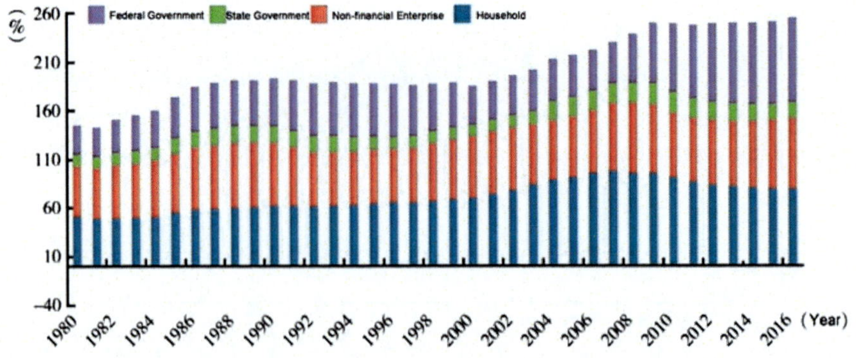

Fig. 10 U.S. Non-financial sector leverage rates from 1980 to 2016. *Source* CEIC

the family sector is the main force of deleveraging—it is easy to understand, because the outbreak of the subprime mortgage crisis itself is due to excessive leverage in the household sector. The non-financial corporate sector was also deleveraging from 2008 to 2011, and the leverage ratio fell from 73 to 66%; however, since 2012, the non-financial corporate sector has started to increase leverage, and its leverage rate has increased to 76% in 2016. As a result of the crisis response, the federal government has been increasing leverage. In 2007, the federal government's leverage ratio was 42%, and in 2016 it reached 86%.

When the leverage shifts around sectors, it has not declined in the entire non-financial sector. However, this kind of maneuver played a crucial role in the recovery of the economy: On the one hand, the excessively indebted household sector gradually repaired the balance sheet. At the same time, the federal government increased leverage and implemented fiscal and monetary expansion together with the Fed's quantitative easing policy to stabilize the market; on the other hand, the corporate sector, which initially had a fairly healthy balance sheet, has been leveraging leverage to promote economic growth after experiencing short-term deleveraging.

For the financial sector, there is an overall financial deleveraging (see Fig. 5). However, even within the financial sector, not all departments are deleveraging. When financial sector is divided into three categories: banks, non-bank financial institutions, and asset securitization products, we find that only asset securitization products have shrunk dramatically.

Further classification of asset securitization products we can see that subprime securitization products have appeared large shrinkage. US securitized products can be divided into two categories by operating agencies: One is the securitized products issued by the GSE (Government-sponsored Enterprises), and the main one is the compliant mortgage loans. Because of the government's credit support, we call it the "public sector" securitization products; the second is the products issued by private financial institutions, which are called "private" securitization products, mainly subprime products. According to this classification, it can be seen (see Fig. 11) that the latter is shrinking dramatically. Its highest scale reached 4.6 trillion U.S.

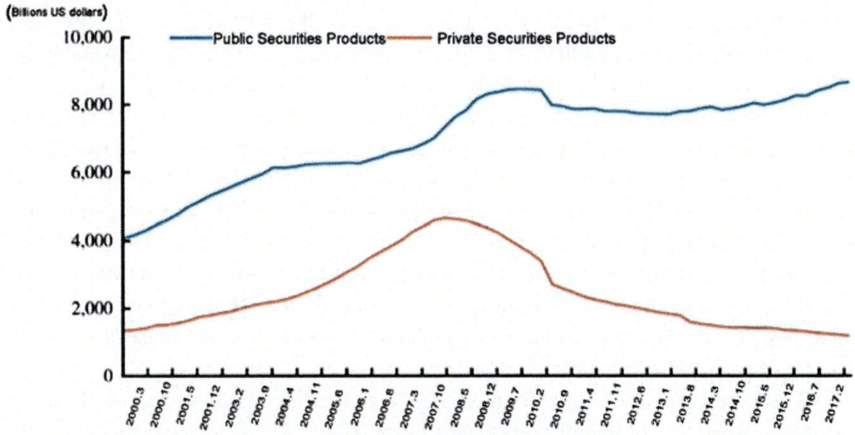

Fig. 11 Scale of U.S. securitization from 2000 to 2017. *Source* CEIC

dollars in 2008 and it is now only 1.2 trillion U.S. dollars; while the scale of the former has dropped since 2008, but it has reached 8.7 trillion U.S. dollars now, slightly higher than the 8.5 trillion U.S. dollars in 2008.

Therefore, a significant feature of the post-crisis U.S. leverage structure changes is that all deleverages is related to real estate, including the household sector and subprime securitization products. Non-financial corporations first go deleveraged and then increase leverage. The financial sector excluding securitizations is actually stabilizing leverage and encourages an upward shift in the economy.

Emerging Industries Need "Money"

The experience of the United States tells us that "money" should at least not embrace "real estate" so enthusiastically. However, in China "money" precisely flew to industries that have been directly or indirectly related to real estate after the 2009 crisis. This is partly due to the fact that the crisis has hit the economy. There is a lack of investment opportunities in the real sector and the return on investment is low. However, there are various indications that the current economic situation in China and even the world is at an upward turning point. After many years of painful adjustments, China's industrial structure has undergone profound changes. Some industries are generating large investment opportunities. These industries need "money".

Since 2015, China's tertiary industry's contribution to GDP growth has largely surpassed that of manufacturing. In 2016, the tertiary industry drove GDP by 3.9 percentage points, and the secondary industry only pulled 2.5 percentage points. China has entered the stage of tertiary industrialization after industrialization. A worrying issue after the economy enters the service-industry stage is "Boomer's disease": As the labor productivity and total factor productivity of the service industry are lower than those of the manufacturing industry, the service industry will lead to slower economic growth and even stagnation. The experience of advanced economies and the so-called middle-income trap countries shows that whether the service productivity of the service industry exceeds the manufacturing industry determines whether the economy can move through the threshold and enter the high-income stage. According to statistics (see Fig. 12), in the comparison of the labor productivity of the secondary industry and the tertiary industry in China, the tertiary industry has always been lower than the secondary industry, but a good sign is that the gap is continuously narrowing. In 2016, the per capita output value of the tertiary industry was already equivalent to 90% of the per capita output value of the secondary industry. If this trend can be maintained, in 2018, labor productivity in the tertiary industry will be equal to the secondary industry.

The improvement of labor productivity in the tertiary industry is closely related to the optimization of its internal structure (see Fig. 13). The tertiary industry can be divided into "traditional service industry" (traffic, warehousing and postal service,

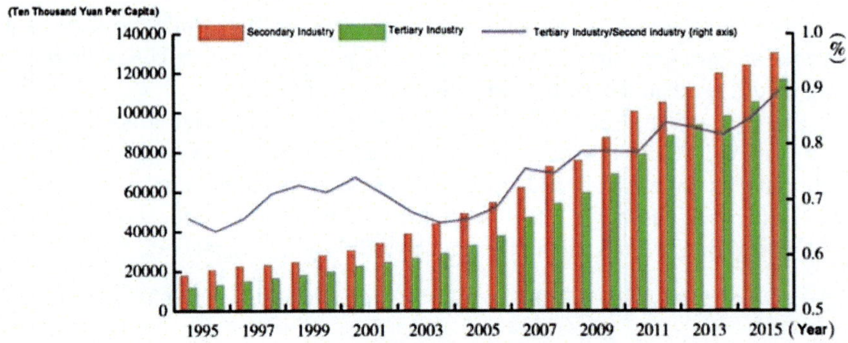

Fig. 12 Per capita output of the secondary and tertiary industries from 1995 to 2016 and the comparison of growth between tertiary industry and secondary industry. *Source* National bureau of statistics

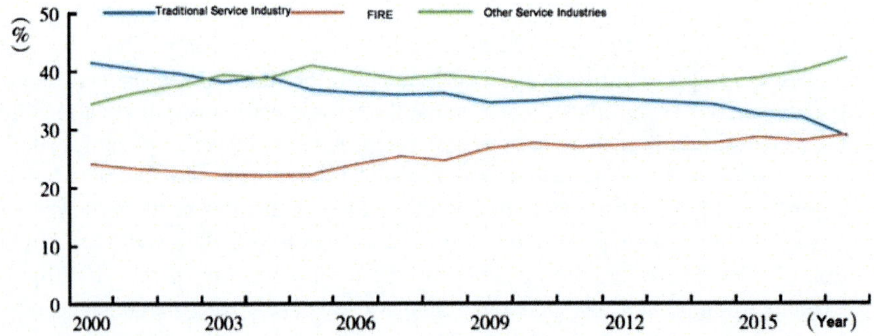

Fig. 13 Internal structure of the tertiary industry from 2000 to 2017. *Source* National bureau of statistics

wholesale and retail, accommodation and catering), "FIRE" (finance and real estate), and "other service industries" (including information technology, computer communications, science, education, culture, and health, etc.). The proportion of "other service industries" remained stable at around 39% of the total added value of the tertiary industry. In the first quarter of 2017, it exceeded 40% to reach 42%. At the same time, the proportion of "traditional service industries" has continued to decline. At present, the key factor constraining the labor productivity of the tertiary industry is that the modern productive services such as science, education, culture and public health are still tie up by the "public institution" system with low efficiency and being overstaffed. If the system reform of public institutions can be accelerated after the 19th National Party Congress, the tertiary industry will usher in faster development.

Emerging Technologies Attract "Money"

No matter which industry is classified as "emerging," the flow of "money" is ultimately determined by the return on investment and the return on investment depends on technological progress. In recent years, China's technological progress has made remarkable achievements. Such as "J-20," "Y-20," "C919," space station, quantum communication, etc. are well known. According to the statistics of the World Intellectual Property Organization, the number of patent applications in China has accelerated since the global crisis and surpassed Germany in 2013. In 2016, it increased by 46% from 2015 to 43131, close to Japan's level.

Behind the accelerating increase in the number of patent applications is a large amount of R&D funding. In 2016, China's R&D expenditure reached 1.55 trillion yuan, which was nearly 3 times that of 2009, and the scale was second only to the United States. From the R&D expenditure intensity (R&D expenditure/GDP) (see Fig. 14), China exceeded 2% in 2015, but compared with the United States (2.74%), Germany (2.84%) and Japan (3.59%), there is still a lot of room for growth. Regarding

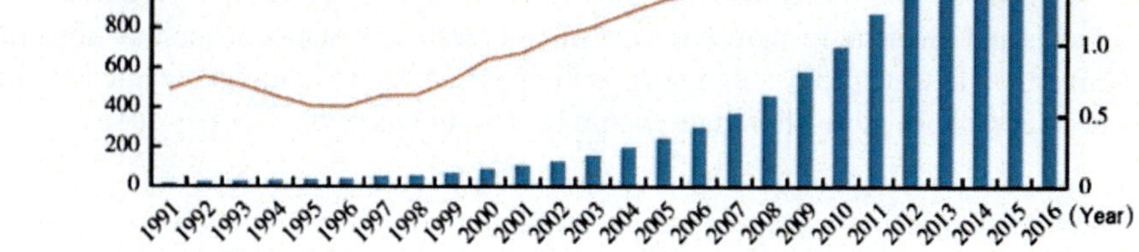

Fig. 14 R&D expenditure and input intensity in China. *Source* CEIC

the sources of R&D funding, the proportion of government funds decreased from 29% in 2000 to 15% in 2015, and the proportion of corporate funds increased from 60 to 77% in the same period. China has become one of the few countries in the world where the proportion of R&D expenditure exceeds 75%.

From the perspective of the manufacturing industry, where R&D investment intensity exceeds the average level of the manufacturing industry are in technology and capital-intensive industries. They are also the most significantly developed industries in technology in recent years. Among them, R&D intensity in railways, ships, aerospace and instrument manufacturing has exceeded the national average. In terms of geography regions (see 15), in 2015, the R&D input intensity of 8 provinces and cities in China exceeded the national average. With the exception of Shaanxi, the remaining seven provinces and cities are all located in the eastern coastal areas. After the global crisis, these regions have undergone profound industrial structural evolution. On the one hand, there are manufacturing upgrades, and on the other hand, their economy has shifted to service industry. Therefore, the higher intensity of R&D investment in these seven coastal provinces and cities reflects the technical progress in the service sector to a certain extent, which is in line with the aforementioned changes in the industrial and investment structure of our country. Take Beijing for example, the input intensity is as high as 6%, and in 2016, the added value of its tertiary industry was close to 2 trillion yuan, while the secondary industry was only 480 billion yuan.

In addition to technological advances, the efficiency of capital investment is also an important factor in determining the return on investment. The efficiency of capital investment, that is, the capital's marginal remuneration decreases with the capital output ratio. The intuitive meaning is very obvious: if there is too much capital, the return on capital investment will be smaller. Take 1970 as the base period, calculating and comparing the growth rate of capital output ratios across countries,[4] China's capital output ratio was 5 times that of 1970 in 2015, while the United States, Germany, and Japan were 6 times, 7 times, and 9 times respectively; among the BRIC countries, Brazil and South Africa are also higher while India is similar to ours. China's lower capital output ratio means a higher capital's marginal return, and capital investment will become the main driving force for economic growth (Fig. 15).

At the end of this foreword, the author wants to emphasize a few points: first, where should the "money" go? It is ultimately determined by the market. The Third Plenary Session of the 18th CPC Central Committee pointed out that the market should play a decisive role in the allocation of resources. While China is about to sprint into a high-income economy, it is better to keep a variety of industrial policies and financial resources allocation policies at a distance when the industrial and economic structure is undergoing profound changes. Second, for macroeconomic financial policies more attentions should be paid to where the "money" comes from

[4] Because the capital-to-output ratio of the United States, Japan, and Germany in the base period of 1970 was much higher than that of China, this kind of comparatively overestimated the current capital output ratio in China and underestimated the capital's marginal return in China.

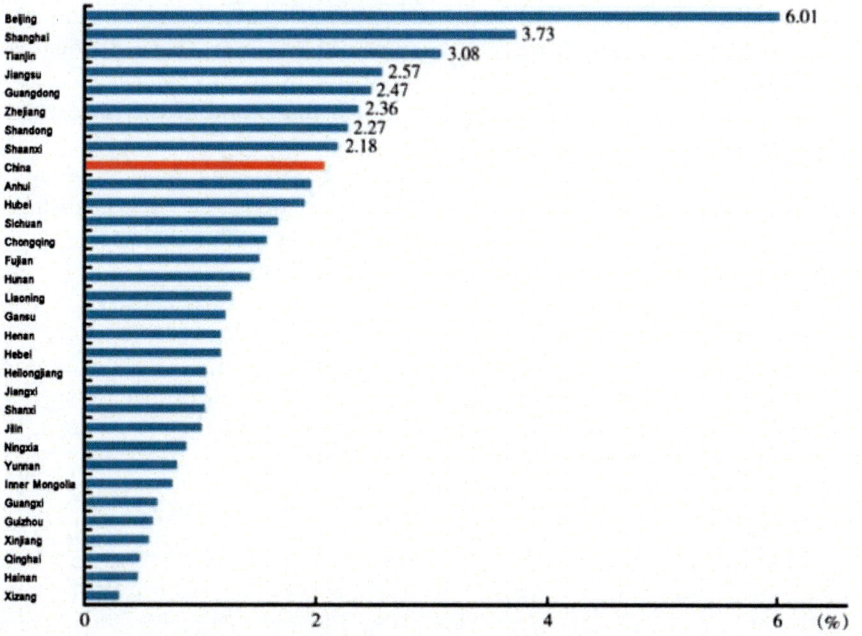

Fig. 15 Regional R&D input intensity in 2015. *Source* CEIC

and where to go. With the development of the economy, the financial system will inevitably become increasingly complicated, which means that it is no longer possible to merely rely on what officials tell us to do to allocate resources. On the other hand, it also reminds relevant departments that it is necessary to closely track and analyzes the move and mechanisms of fund, establish cross-regional, cross-sectoral, and real-time data monitoring systems to prevent regional and systematic risks from occurring. Third, for the various financial innovations mentioned in this book, we need to analyze them dialecticly. We shall not blindly condone them, or simply "killed on one stick." Over the past few years, our country's financial innovations have reflected dazzling progress of financial institutions in areas such as management, technology, and business development. They even evoked admirations from peers in advanced economies who devalued China's finances a decade ago. Some people criticize these innovations as "profit seeking," but what is wrong with craving for profit? Once upon a time, the biggest problem that hindered China's economic and financial development was that all economic parties did not seek profits, and did not even work or want to make progress. Without profit-driven innovation, the cost of supervision attached to social and economic operations cannot be minimized, therefore, the supervision itself will be solidified, which means the necessity of supervision does not exist.

In the end, I am very grateful to the readers. You forgave us for all the mistakes that we made in the report. It was your support that our past reports could be republished several times and sold out. I am also very grateful to the collaborators of this book.

We have been working together for ten years. We might have never been glorious or have been too proud to think we could be surpassed. At least we have experienced it together.

Life is nothing more than an experience in this world. We wish everyone happiness!

Beijing, China Jianfeng Yin

Contents

Chapter 1
Analysis of Flow of Bank Wealth Management Fund and Its Mechanism

In this article we use "broad-caliber" principal-protected wealth management, non-principal-based wealth management and structured entities as benchmarks to analyze the flow of funds and its mechanism in bank wealth management. Based on the annual report data of 31 listed banks, we measure and analyze the scale of bank wealth management and its structure. The overall scale of bank wealth management increased from 5.58 trillion yuan in 2012 to 33.64 trillion yuan at the end of 2016. Among them, funds from principal-protected and non-principal-guaranteed wealth management were mainly invested in liquid assets and bond markets, investment in non-standard and equity assets is supplemental; structured entities mainly invested in non-standard product such as "accounts receivables", supplemented by other investments. The aggregated scale of non-standard asset investment was 12.55 trillion yuan, accounting for 37.31% of the bank's wealth management scale at the end of 2016, much higher than the second-ranked bond market investment. In the process of gaming with regulatory policies, the investment model of non-standard asset business is also being innovated. The basic path is "interbank wealth management - bank and trust cooperation - bank and security channel". The latter is mostly the substitution of the former due to the regulatory environment. Looking into the future, the prospects for the development of bank financing can be expected and the standard will become clearer. The essence of regulation is to standardize the investment of "non-standard assets". At the end of this paper, three questions will be given for discussion.

1 Analysis of Flow of Funds: Non-standard Dominant

In order to comprehensively analyze the flow of bank wealth management fund, we divide the business into three categories: principal-protected, non-principal-guaranteed and structured entity. The main reason why the structured entity is

---

Written by Zengwu Wang.

J. Yin et al., *Whither has the Money Gone*,
https://doi.org/10.1007/978-981-16-4931-8_1

included in the scope of investigation is that the commercial bank's annual report explicitly states that the source of funding for the structured entity is the direct investment of the commercial bank or the transaction of shares of its splitting product. "Share of splitting product" means to split the bank investment into wealth management products and sell them to investors. Even with direct investment, the fund flows to financial instruments issued by non-bank financial institutions, such as the trust plan or the asset management plan of the securities company or of the subsidiary of fund company, which we called the "grand asset management." The level of incomes and risks of these three types of products or businesses, principal-protected, non-principal-guaranteed and structured entity, gradually increases in this order, while the degree of entry into the balance sheet, and the degree of dominance of commercial banks decreased in turn (see Fig. 1). For example, the out-of-balance-sheet structured entity business of the share-based transaction ranks first in terms of its income level and risk level, while commercial banks have the lowest degree of dominance in this type of business. The aggregate stock size of the three groups increased from 5.58 trillion yuan in 2012 to 33.64 trillion yuan in 2016, an increase of approximately 5.02 times. Among them, non-principal protected products and structured entities are the major growth points of bank wealth management business in recent years. The increase of non-principal-guaranteed products was 4.77 times, while the structured entities increased by 12.17 times from 881.68 billion yuan in 2012 to reach 11.61 in 2016. Trillion yuan (see Fig. 2).

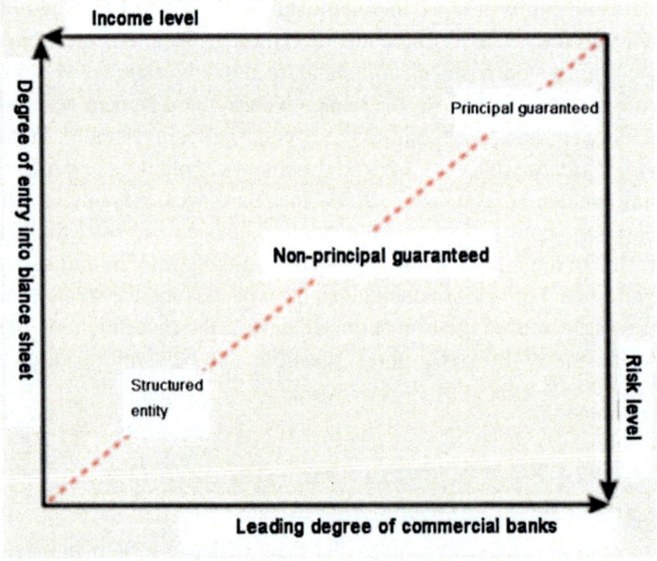

Fig. 1 Bank wealth management classification and main features. *Source* Author's drawing

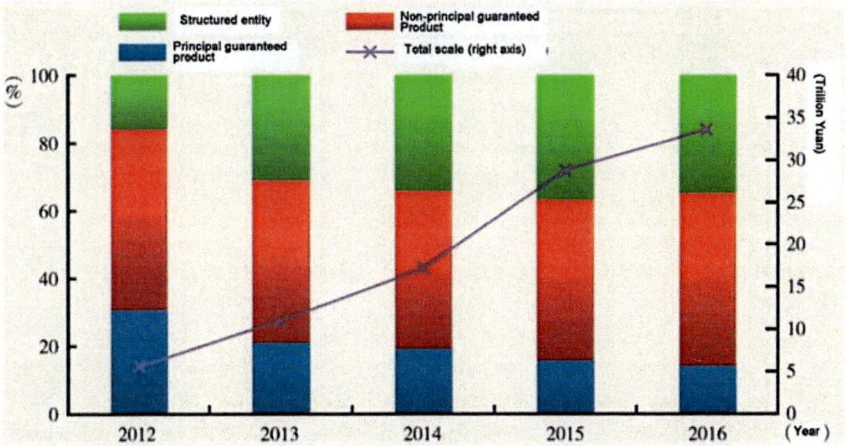

Fig. 2 Aggregate scales of bank wealth management market and proportion by types

1.1 Calculation of Fund Flow: Structured Entities

In order to thoroughly analyze the flow of funds in bank wealth management, we used the annual report data of 31 listed banks as the benchmark and combined sources that were disclosed by China Debt such as the bank' annual reports on wealth management and the data from Wealth Management Research Center. The above and the following sources of chart data will not be explained individually. We also included measurement standards for relevant data here once and for all for conveniences.

- Data length selection is from 2012 to 2016, those without published 2016 annual report will be measured at the periodically released data by April 15, 2017.
- For missing data supplements, we used the full data performance average as a benchmark or interpolation methods, such as utilizing the average of complete non-principal-guaranteed products or their balances to calculate missing data.
- The classification data is estimated based on the average of the aggregated data, for instance, if the total amount of trust plan and the asset management plan were included in the annual report, half of the total will be listed in the trust plan and asset management plan respectively.
- Account receivables are measured based on the data published in the annual report. Those unpublished or with incomplete information will all be accounted as accounts receivable.
- Unmeasurable or unpublished data are all recorded as zero.

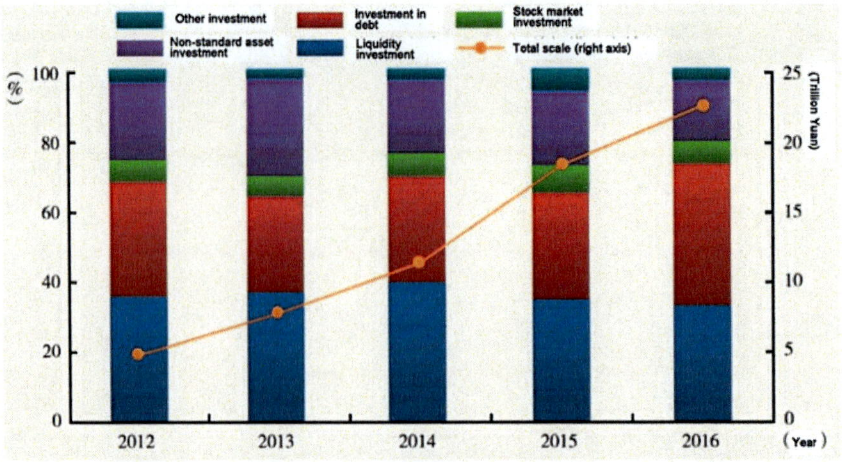

Fig. 3 Funds investment targets of capital-protected and non-principal guaranteed wealth management

First, we estimate the capital flow for principal-protected and non-principal-guaranteed products. Based on the annual report data released by China Debt (see Appendix 1), cash and bank deposits and money market instruments are classified as liquidity management investment vehicles (liquid assets), bond investments as bond market investments, and equity investment as stock market investment. The non-standardized debt investment is classified as non-standard asset investment, and the remaining public funds, financial derivatives, industrial investment funds, newly added investable assets, wealth management direct financing tools, and QDII (qualified domestic institutional investor) management and alternatives assets are classified as other investment items. According to statistics, as of the end of 2016, the total amount of principal-protected and non-principal-guaranteed wealth management of the 31 listed banks was 22.02 trillion yuan, accounting for 83.41% of the total 26.4 trillion yuan in the bank's wealth management market. Therefore, the data analysis of 31 listed banks is quite representative. From the overall data performances, liquidity assets accounted for about 36% in average, bond market investment was about 32%, the stock market investment about 7%, non-standard assets investment about 22%, and other assets investment was less than 5%. In terms of time order of the data, the proportion of investment in liquid assets and non-standard assets rose first and then decreased, while the bond market investment fell first and then rose, a peak of 40.42% occurred in 2016 which coincided with timing of the leveraged outsourced investment and default in bond market (see Fig. 3). This indicates that the flow of funds for principal-protected and non-principal-guaranteed wealth management is dominated by liquidity tools and bond markets.

Second, we measure the flow of funding for structured entities. The public data from annual reports shows that the structured entity invests in four major entities: interbank wealth management, securities funds, trust plans, and securities asset management. The inter-bank wealth management and bank-trust cooperation are the two long-term investment directions of the structured entity, while the securities asset management is the new growth pole. This is closely related to the "Regulation No. 8" and other regulations that delimit the bank-trust cooperation. At the end of 2016, the size of securities investment in structured entities was 5.26 trillion yuan, accounting for 42.39% of the total structured entities (see Fig. 4a). Further, due to the "penetration principle", the structured entities' accounts in the commercial bank statements include "accounts receivable investment", "reverse purchase investment", "hold-to-match investment", "financial assets that were measured at fair value and included in the current period profit and loss and etc. In view of this, we have summed up "accounts receivable investment" and "reverse purchase investment"

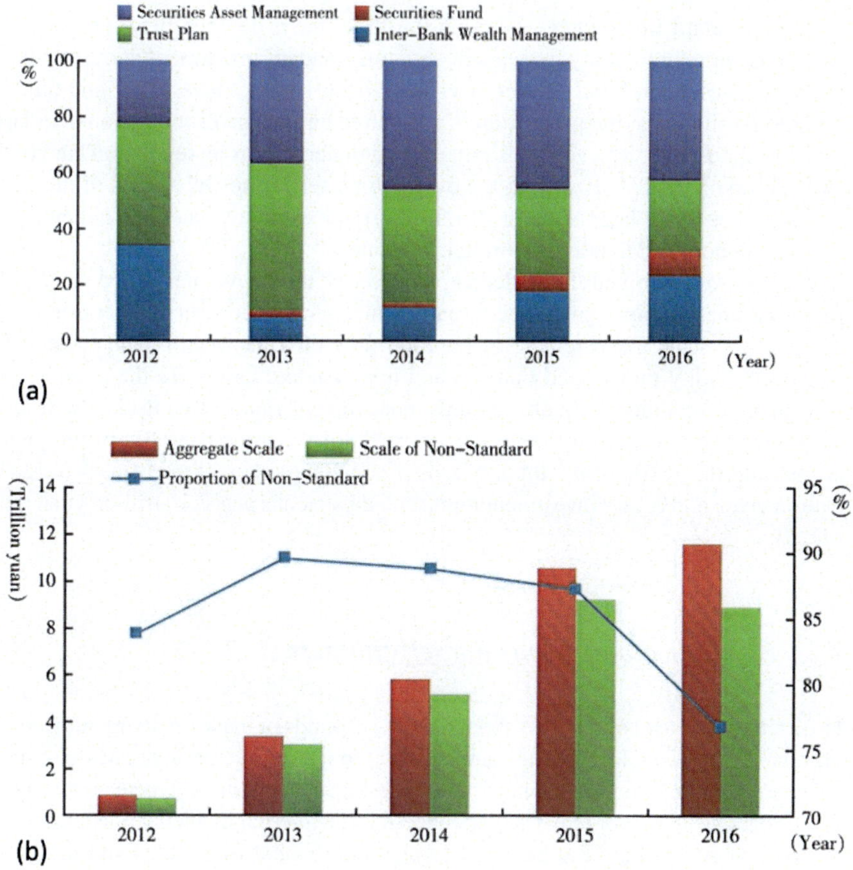

Fig. 4 Investment direction of structured entities

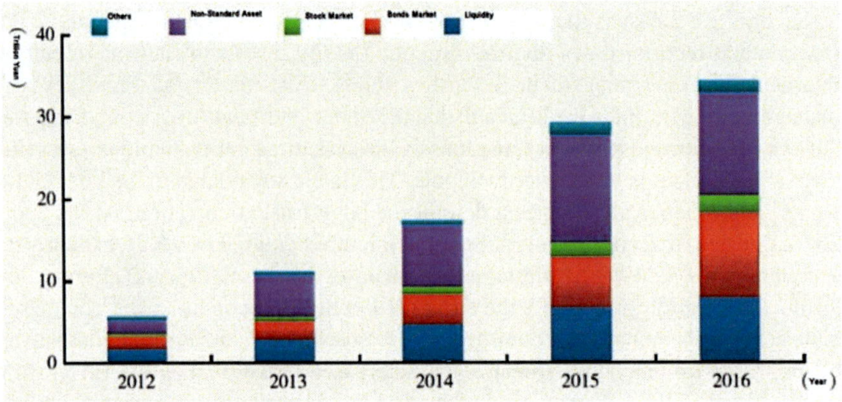

Fig. 5 Flow of funds of bank wealth management

as "non-standard investment", and one-fourth of the difference between the total amount of structured entity investment and non-standard investment corresponds to liquidity investment, bond market investment, stock market investment and others. The results show that the proportion of structured entities investing in non-standard assets is almost over 80%, only a slight exception under "strong regulation" in 2016, with a ratio of 76.72%. However, the overall time series showed a trend of increase at first and decrease later (see Fig. 4b). In short, the essence of a structured entity is to invest in non-standard assets through "channels."

Finally, we combined the scaled capital flow of the above-mentioned principal-protected/non-principal-guaranteed wealth management and structured entities, and obtained the scale measurement of the total flow of bank wealth management. In general, liquidity tools, bond markets and non-standard assets are the three major investment directions for banks' wealth management funds. Taking the 2016 data as an example, the sum of the investment scale of the three is 30.81 trillion yuan, accounting for 91.6% of the total, of which non-standard asset investment is 12.55 trillion yuan, and equity investment represented by stocks was 2.16 trillion yuan (see Fig. 5).

1.2 Key Indicators: Focus on Self-financing

In fact, there are a lot of theories about the flow of funds of bank wealth management. Now we use the sample data in the annual report to measure some key indicators, such as outsourcing investment, capital pool, real estate investment and local government financing. One indicator of particular concern is the internal financing of commercial banks, that is, the liquidity between commercial banks' own funds and the bank wealth management market.

First, at the end of 2016, the liquidity input from commercial banks to non-principal-guaranteed wealth management reached 1.8 trillion yuan. ICBC, Bank of Communications, China Merchants Bank, CITIC Bank and Bank of China disclosed the complete samples of internal financing data. The main tools include funds lending, reverse purchase or bond sales and etc. Taking the ratio of their financing scale to their non-principal-guaranteed wealth management scale as the sample, we use the minimum, average, and maximum percentages as the calculation basis for the three scenarios of low, medium, and high ratios of internal financing, and measure the scale of funds lending between bank's own funds and non-principal-guaranteed wealth management in the bank's wealth management market. The scale is about 1.8 trillion yuan (see Fig. 6) at the end of 2016. Further, the average ratio of internal financing to non-principal-guaranteed wealth management declined from the previous year to 2016 and then rose. The average for 2016 was 8.19% and the maximum was 13.69%. In fact, this type of "blood transfusion" from bank wealth management to non-principal-guaranteed wealth management is equivalent to investing bank's own funds to non-principal-guaranteed wealth management or supplying off-balance sheet credit. Whether or not it is in compliance with regulations, the potential liquidity risks arising therefrom cannot be ignored.

Second, in 2016, the balance of outsourcing investment in commercial banks' wealth management market was approximately 5.61 trillion. In the market, only CITIC Bank announced the outsourcing size of its guaranteed principal/non-principal-guaranteed wealth management and structured entities. Setting the ratio of CITIC bank's outsourcing size to the principal-protected/non-principal-guaranteed wealth management balances and structured entity balances as the standard, 1/2 of the ratio is the low case of scenario and 2 times of it is the high case. Using the aforementioned benchmark as the calculation basis for the medium case scenario (i.e., the medium scenario), the estimated medium-sized outsourcing scale at the end of

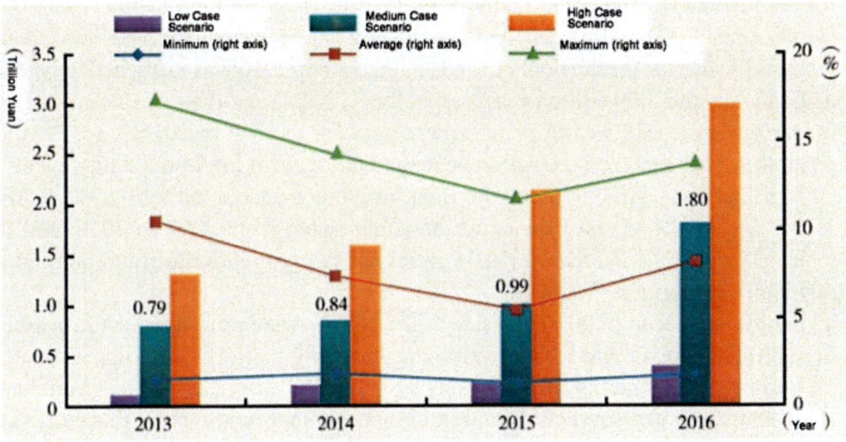

Fig. 6 The lending of the bank's own funds to non-principal-guaranteed wealth management

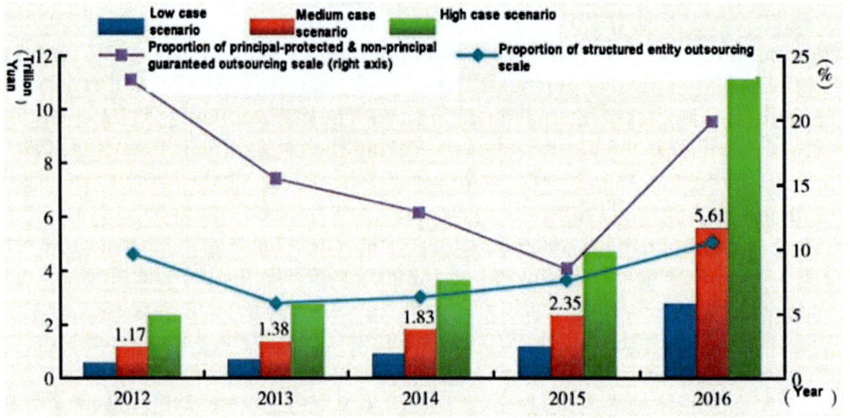

Fig. 7 Estimates of outsourcing investment by bank wealth management

2016 was approximately 5.61 trillion yuan (see Fig. 7). In general, the proportion of outsourcing scale of principal-protected/non-principal-guaranteed wealth management is significantly higher than the proportion of outsourcing scale of structured entities except for 2015 when the two were basically the same; the former is almost twice as large as the latter in other years. The main reason for this phenomenon is that the structured entity itself is a kind of "outsourcing".

Third, the operating balance of capital pool of principal-protected/non-principal-guaranteed wealth management business at the end of 2016 was around 3 trillion yuan. Among the 31 listed banks, only Bank of Ningbo announced the balance of its capital pool. Setting the ratio of this balance to its principal-protected/non-principal-guaranteed wealth management scale as the standard, and 5, 10, and 20 times of the value as low, medium, and high scenarios, respectively, the calculated time series for the medium-sized capital pools from 2013 to 2016 are 0.68 trillion yuan, 0.56 trillion yuan, 3.27 trillion yuan, and 2.55 trillion yuan respectively. The low-end and high-end scenarios for the pool of funds at the end of 2016 was estimated to be 1.27 trillion yuan and 5.09 trillion yuan respectively, indicating that the minimum limit for the scale of bank wealth management pools at the end of 2016 is 1.27 trillion yuan, the upper limit is 5.09 trillion yuan, and the scale of high-probability events is 2.55 trillion yuan. Among them, the Bank of Ningbo accounted for 0.89%, 0.50%, 1.79% and 1.16% of the balance of the capital pool from 2013 to 2016, and the main reason for the decrease in 2016 ratio was the prohibition of fund pooling by regulatory authorities.

Fourth, at the end of 2016, the size of the bank's wealth management investment in real estate market and local government financing platform were approximately 1.66 trillion yuan and 0.97 trillion yuan respectively. At present, China Merchants Bank announces the sources of its wealth management funds for its real estate and local government financing platforms. The original text of its real estate investment described "the company's balance of generalized domestic real estate risk business is

33,162,100 yuan (including real and contingent loans, bonds financing, self-operated and wealth management investment of non-standard products"). In view of this, we use a quarter of the 331.621 billion yuan as the scale of real estate investment for wealth management of non-standard business, setting its ratio to the total scale of non-principal-guaranteed and principal-protected products as the base and taking $1\times$, $2\times$, and $3\times$ of the base for measurement caliber, in medium case scenario the estimated size of real estate investment for bank wealth management fund from 2014 to 2016 was 1.93 trillion yuan, 1.66 trillion yuan, and 1.66 trillion yuan respectively. At the end of 2016, the scale of bank wealth management investment in real estate fluctuated between 0.83 and 2.49 trillion yuan. The original text of annual report on the wealth management investing in local government financing platforms was "the balance of generalized risk business of local government financing platform business is 358.694 billion yuan (including real and contingent credit, bond investment, self-operated and wealth management investment of non-standard products, etc.) Similarly, it can be calculated that the proportion of wealth management funds invested in local government financing platforms from 2014 to 2016 is 6.57%, 3.54%, and 2.21%, respectively. Taking the aforementioned proportions as the base and setting $1\times$, $2\times$, and $3\times$ of the base for low, medium and high scenario, respectively, in medium scenario, the estimated time series scales of bank wealth management investment in local government financing platform from 2014 to 2016 was 1.49 trillion yuan, 1.29 trillion yuan, and 0.97 trillion yuan, respectively. In 2016, the lower and upper limit of bank wealth management investment in local government financing was 0.49 trillion yuan and 1.46 trillion yuan respectively.

Fifth, how does the statistics of non-standard investment of bank wealth management come from? In the 31 commercial banks, China Merchants Bank and Harbin Bank announced the scale of non-standard investments since 2013, and calculated their ratio of non-principal-guaranteed/principal-protected wealth management scales and compared with the proportions of non-standard investment announced by China Central Depository & Clearing Co., Ltd (CCDC). A distinct feature is that the calculated ratio of non-standard investment of Harbin Bank and China Merchants Bank is smaller than the one announced by CCDC, and the gap between the two in 2015 and 2016 has increased significantly (see Fig. 8). There are at least three reasons: first, the annual report data is distorted, that is, the non-standard investment announced by the two banks is smaller than the actual investment scale, which is quite unlikely; second, the ratio of non-standard investment in state-owned banks is significant, and China Merchants Bank is a joint-stock bank, Harbin Bank is a municipal commercial bank, and the overall size of rural commercial banks is not large enough, so one explanation is that the proportion of non-standard investment in state-owned banks accounted for too high; Third, the other 29 banks' non-standard investment is in excessive scale, of course, in terms of data performance, this is a fact, otherwise it is impossible to have these two individual ratio is less than the overall situation of the industry.

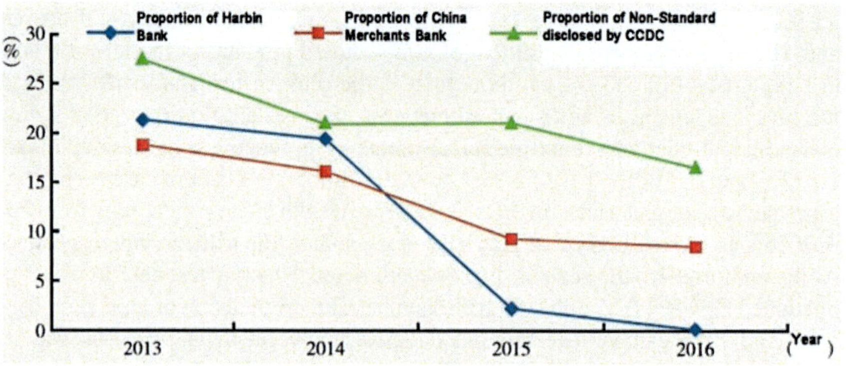

Fig. 8 The proportion of non-standard bank wealth management data

Sixth, the main business of wealth management investment in the stock market is beneficiary right of margin trading and short selling, secondary market allocation and stock pledge financing business, etc. In 2015, China Merchants Bank's annual report data showed that the balance of the wealth management fund investment in margin trading and short selling beneficiary rights business was 27.57 billion yuan, a decrease of 39.007 billion yuan from the end of 2014; the scale of investment in the secondary market stock financing business of wealth management funds was approximately 300 billion yuan; The scale of investment in stock pledge financing business was 24.442 billion yuan. No other banks have published the scale data of the investment in stock market for wealth management funds in public channels.

2 Capital Flow Mechanism: Innovation in Evolution

For bank wealth management funds investment in relevant market, there are nothing more than direct and indirect investment. Indirect investment can be divided into two forms: structured notes and structured entity. Take the stock market investment as an example, direct investment includes new share subscription products or secondary market investment products and etc., and indirect investment includes structured products linked to stock indices, bank-trust, bank-private, bank-capital cooperation or FOF, MOM, etc. Typical cases include, for example, umbrella trusts with market financing allocation as the main function. Direct investment and structured notes are the main manifestations of the bank's wealth management market business before 2012 and even 2008, but after 2013 it changed to the structured entity. The evolution of structured entities follows the path of inter-bank wealth management, bank-insurance cooperation, and bank-security cooperation. The internal reasons for this change are related to the regulatory perspective. Just like the development of inter-bank wealth management is due to the regulations of the China Banking Regulatory Commission that commercial banks must not use wealth management funds to purchase the bank's credit assets, the development of bank-trust cooperation is due to the CBRC regulation that commercial banks cannot implement loan reversal services. As for the origin of bank-security cooperation, it is the need for bank-trust cooperation to enter the balance sheet and accrue risks according to regulations. Of course, circumventing industrial policy regulation is also one of the reasons for changes in wealth management structure. These policies, such as restricting loans to industries with high energy consumption, high pollution and overcapacity were implemented in 2008, and a new round of control of real estate control and local financing platforms in 2010. In the following, we mainly introduce the transaction structure model of interbank wealth management, bank-trust cooperation and bank-security channel business.

2.1 *Interbank Wealth Management Models: Investment in Non-standard Assets*[1]

From the transaction model, the outright sell transaction mode, outright repo transaction mode, and pledged repo transaction mode are the three common modes of inter-bank wealth management. Given that there is no clear legal basis for the pledge of the trust beneficial right, with no legal effect there may be a legal flaw in the pledged repurchase trading model for non-standard asset transactions. Therefore, the outright sell transaction mode and the outright repo transaction mode are the two main types of interbank wealth management in the market. Outright sell transaction is a business activity in which A Bank's wealth management ("Transferor") transfers the non-standard assets they invest into B Bank's wealth management ("Transferees") and B bank pays the corresponding transfer price. Through outright sell transaction, all rights related to the non-standard assets are transferred from the transferor to the transferee; the risks that may occur in the future to the non-standard assets also transfer to the transferee at the same time.

The outright repurchase transaction is different. It means when A-bank's wealth management ("repurchaser") sell their non-standard assets to B-bank's wealth management ("reverse repurchaser") and at the same time the reverse repurchaser pays the down-payment of the settlement amount to the repurchase on the first settlement date (transfer date), both parties agree that the repurchaser will buy back the non-standard assets from reverse repurchasers at the agreed-upon price(due date settlement amount) at a certain time in the future (the due settlement date). An outright repurchase transaction is a transaction that includes two settlements. After the initial transaction, all rights related to the non-standard assets are transferred from the repurchaser to the reverse repurchaser. However, according to the contract, the repurchaser will buy back the non-standard assets from the reverse repurchaser at the agreed price on the due date. And since both parties to the transaction are bank

[1] Jieyi Li, Editor-in-Chief, "Understanding and Case Analysis of Bank Non-standard Asset Transactions", CITIC Publishing House, 2015.

wealth management products and have bank credits, the outright repurchase transaction model reduces the risks borne by the reverse repurchasers in non-standard assets to a certain extent, which facilitates the bank's internal approval process. The internal approval time was shortened, which in turn improved the liquidity of non-standard assets of bank wealth management.

In the following, we analyze the transaction structure of non-standard assets of interbank wealth management by taking notes assets, trust loan assets, equity financing with repurchase terms (outright sell transactions), equity financing with repurchase terms (outright repurchase transactions) and direct investment as examples. First, the transaction structure of notes assets, the transaction process is as follows (see Fig. 9): A bank initiates the wealth management product A as the product manager and raises funds to invest in the commercial draft; When A bank intends to sell the wealth management product A, the notes asset package will be registered on CCDC's platform for non-standard assets of bank wealth management; Bank B sets up wealth management product B, and raises funds to purchase the notes asset package registered by Bank A on the exchange platform; The initial transferor, that is, Bank A conducts inspections, custody, collection and collecting funds, and finally repays the principal and income to Product B investors based on the cash flows generated by the notes asset package.

Second, the transaction flow of trust loan assets (see Fig. 9). C Bank's wealth management transferred the invested trust single fund plan's beneficiary rights B to E Bank's wealth management through outright sell. E Bank's wealth management products paid C. Bank's f products at the transfer price. At the same time, E Bank entrusted C Bank (initial transferor, i.e. the administrator of its initiated non-standard asset) to carry out subsequent management of this project.

Third, the equity financing with repurchase terms (outright sell transactions) (see Fig. 9). E bank wealth management transfers its beneficial rights of single-fund trust plan to G bank's wealth management. G Bank's wealth management products pay the transfer price to E Bank's wealth management products. At the same time, G Bank entrusted E Bank (the initial transferor, i.e. the administrator of its initiated non-standard asset) to manage the project. Different from outright sell transactions, the outright repo transaction agrees at the time of transaction that E bank wealth management products will repurchase from G bank the said trust beneficiary rights at an agreed upon price on a certain date in the future. At the time of maturity, E Bank's wealth management products will pay the contract price for G Bank's wealth management products and the trust beneficiary rights will be returned to E Bank's wealth management products.

Finally, the case of direct investment in non-standard assets (see Fig. 9). Bank B's wealth management products transfer their claims on company A to C Bank's wealth management product manager through outright sell, and C Bank's wealth management product manager pay the transfer price to B bank. When the claim expires, Company A pays the investment principal and income to C Bank's wealth management product manager.

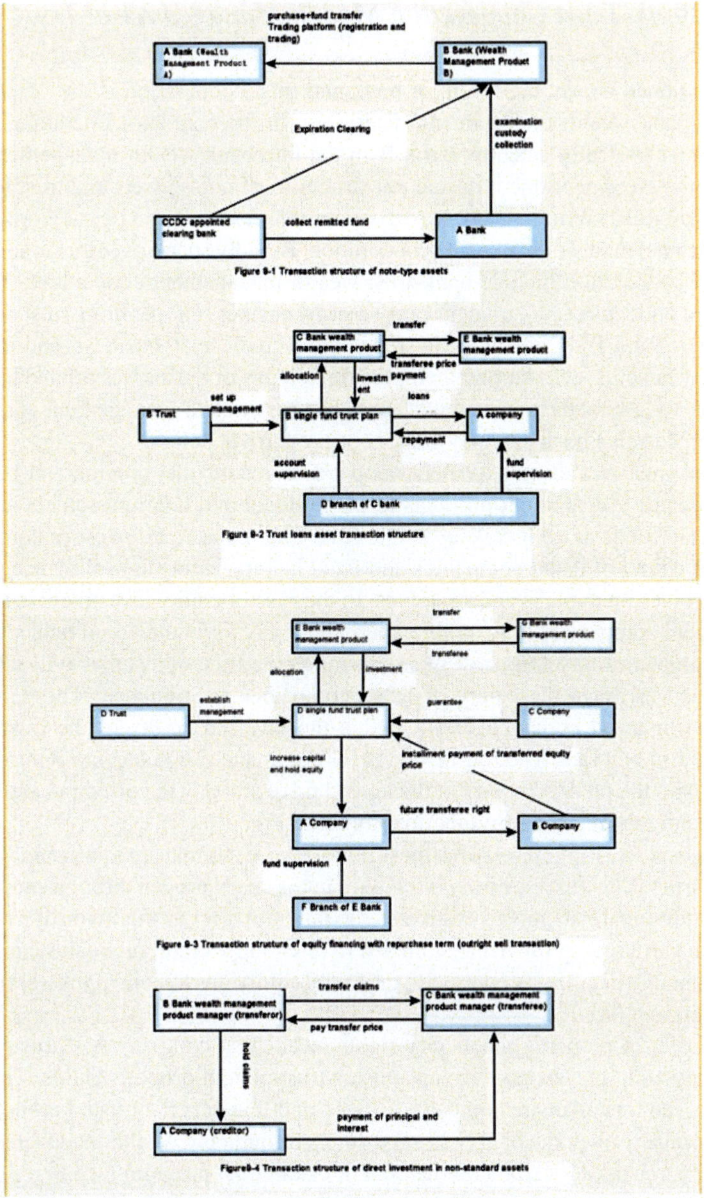

Fig. 9 Schematic diagram of non-standard investment trading structure of inter-bank wealth management. *Source* Author's drawing

2.2 Bank-Trust Cooperation Model: Managed Asset Trust

As mentioned above, the origin of bank and trust cooperation is the "supervision" of interbank wealth management. Therefore, in the course of operation, the trust companies basically acted as Bank B in the interbank wealth management, which means the aforementioned transaction structures of notes assets and trust loan asset can all established in the bank-trust cooperation model. It can be categorized as the trust channel model of bank-trust cooperation. Broadly speaking, other models of this kind of cooperation include bank-trust wealth management cooperation, trust plan proxy of collective fund, trust property escrow business cooperation, trust projects of collective fund Trust guarantee business, bank credit relay business, and transfer of property benefits, etc. Among them, the three types of businesses related to the flow of bank wealth management funds are bank-trust wealth management cooperation, bank credit relay business, and transfer of property benefits.

Bank-trust wealth management cooperation means that commercial banks will issue wealth management products to institutional and retail customers and set up the raised funds as collective or single fund trust plans, and invest in equity assets such as equity of listed companies and fixed income assets in accordance with pre-agreed investment plans and strategies. In the case of equity investment in the above municipal companies, for example, the first step is for commercial banks to entrust trust companies to set up trust plans, and then the trust companies will set up trust plans and invest in the equity of listed companies as stipulated. The third step is that the financed companies will pledge the invested equity to the trust plan on certain discount rate. The fourth step is for the financed company or a third party to repurchase the pledged equity at the agreed price and pay the principal and return to the wealth management product investors (see Fig. 10).

The bank-trust credit relay business refers to projects that are jointly recognized by both parties. The trust company intervenes in the target project through equity investment in prophase stage and cultivates the target project to the maturity recognized by both parties, then the bank promised to pitch in by credit or wealth management funds, mainly in order to repurchase the initial equity investment of the trust company at a premium (see Fig. 10).

Transfer of property beneficiary rights means that company A entrusts the trust company with its own assets to establish a trust plan of property rights. The beneficiary of the trust plan are company A itself, and transfers the trusted property to the trust company, then the bank will raise funds through the wealth management products to purchase A's claims on the benefit of the trust program (see Fig. 10). By its very nature, the model is still that company A obtains loan financing (wealth management fund) from banks, only with the addition of property, company A doubles as a financing company and a "bridge" company in the similar form of pledge financing. Among the three types of business, bank-trust wealth management cooperation, bank credit relay business and transfer of property benefits, the last one is worthy of most attention because of the essence of the business is basically the implementation of

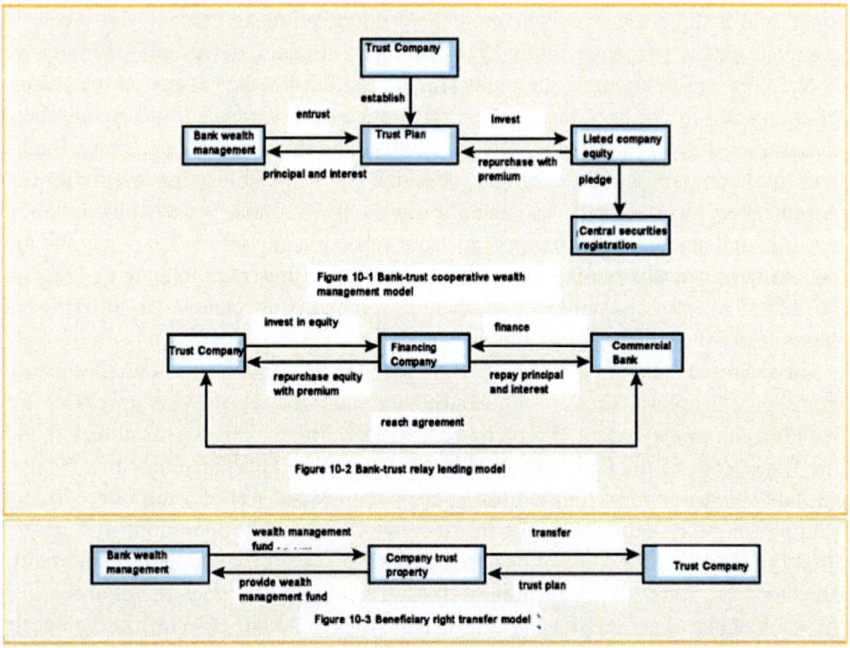

Fig. 10 Three types of business models for bank-trust cooperation. *Source* author's drawing

credit in the name of the managing property trusts, and causes the increase of the amount of property trust in decrease in the capita accrual in trust industry.

2.3 Bank-Security Channel Business: Substituting Bank-Trust Cooperation

Bank-security cooperation is an alternative to bank-trust cooperation. The reason is that in July 2011, the CBRC requested that trust loans, transferred credit assets and notes assets issued by the bank wealth management products through the channel of trust company to be included in the balance sheet at the end of 2011 as risk assets and accrue provisions. In order to have credit assets outside balance sheet, commercial banks have added the security company links to the original bank-trust cooperation chain. In the following, we take trust beneficiary rights transfer as an example to illustrate this model. Assume that bank A's corporate customers apply for a loan from bank A, for this purpose, bank A uses the trust beneficiary right as a platform to join trust company, bank B, and securities company and set up a financing channel between the funder and the financing party. Bank A contracts with bank B to conducts inter-bank wealth management. Bank B and securities companies enter into a directional asset management cooperation agreement. The securities company entrusts the trust company to establish a single fund trust plan. Finally, trust companies and financing companies sign a contract for the claims on the incomes of equity and the right of buy-back. The essence of this transaction structure lies in the process of loan placement between Bank A and the financing company, Bank B, securities company and trust company are added in as three links. In view of this, Bank A pretended investing but was actually issuing loans, Bank B pretended managing wealth but it actually was channeling, securities company pretended managing asset but actually was channeling as well, trust company pretended managing trust plan but actually is also channeling, and financing company ultimately was utilizing bank funds under the cover of trust funds (Fig. 11).

In addition to the trust beneficiary right transfer transaction structure, the entrusted loans and the notes asset transaction structure under the original framework of inter-bank wealth management and bank-trust cooperation can also be established under the framework of the cooperation between bank and securities company. Next, we explain the structure of transactions such as money transfer of letter of credit, bond trading, one-day deposits, and bank-security-insurance cooperation. The letter of credit money transfer channel business under bank-security cooperation basically is an inter-bank letter of credit money transfer business that does not squeeze quota for on-balance-sheet credits and thus expand deposits scale, and utilize the broker's directional channels of asset management. The ultimate purpose of this is to break through the restrictions on the scale of loans and expand the size of out-of-balance-sheet assets. The main process is as follows: first step, bank A entrusts the securities company to establish a directional asset management plan with its wealth management funds; second step, the securities company invests the entrusted assets in bank B's right of benefit of account receivables under the letter of credit as the manager of the directional asset management plan; third step: after the letter of credit expires, the issuing bank C will honor the letter of credit, and the funds due will be collected by bank B and will be returned to the directional plan, and then the directional plan will pass it to the entrusting bank, where the entrusting bank usually requires the

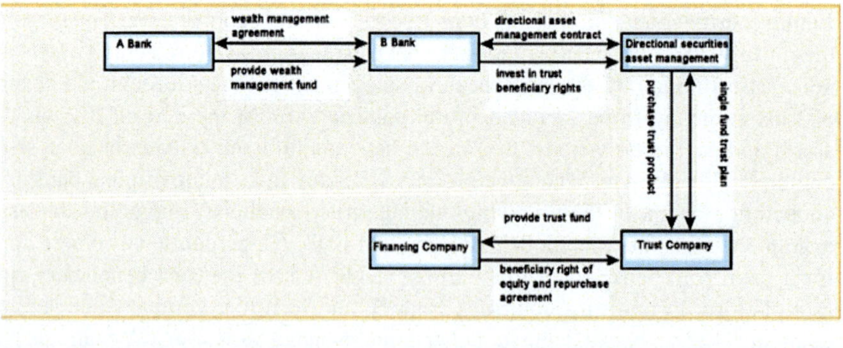

Fig. 11 Transaction structure of trust beneficial rights transfer through bank-securities cooperation. *Source* Author's drawing

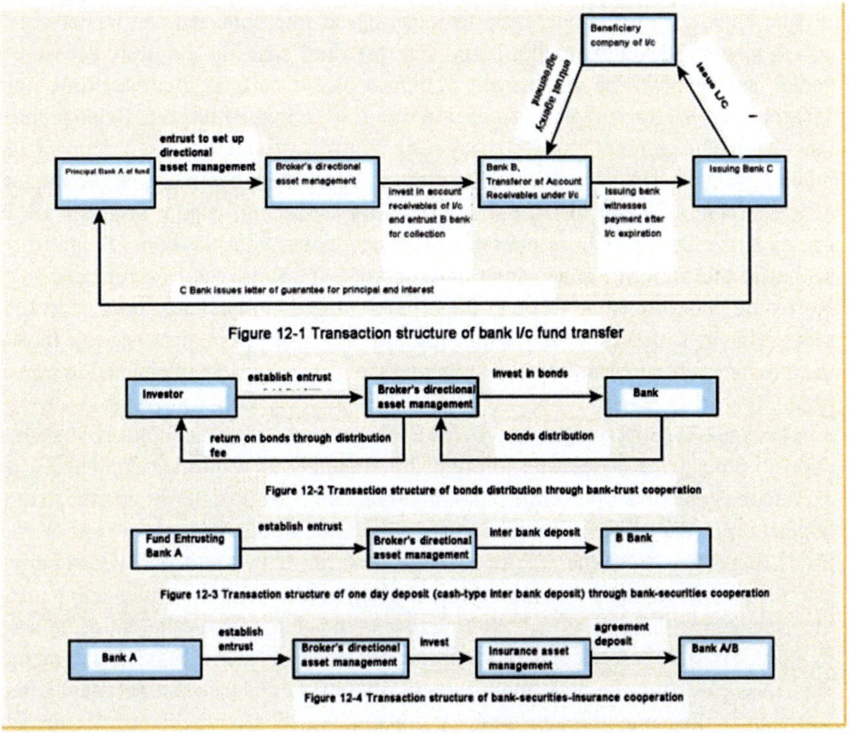

Fig. 12 Types of major transaction structures for the bank-securities cooperation. *Source* Author drawing

issuing bank to provide the bottom line guarantee through letter of guarantee or a prospective transfer of the plan's income rights (see Fig. 12).

The essence of bond trading business under the bank-security cooperation lies in the fact that securities companies participate in the distribution of bank bonds through the issuance of orientated plans to provide customers with higher fixed-income products and pledged financing services. The main advantages of this business are: First, it can obtain higher benefits than buying bonds directly from banks; second, it can break the 10% constraint; third, customers can engage in repurchase finance through the purchased bonds as pledges. The operation process is that the investor first entrusts the securities company to establish a oriented asset management plan, and then the securities company, as the manager of the plan, invests the entrusted assets in the bonds distributed by the bank (see Fig. 12).

The bank-security cooperation for cash-based interbank deposit business is to attract savings through market-based interest rate, ease the liquidity pressure of banks, and achieve the assessment of interbank deposits at a certain time point. The transaction structure is completed in three steps: in the first step, Bank A entrust the wealth management funds to the security company to establish a directional asset management plan; and in the second step, the securities company, as the manager of the directional asset management plan, invests the entrusted assets in bank B's interbank certificates whose interest rate is negotiated with the bank; the third step is that at the maturity of the interbank deposit, the funds will be returned to the entrusting bank's account through the broker's oriented plan (see Fig. 12). In short, this is a business that Bank B will take to achieve the time point deposit scale through the agreement of interbank interest rate and the broker's oriented channel to transfer funds.

The bank-security-insurance cooperation business aims to convert inter-bank deposits into general deposits through the channels of securities companies, and expand the general deposit scale of commercial banks while determining the loan-to-deposit ratio. There are four steps in the cooperation of the bank-security-insurance: First, Bank A entrust the wealth management funds to the security company to establish a directional asset management plan; second, the securities company, as the manager of the directional asset management plan, invests the entrusted assets in the assets management plan of the insurance company; third, Bank B's agreement deposit is placed in the asset management plan of the insurance asset management company in the name of the insurance company; fourth, after the deposit expires, the funds are returned to bank A account through the insurance asset management plan and the oriented asset management plan of security company (See Fig. 12).

3 Future Outlook: Who Is the Next?

In order to measure and analyze the scale and mechanism of the flow of bank wealth management product funds, we will examine principal-protected, non-principal-guaranteed wealth management and structural entities under a unified framework. In general, the fund from principal-protected, non-principal-guaranteed wealth management mainly flow to liquid assets and bond assets, complemented with products such as non-standard asset investment. The capital flows of structured entities are dominated by non-standard asset investments. In the calculation of key indicators, we need to focus on the two data of self-financing scale and commissioned investment scale, because the two correspond to liquidity risk and counterparty risk respectively.

Direct investment and indirect investment are the two main investment vehicles for wealth management funds. Structured notes and structured entities are two ways of indirect investment. Structured notes have been decreasing in the market. Structured entities are mainly based on interbank cooperation and their funds are mostly invested in non-standard assets such as accounts receivables. On the issue of stock market investment, direct investment methods include new stock subscriptions and secondary market investments, and indirect investments include stocks or structured notes linked to stock indices, and pertaining cooperative businesses of banks and non-banking financial institutions, such as Shushing Bank's cooperation with security or fund companies, cooperation of commercial banks and private equity funds, and of commercial bank and asset management companies. In the annual report of commercial banks, there is little disclosure of information on stock markets investment of wealth management funds. In practice, structured entities invest more in the stock market, and the "penetrated" structured entities' investment mostly is presented in non-standard assets such as "accounts receivable", which indicates that from the perspective of regulatory rules, in order to achieve the "penetration supervision," at least the commercial banks should be required to provide "penetrated disclosure" or "penetrated declaration."

In fact, in the aforementioned analysis of the flow of wealth management funds, we have overlooked the analysis of an important investment channel—global asset allocation or overseas investment of wealth management funds and its mechanism. The major breakthrough in realizing this function is private banking, the "jewel" on the crown of wealth management. Since Bank of China began its private banking business in 2007, the organizational structure, business model, profit model, product system, value-added service, risk control system, IT system and human resources of the private banking business have become increasingly mature and have Chinese characteristics. The scale of private bank asset management also increased from 292.6 billion yuan in 2008 to 8.35 trillion yuan in 2016 (see Table 1). Further, if we analyze the positioning of the top five commercial banks in their asset management scales for their private banking business, we can see that the family business governance services and global asset allocation are the two major positioning of each banks' private banking services, and one representative mechanism of global asset allocation is the "private sharing" business of China Construction Bank's private banking section, which is through the business model of "domestic insurance and overseas loans" of dual-legal person. Taking Hong Kong as an example, the main ways in which mainland residents can utilize the wealth management services to allocate funds in Hong Kong are high-end insurance, Shanghai-Hong Kong stock connect, Shanghai-Hong Kong Bond Connect, Shanghai-Hong Kong fund Connect, investment banking, and private banking. According to another estimate, from 2011 to 2016, China's average outflow of funds through private banking was approximately US$34 billion each year.

Table 1 Scale of Private Bank Asset Management and Incomplete Institutional Data Unit: 100 million yuan

Year	Total asset management	Merchants Bank	Industrial and Commercial Bank	Construction Bank of China	Bank of China	Bank of Agriculture
2008	2926	1299	749	878	3000	3000
2009	8186	1814	2550	1308	1500	3000
2010	10952	2703	3543	17931	1667	3000
2011	18818	3699	4345	2241	3000	3400
2012	26341	4342	4732	2918	4500	3960
2013	35985	5714	5413	3968	5700	5050
2014	46621	7526	7357	4687	7200	6400
2015	63200	12500	10600	6231	8100	8077
2016	83515	16595	12100	7863	10000	8184

Source Annual report data of commercial banks in the table

Adhering to the basic guiding ideology of preventing financial risks, "Central bank, securities, insurance and bank commissions, ministry of finance, finance council and administration of foreign exchange" and other relevant departments have successively issued guiding principles or regulatory rules relating to asset management, such as "Guiding Opinions on Regulating the Asset Management Business of Financial Institutions" and the CBRC's supervision on "three arbitrages". At the micro level, the supervisory management also regulates related businesses in the bank's wealth management market through industry associations or quasi-government organizations. For example, on May 15, 2017, China Wealth Management disclosed "Notice on Further Regulating the Bank's Financial Products through Penetration Registration." (Wealth Management Center [2017] No. 14) and requested further standardization of the penetration registration of bank wealth management products. For the cases where bank wealth management funds purchase various kinds of asset management plans and invest through commissioned investment agreements with other financial institutions, the underlying foundation assets or liabilities must be registered through the wealth management registration system, i.e., the "penetration registrations" that is compatible with "penetration supervision", "penetration disclosure" and "penetration declaration". For another example, the "private sharing" overseas asset allocation business of China Construction Bank Private Bank has also received the attention of the SAFE.

Whether it is the development trend of the international market, or the development prospects of the domestic market, or even comparative analysis of individual cases, they all prove one point: The development of domestic asset management business is a general trend and has huge potentials. As of the end of 2015, the assets of ICBC and JP Morgan Chase were US$3.42 trillion and US$2.35 trillion respectively, the former being 1.45 times that of the latter, and the AUM being US$0.57 trillion and 1.72 trillion US dollars respectively, the former accounted for only 33.13% of the latter which is less than ¼. The gap is obvious. Further, if we analyze the AUM scale of the unit assets, we can see that the size of the AUM unit assets of JPMorgan Chase is 0.73, while the AUM scale of ICBC's unit assets is only 0.17. From the perspective of time series data, the average unit asset size of AUM for JPMorgan Chase from 2006 to 2015 was 0.65, while the corresponding index of ICBC was only 0.18. In particular, if only the data performance for the two years of 2014 and 2015 is taken into account, the corresponding index value of ICBC is only 0.14. In short, ICBC's asset size is 1.45 times the size of JPMorgan Chase's assets, while JPMorgan Chase's AUM unit asset size is nearly five times of ICBC. The difference in asset management between the two is quite apparent (see Fig. 13).

Looking into the future, there is a huge potential for the development of domestic asset management businesses represented by bank wealth management. The new policy "The Measures for the Supervision and Administration of Wealth Management Services of Commercial Banks" (opinions solicited twice and reported to be launched soon) will boost and guide it. In general, the supervisory management aims

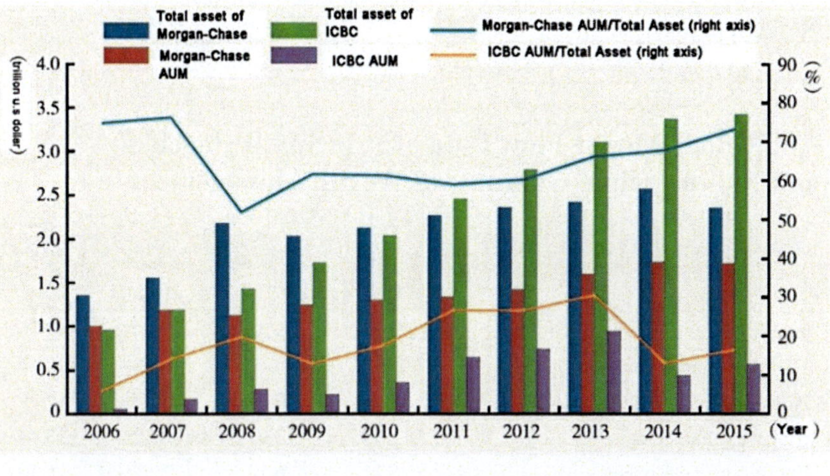

Fig. 13 Comparative Analysis of Asset Size and AUM of ICBC and JP Morgan Chase. *Source* Annual reports of respective banks, organized by the authors. *Note* (1) The statistics of ICBC shows that from 2008 to 2013, the asset management scale is based on its consigned sales. In 2014 and 2015, it is based on the sum of the balance of its wealth management products and the private bank AUM. (2) Based on the exchange rate of the US dollar against the RMB at the end of the year

to guide the bank's wealth management business to the net worth asset management while breaks up the "rigid redemption" situation, so as to better serve the real economy while undertaking the asset management transformation. Since the bank's wealth management business started in 2005, it has undergone two rounds of "strong supervision and regulation" around the 2008 global financial crisis and "preventing financial risks" in 2017. The result of the first round of "strong regulation" was the disappearance of "structured products/notes", because the stock market and commodity market's retracement after the global financial crisis triggered zero or negative returns on a large number of equity-linked and commodity-linked structured products, even leading to large amount of debt beard by some investors who bought "Accumulator" products. Current round of "strong supervision" may cause the disappearance of "structured entities or nested businesses" since this type of business results in idling wealth management funds within the financial system, reducing the efficiency of fund use, raising price of funds and accumulating potential financial risks. Looking at the wealth management innovations from 2005 to the present, other than the structured products/notes that represents asset management capabilities, one of the central objectives of business cooperation or nested business between bank-trust, bank-securities, bank-funds, bank-securities-insurance, and other institutions is to avoid the scale limit of commercial banks credit, i.e. the 12.55 trillion yuan of non-standard investment estimated in the article. Imagine if we can add 12.55 trillion yuan of credit a reasonable extent, can we substantially solve the problem? If the "structured entity or nested business" disappeared under "strong supervision" in this round, what kind of new faces will they be wearing or what kind of new business model will replace them? And in what way will the "new faces" or "new business" be "disappeared"?

Appendix 1 Money Flow Data of Principal-Protected and Non-principal Guaranteed Wealth Management

Time	2013 (%)	2014 (%)	2015 (%)	2016 (%)
Bonds	27.09	29.78	29.94%	43.76
Cash and band deposit	25.62	26.56	22.38%	16.62
Non-standard bond-type assets	27.49	20.91	21.05%	17.49
Monetary market tools	11.55	13.97	13.12%	13.14
Equity-type investment	6.14	6.24	7.84%	6.16
Public fund	–	1.27	–	–
Financial derivatives	1.12	0.50	–	–
Wealth management direct financing tool	0.16	0.25	–	–
Proxy overseas wealth management QDII	0.44	0.30	–	–

(continued)

(continued)

Time	2013 (%)	2014 (%)	2015 (%)	2016 (%)
Alternative assets	0.37	0.02	–	–
Others	0.02	0.02	5.67%	2.83

Note The "other" is non-CCDC published data. In order to ensure that the sum of all data in the year is 100%, the author adds this
Source of data "Report on China's banking wealth management products" published by CCDC

Appendix 2 Overview of Bank Wealth Management Market Development (2004–2017)

See (Fig. 14).

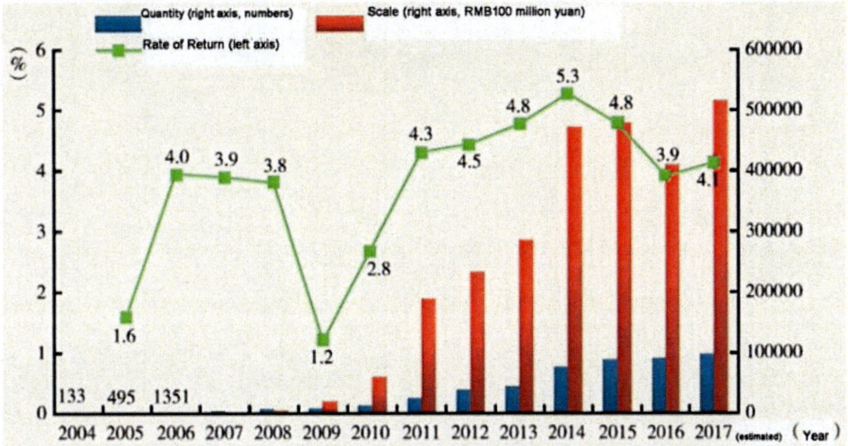

Fig. 14 Issuance quantity, fundraising scale and yield performance of banks wealth management market. *Source* National Institute of Finance and Development Laboratory Wealth Management Research Center, the same below, no longer be marked. *Note* The method of 2017 data estimation is to set the monthly average performance of the quantity and scale in 3 months as the benchmark, multiplied by 12 to obtain the annual data, the unit of quantity is number, the unit of scale is 100 million yuan, and the rate of return is the previous 3 months' average performance. The same as below, no longer be marked

Schedule 1 Quantity of bank wealth management issuance (by issuing institutions)

Year	City commercial bank	State-owned commercial bank	Rural cooperative bank	Rural commercial bank	Rural credit cooperative	Listed joint-stock commercial bank	Foreign bank
2004	39	12				81	1
2005	36	127				301	31
2006	149	321		1		734	146
2007	277	838	5	6		1378	469
2008	676	1332	8	45	5	3434	587
2009	702	2354	11	113		3752	326
2010	1165	4252	6	178		4682	1422
2011	3677	8744	25	449		9953	1236
2012	10397	12813	137	1838	33	11432	1363
2013	13489	12139	353	3433	112	12086	1544
2014	25384	20165	716	7664	208	19718	1936
2015	31119	21040	1354	10919	523	20522	1878
2016	34949	17934	1576	14371	702	17879	2216
2017 (est.)	36180	24648	1962	15432	786	15294	2250

Schedule 2 Quantity of bank wealth management issuance (by investment currency)

Year	Australian Dollar	Hong Kong Dollar	Canadian Dollar	US Dollar	Euro	RMB	Japanese Yen	Singapore Dollar	New Zealand Dollar	Pound Sterling
5922004	1	24		86	3	19				
2005	6	68	1	274	17	123				6
2006	21	215		592	36	479			2	6
2007	40	364	4	970	102	1484	2			7
2008	274	242	5	710	203	4661	4			32
2009	204	100	15	512	101	6349		1	1	14
2010	385	420	22	871	210	9766	36	3		65
2011	613	599	25	1091	472	21238	85	1	9	114
2012	571	488	20	926	388	35653	95		21	94
2013	338	324	7	638	119	42107	16		34	32
2014	396	370	7	1065	195	74493	1		49	85
2015	356	287		1081	153	86887			51	50
2016	167	110		1179	6	88829	1			90
2017 (est.)	156	120		990		95616				114

Schedule 3 Quantity of bank wealth management issuance (by structure type)

Year	Fluctuation type	Bearish type	Bullish type	Interval type	Connection type
2004		15	97	21	
2005			455	36	
2006	2	7	1239	98	5
2007			2965	8	
2008	2		5887	58	8
2009	2	12	7142	133	2
2010	4	20	10738	1009	1
2011	7	110	23361	599	5
2012	2	320	37183	405	12
2013	4	458	42655	462	36
2014		653	74700	584	3
2015		529	87424	714	
2016		595	89150	605	
2017 (est.)		522	95478	2430	

Schedule 4 Quantity of bank wealth management issuance (by linked target)

Year	Stock	Fixed income	Exchange rate	Mixed	Interest rate	Alternatives	Commodity	Credit	Asset pool
2004	1	91	4		37				
2005	3	421	39	2	20		9	1	
2006	116	721	91	1	66	4	23	307	22
2007	913	1151	33	7	108	9	59	599	94
2008	393	2357	46	10	139	3	112	2920	151
2009	176	2482	58	5	137	1	56	3128	1254
2010	146	5436	75	1	1096		48	1348	3628
2011	205	13322	251	2	864	1	58	1721	7823
2012	356	24005	691	13	408	2	217	389	12175
2013	426	29169	641	26	330	5	211	282	12525
2014	983	54764	875	38	586	5	390	33	18977
2015	1535	67166	662		591		434	4	18473
2016	1653	69279	323		517		744		17866
2017 (est.)	1410	78102	354	0	390	0	942	0	15798

Schedule 5 Quantity of bank wealth management issuance (by income type)

Year	Principal-protected floating	Interest-guaranteed floating	Interest-guaranteed fixed	Non-principal guaranteed floating
2004	100			33
2005	85	6		404
2006	680	53	333	285
2007	929	5	561	1478
2008	949	75	410	4697
2009	1731	94	728	4744
2010	3665	187	1878	6048
2011	5597	350	2188	16112
2012	9363	612	4201	24080
2013	9601	757	3210	30044
2014	15970	2263	5431	52993
2015	20151	2411	5744	60556
2016	20452	1897	3566	64467
2017 (est.)	22140	1332	2976	70548

Schedule 6 Quantity of bank wealth management issuance (by Cooperation Mode)

Year	Bank-insurance	Bank-trust	Bank-bank	Bank-securities	Bank-fund	Bank-intersected	Bank-asset	Nesting[a]
2004								
2005								
2006		44						
2007		233						
2008		499						
2009	1	2081		3				
2010		500						
2011		391						
2012		453	4	14				
2013	3	1795	2	129	50	1	1	76
2014		792	9	562	19		81	35
2015		949	8	703	26		40	38
2016		362		621			267	45
2017 (est.)		378		720			372	

[a] *Source* Editor-in-chief, Li Jieyi, "Understanding and Case Analysis of Bank Non-standard Asset Transactions", CITIC Publishing House, 2015

Schedule 7 Scale of fund raised by bank wealth management (by distribution entity)

Year	City Commercial Bank	State-Owned Commercial Bank	Rural Cooperative Bank	Rural Commercial Bank	Rural Credit Cooperative	Listed Joint-Stock Commercial Bank	Foreign Bank	Post Office Savings Bank
2004						41.4		
2005		82.8				24.8	48.6	
2006	474.0	23793.6				1320.1	199.1	
2007	320.0	5375.1	300.0	415.0		14864.8	2108.0	
2008	49382.1	100853.2	650.0	3667.5	50.0	278260.7	17220.8	5943.8
2009	50086.0	1310687.5	675.0	10548.0		614531.8	14637.2	5406.8
2010	100249.1	4459995.9	650.0	28856.0		1401700.3	33739.8	18651.1
2011	528462.8	11560963.3	2345.0	97157.7		6645019.4	41266.7	34514.9
2012	1887187.6	13075662.4	24863.0	369136.9	2710.0	7844465.1	100967.3	144237.5
2013	2675790.9	13922878.1	23185.7	892478.9	16285.2	10804196.5	165488.6	238733.7
2014	6757655.8	21016258.3	58654.7	2122138.2	52244.7	16578800.7	258924.1	469963.7
2015	6931761.0	22144244.1	97793.7	2357901.2	23399.0	15604351.8	264574.8	533450.6
2016	7664716.0	16040906.3	87067.6	2441956.3	19528.8	14257980.0	218912.3	299814.2
2017 (est.)	9937394.5	19911795.9	148704.4	3415570.0	31140.0	17686269.8	258638.4	298867.2

Schedule 8 Scale of fund raised by bank wealth management (by linked target)

Year	Stock	Fixed income	Exchange rate	Mixed	Interest rate	Alternatives	Commodity	Credit	Asset pool
2004		41.4							
2005		24.8			131.4				
2006	897.9	1614.7	6268.0	23.7	134.5		2492.1	992.0	13363.0
2007	7386.9	2547.6				70.0	450.3	900.0	12028.0
2008	14833.8	150255.2	849.2	465.4	2880.9		3724.2	247584.3	35435.2
2009	16237.2	571528.5	5296.0	296.6	11219.7	100.0	4152.9	683970.9	713770.6
2010	13965.0	1948468.2	17702.9	20.0	32228.3		10713.5	466912.8	3553831.4
2011	8908.3	6151176.3	54169.0	43.9	138799.7	10.0	28553.1	739715.7	11788353.7
2012	28038.9	11197211.1	115549.1	1170.1	449601.6	210.0	304827.8	70304.2	11282317.2
2013	42383.9	14496136.5	192096.1	13110.0	78301.0	600.0	392387.7	12487.7	13511534.6
2014	288073.2	27636294.0	288810.0	21780.0	220482.7	625.0	548081.2	6899.7	18301414.4
2015	562419.9	32110385.3	121241.4		341689.5		422170.5	650.0	14398920.0
2016	622792.7	28084236.4	158096.7		270401.2		474544.0		11420810.5
2017 (est.)	420617.3	36826865.3	69780.0		97884.9		386034.0		13887198.7

Schedule 9 Scale of fund raised by bank wealth management (by cooperation model)

Year	Bank-insurance	Bank-trust	Bank-bank	Bank-securities	Bank-fund	Bank-intersected	Bank-asset	Nesting
2006		44.0						
2007		50.0						
2008		31571.2						
2009	110.0	336089.4		150.0				
2010		125287.4						
2011		146539.1						
2012		214534.8	400.0	7360				
2013	1256.0	950756.6	478.6	28308.5	24472.8	150.0	660.0	47480
2014		389440.0	4900.0	113261.6	17621.2		35715.8	24198
2015		298909.5	2520.0	133581.1	28248.5		21395.1	11082.49
2016		118243.0		106855.6			14335.4	7255.66
2017 (est.)		378000.0		100597.8			28728.0	

Chapter 2
Interbank Business and Outsourcing Investment

In the past five years, the grand asset management industry has become the fastest growing and most widely expanded area within the Chinese financial system. According to the data, the total size of domestic asset management was 21 trillion yuan at the end of 2012[1]; by the end of 2016, the scale of asset management in the grand asset management industry had exceeded 100 trillion yuan. If the channel-related business is excluded, the real asset management business in the Chinese market will be 60 trillion to 70 trillion yuan.

Domestic financial institutions engaged in asset management mainly include commercial banks, securities companies, trust companies, insurance companies, fund and fund subsidiaries, private equity funds, and futures companies. Among them, commercial banks are the most important operational entity in China's asset management market. On the one hand, in terms of volume, banks are the absolute leader and dominator in the domestic asset management market. According to the data released by the Banking Wealth Management Services Registry and Trusteeship Center, by the end of 2016, the balance of bank wealth management products was 29.05 trillion yuan, accounting for approximately one-third of the total market capitalization scale; on the other hand, the rapid expansion of the asset management scale of other financial institutions is closely related to the increase in the volume of outsourced bank investments. According to our estimation, by the end of 2016, the scale of wide-caliber outsourcing business including "channel services" and "commissioned investment", reached 25.75 trillion yuan, which means that 25.75 trillion yuan in the funding sources of other financial institutions' asset management products came from commercial banks. Therefore, this chapter focuses on the source and use of bank funds, interbank business, and analysis of bank outsourcing with

[1] Jianfeng Yin and Zengwu Wang: "The Shadow Banks and Banks' Shadow: Market Development and Evaluation of China's Wealth Management Products (2010–2012)", Social Sciences Academic Press, 2013.

Written by Lijun Fan.

J. Yin et al., *Whither has the Money Gone*,
https://doi.org/10.1007/978-981-16-4931-8_2

focal points on bank's fund flow based on outsourced assets scale and direction, and concludes with bank outsourcing risk analysis and suggestions.

1 Source and Direction of Bank Funds

Sources of bank funds consist of customer deposits, interbank liabilities, central bank loans, bonds, and issuance of wealth management products. The investment of bank funds is mainly made from deposits with central banks, various loans, interbank assets, bond markets, and non-standardized debt and equity products that cannot be directly invested by banks. In order to accurately and clearly explain the source and direction of bank funds, we summed up the funds sources and applications published in "Chinese-funded national large-scale bank Renminbi credit balance sheet" and "Chinese-funded small and medium-sized banks' Renminbi credit balance sheet" by the People's Bank of China and made minor adjustment based on the "balance sheet of other depository companies", the "balance sheet of deposits and withdrawals of depository financial institutions' local and foreign currencies" and the "balance sheet of monetary authorities," to deposits, loans data. On this basis, adhering to the "penetration" principle, we calculated the scale and analyzed the final destination of the "other investments" that are not clearly defined in the use of funds in the balance sheet per annual reports of 37 banks.[2]

Figure 1 shows the source and application of funds in China's banking sector. According to the data, as of the end of 2016, domestic banks have a total of 207.71 billion yuan of funds (used) in the credit balance sheet. In terms of funding sources, although deposits are still the bank's main source of funds, its share has fallen from 85% at the beginning of 2010 to 68%. Correspondingly, the proportion of other sources of funds such as loans to the central bank, interbank liabilities, issuance of bonds, etc. have different degrees of improvement. With regard to the use of funds, the proportion of loans also showed a downward trend, from 60% at the beginning of 2010 to 52% at the end of 2016; the share of equity and other investments in the use of funds rose rapidly after the fourth quarter of 2014. At the end of the 4th quarter of 2014, this proportion only increased from 1% at the beginning of 2011 to 4%, But by the end of 2016, the scale of equity and other investments reached 21.30 trillion yuan, accounting for more than 10% of the funds used.

Specifically, the sources of funding for banks shows the following changes: First, after 2013, the central bank created a variety of monetary policy instruments to provide financial institutions with liquidity. In 2016, the bank's source of funds "borrowed from the central bank" greatly increased. Since financial tools such as

[2] Including 5 large state-owned banks, 10 joint-stock banks, 17 city commercial banks and 5 rural commercial banks. We compiled the annual reports of 40 banks for the period from 2013 to 2016. Two of the joint-stock banks and one city commercial bank only released the summary of the bank's annual report, not including the bank's "equity in the structured entity initiated by a third-party organization". Therefore, it is impossible to know the situation of off-balance-sheet funds in the three banks.

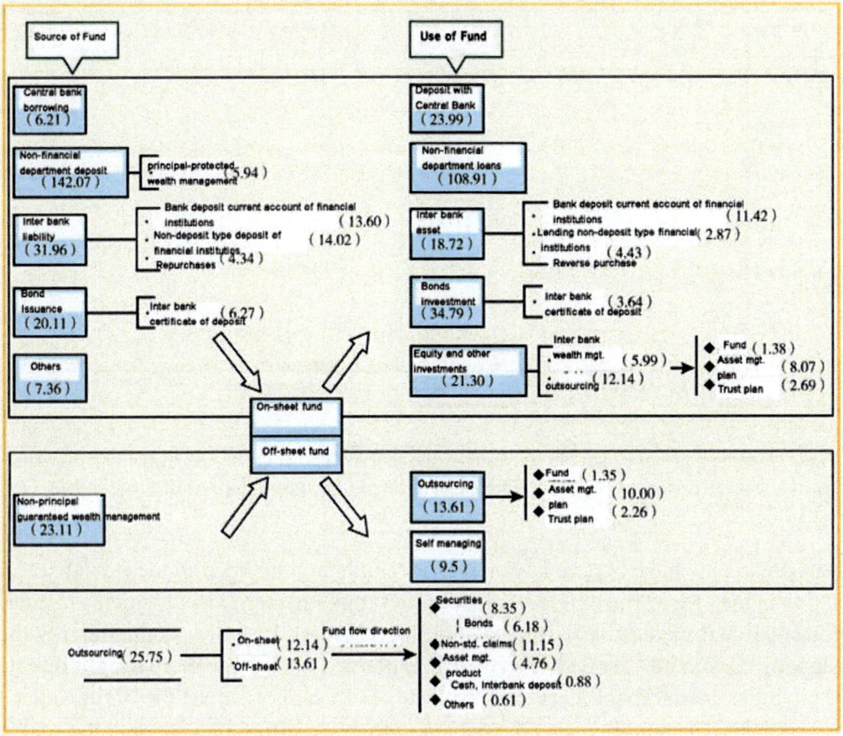

Fig. 1 Fund sources and investment directions for China's Banks in 2016 (Unit: trillion yuan). *Source* Authors compiled from the central bank data

SLF, MLF, and PSL all require banks to pledge their assets to obtain financing from the central bank, large banks with large amounts of pledges and collaterals are more likely to get adequate low-interest liquidity funds. At the end of 2016, the 40 banks we counted borrowed a total of 4.01 trillion yuan from the central bank. Among them, five state-owned banks borrowed 2.04 trillion yuan, and 12 joint-stock banks borrowed 1.59 trillion yuan from the central bank. The sum of the two types of bank borrowings among the 40 banks accounts for more than 90% of the total, and almost 60% the total bank loans borrowed from the central bank.

Second, the issue of interbank deposit certificates for joint-stock banks and city commercial banks showed an explosive growth. At the end of 2016, the stock size of interbank deposits of 12 joint-stock banks was 2.90 trillion yuan, and its share in total liabilities increased from 1.2% in 2014 to 7.0% in 2016; the interbank deposits of 18 city commercial banks amounted to 1.31 trillion yuan, accounting for 10.2% of the total liabilities. During the same period, the total amount of interbank deposits of 5 state-owned banks was only 7.736 billion yuan. (See Fig. 2). On the one hand, interbank certificates of deposit are tradable, pledgeble, and highly liquid, and in

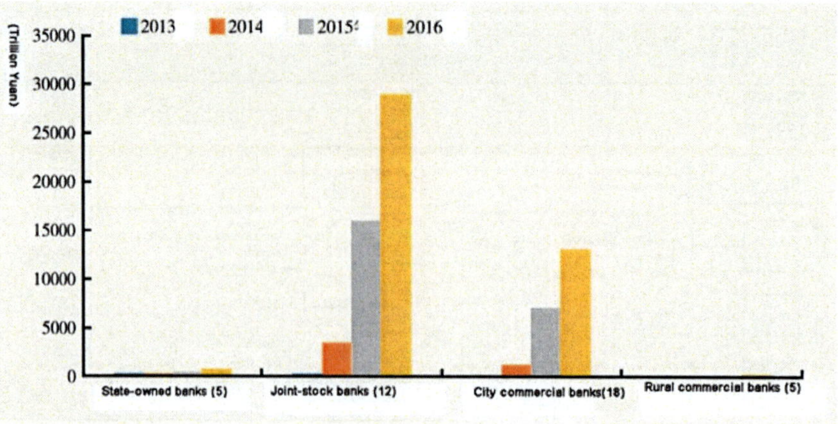

Fig. 2 Changes in stock size of inter bank certificate of deposit at the end of the year for various types of banks from 2013 to 2016. *Source* According to the annual reports of the 40 banks

particular, they have system advantages for not being included in the statistic calculation of the proportion of interbank liabilities, making them ideal financing channels for small and medium-sized banks. On the other hand, as the economic growth is slowing down and "asset shortage" occurs, large banks have increasingly invested their funds in interbank deposit certificates with higher safety factors in order to avoid risks. The supply meets the demand nicely, resulting in a surge in the scale of interbank certificates of joint-stock banks and city commercial after 2015.

Third, after 2012, the scale of deposits in banks of non-banking financial institutions such as securities, funds, trusts, insurance, bank wealth management, etc. continued to increase sharply (see Fig. 3). The sources of the increase come from two sides: first, residents and enterprises purchase wealth management products and asset management plans and resulted in the "deposit relocation"; second, banks use their own funds to purchase asset management products from various financial institutions. However, when the asset management plan is only used as a channel for banks to invest in non-standard credits, it will not result in an increase in non-bank deposits. The bank's balance sheet will ultimately reflect only as "debit: accounts receivable investment; credit: corporate deposits". The increase in non-bank deposits after 2012 indicates that residents, companies, and banks' own funds are increasingly invested in various types of wealth management products and asset management plans. It also indicates that the funds that banks pass through the channel services of non-banking financial institutions to enter into the real economy are declining, a large part of the funds remains in the financial system.

Fourth, the scale and proportion of non-principal-guaranteed financial management continued to expand. According to the statistics of the Banking Wealth Management Service Register and Trusteeship Center, by the end of 2016, the balance of bank wealth management products was 29.05 trillion yuan, of which, the balance of non-guaranteed products was 23.11 trillion yuan, accounting for 79.56% of the

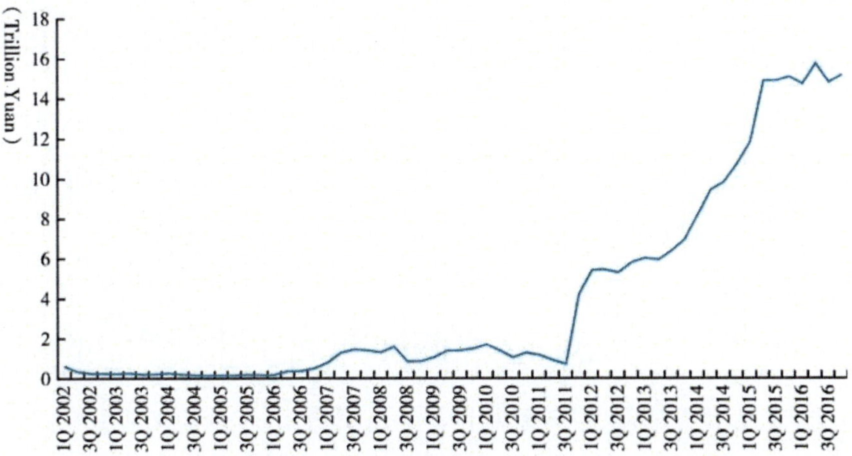

Fig. 3 Deposit scale of Non-Bank Financial Institutions (2002–2016). *Data source* "Liability to other financial companies: deposits included in broad money" in the "Balance Sheet of Other Deposit-taking Companies" of the People's Bank of China

total, increased 15.79 percentage points from the end of 2013; the remaining balance of principal-protected products was 5.94 trillion yuan, accounting for 20.45% of the balance of all wealth management products. Non-principal-guaranteed wealth management products do not need to bear the corresponding risk because they do not guarantee the safety of the customer's principal, and are not included in the internal supervisory system. However, in fact, most non-principal-guaranteed wealth management has an implicit guarantee of the bank's rigid payment. Once there is a problem with the assets, the banks will inevitably carry out "bottom line protection". With the expansion of non-principal-guaranteed wealth management, risks are accumulating within the banking system.

The most important change in the use of funds is that the scale and proportion of bank equity and other investments have shown a rapid increase since November 2014. By the end of 2016, the scale of "equity and other investment" reached 21.30 trillion yuan, accounting for more than 10% of the funds used (see Fig. 4). Among them, "other investment" is mainly the bank's interbank investment, which includes banks investing in trust plans, asset management plans issued by securities companies and insurance companies, specialized account of fund and fund subsidiaries, and other structured entities such as other bank's wealth management products. We estimated the interbank investment scale of the entire banking industry based on the 2016 annual reports of 37 banks, on this basis, we considered the bank funded broker's directional asset management plan, specialized account with fund and the scale of trust, and finally calculated the outsourcing size of off-balance sheet non-principal-guaranteed wealth management. The specific estimation method will be introduced in the third part of this chapter. The calculation results show that, as of the end of 2016, the scale of interbank investment within the balance sheet was approximately 18 trillion yuan, of which 6 trillion yuan was for interbank wealth management, that

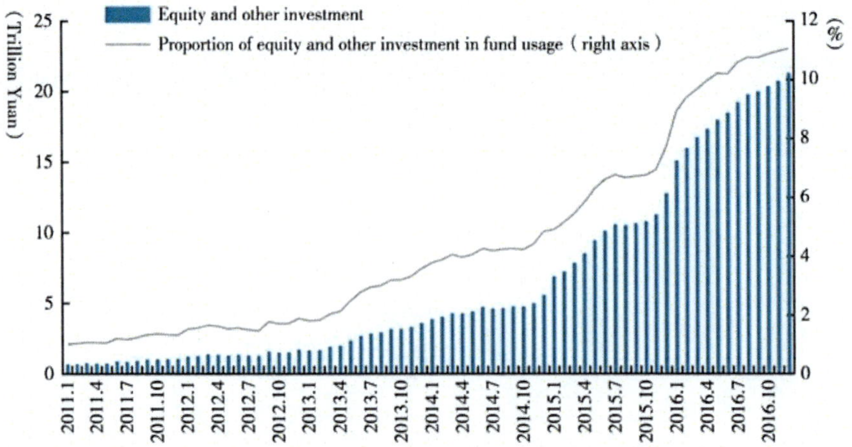

Fig. 4 Changes in the size and proportion of bank equity and other investments. *Sources of data* People's Bank of China, "Chinese-funded national large-scale banks' RMB credit receipts and disbursement sheet" and "Chinese-funded small and medium-sized banks' RMB credit receipts and disbursement sheet."

is, investment in other banks' wealth management products; 12 trillion yuan was for bank outsourcing (including channel services). The outsourced off-balance-sheet non-principal-guaranteed wealth management investments amount to approximately 14 trillion yuan, bank self-managed such type of investment is approximately 9 trillion yuan. Taking account of the proportion of outsourced banks' wealth management product and other types of asset management products, we further estimated the ultimate direction of the bank outsourcing direction: of the nearly 26 trillion yuan outsourced wide-caliber bank investment within and out of the balance sheet, about 8 trillion yuan flowed to exchanges house and standard securities in the interbank market, among them investment in bonds was over 6 trillion yuan; 11 trillion yuan invested in non-standardized credits; 5 trillion yuan for repurchasing bank wealth management and trust as well as asset management plans; nearly 1 trillion yuan is interbank deposit. It can be seen that more than 30% of banks' outsourced investments inside/outside the balance were standard securities such as bonds and money funds. Since such investments are easier to be redeemed, they will bear the brunt of the escalation of supervision and pass the impact to the bond market and liquidity.

2 Review of the Development of Interbank Business

The interbank business initially served as a short-term liquidity tool and played the role of adjusting capital positions and smoothing liquidity fluctuations. Its counterparties include various types of financial institutions such as banks, securities,

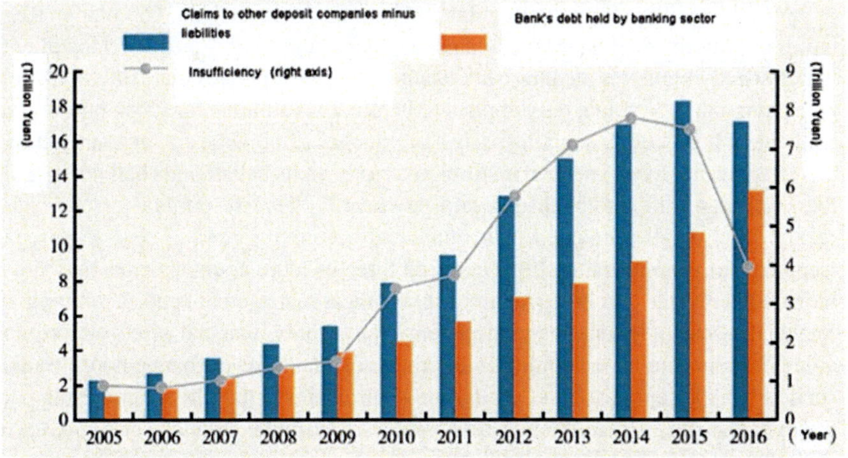

Fig. 5 Net creditor's rights in the banking sector. *Source* People's Bank of China, "Balance Sheet of Other Depository Companies", China Bond Information Network

insurance, trusts, funds, and leasing companies. Its business types include interbank lending, interbank deposits, interbank borrowings, interbank delegate payment, interbank reverse purchase (repurchase), and interbank investment and so on.

The rapid expansion in the size of the interbank business began in 2010. At that time, regulatory agencies implemented credit line management, principal constraint, loan-to-deposit ratio control and introduced credit policies in key monitoring areas such as local government financing platform and real estate, in order to optimize the structure of credit and curb the rapid growth of credit scale. However, the financing needs in the market are still exuberant, interbank business developed along the way and found other paths for evolution such transmuting the traditional capital business into quasi credit business by means of reverse purchase, delegate payment and other approaches. The scale of this new business form increased rapidly. Figure 5 shows the interbank net creditor's rights in banking sector since 2005. The amount of net creditor's rights is calculated by subtracting both the amount of liabilities to other depository companies and the balance of bank debt held by the banking sector from the amount of creditors' rights to other depository companies.

Strictly speaking, the "liabilities to other depository companies" and the "creditors' rights to other depository companies" of the banking sector are two subjects that correspond to one another. The former plus bank bonds held by banks should be exactly the same as the latter. However, in reality there is a large difference between the two. For this difference, it can be explained as the amount of non-standard creditor's rights between created by interbank investments such as delegate payment and interbank reverse purchase, i.e. the "shadow of bank". Since 2010, the net interbank claims in the banking sector have continued to soar, rising from 1.52 trillion yuan at the end of 2009 to 7.81 trillion yuan at the end of 2014, representing a compound annual growth rate of 39% (see Fig. 5).

In 2014, the China Banking Regulatory Commission issued the "Circular on Regulating the Interbank Business of Financial Institutions" (i.e. "No. 127 Document") which strictly regulates the interbank business of and stipulates that "interbank delegate payment in principle only applies to banking institutions for cross-border trade settlement. If the commissioning party has branches in the same city or county, it shall not entrust other local financial institutions to pay on its behalf and shall not disguise the financing with interbank delegate payment."; "reverse purchase (repurchase) related funds shall accounted under financial accounting item of reverse purchase (repurchase), similar transactions between three or more counterparties may not be included in reverse purchase (repurchase) business management and accounting, the financial assets under this accounting item shall be only financial assets with reasonable fair value and high liquidity in interbank or securities exchange house trading, such as bank acceptance bills, bonds, and central bank bills. The repurchasing party may not transfer finance the business assets out from the balance sheet." After the issuance of "No. 127 Document", the expansion of interbank funds investing in non-standard creditor's rights was inhibited. Figure 5 shows the banking sector's net creditor's rights significantly decreased after 2014 after reaching a high level, at the same time, the interbank investment appears on stage.

In "No. 127 Document" the concept of "inter-bank investment" was proposed, which is intended to guide financial institutions to transform from investing non-standard assets to financial bonds, subordinated bonds, asset securitization products, interbank deposit certificates and special purpose vehicle tools, etc. But in fact, the interbank investment has become a new channel for non-standard products for banks. Banks use self-operated funds to transfer non-standard assets to self-operated investments through mutual purchases, rearrangement and other methods, usually accounted as "investments in receivables". Assets management plan, fund subsidiary accounts and trust plans has become the main channel of banks' quasi credit operations.

After 2015, the interbank investment has once again changed to a new format. Outsourcing investment has risen. Investment assets are no longer confined to non-standard assets. Standard assets such as bonds, money funds, and stocks have increasingly appeared in underlying assets; interbank investment partners have grown from trust companies to broker's asset management, fund subsidiaries and public funds, the structure of financial products becomes more complex, and the parterre chain is getting longer (see Fig. 6).

There are three major reasons why banks conduct outsourcing investments: First, some city commercial banks and rural commercial banks are lack of the personnel, capabilities, and experience of professional investment teams. Many small banks do not even have independent asset management departments, so they need to commission external agencies to manage; second, banks have to entrust other institutions to invest because of restricted licenses. For example, bank wealth management cannot open securities accounts at the exchange, and the stock market has started to rise in the second half of 2014. In order to enter the stock market, banks must rely on securities firms, funds or trust plans and other channels to open accounts, and then nest a layer of brokerage directional asset management plans or fund specialized account to

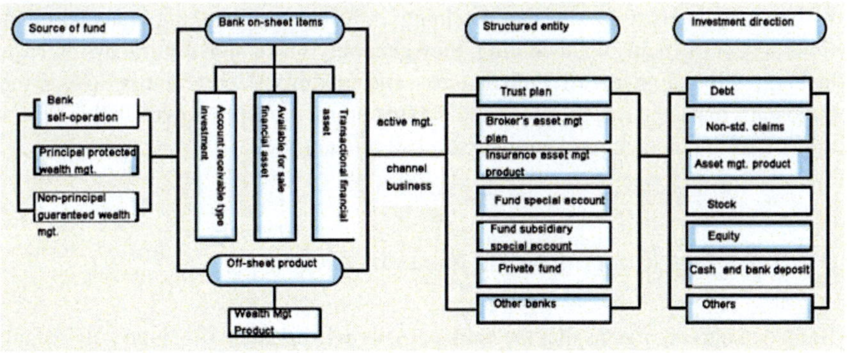

Fig. 6 Bank outsourcing business operation modes. *Source* Author finishing

invest in stocks and bond markets; Third, after 2015, as the economic situation weakened, the investment needs of real entities have been severely contracted, "shortages of assets" occurs, high-quality, high-yield assets are increasingly difficult to find, the default rate of bad credit assets and bonds rises, therefore, it is more and more difficult to find asset income to cover capital costs and labor costs. In this case, banks choose not to directly invest in basic assets such as bonds, but instead entrust funds to interbank organization for fixed income.

Figure 7 shows that after the first quarter of 2015, the year-on-year growth rate of non-financial corporate bonds held by banks continued to decline. The year-on-year growth rate after 1Q16 was negative; after 3Q15, the growth rate of loans issued

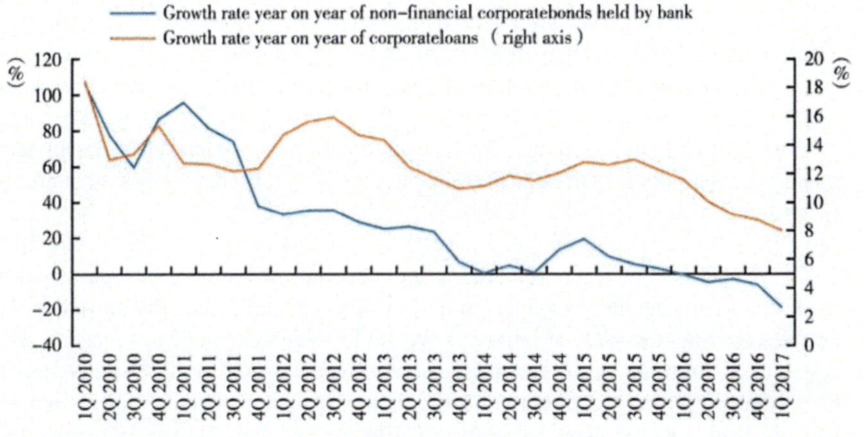

Fig. 7 Growth rate year on year of corporate loans and non-financial corporate bonds held by banks. *Source of data* The non-financial corporate debt data held by banks is compiled by the author according to the bond investor holding structure announced by China Bond Information Network and Shanghai Clearing House; the corporate loan data comes from the "local deposit and withdrawal foreign currency credits issued by the People's Bank of China". "Balance sheet"

by banks to enterprises was also declining. After the non-banking financial institutions accept the bank's outsourcing, they generally make high returns by increasing leverage, expanding maturity mismatches, and sinking risk preferences, so as to meet the bank's expected rate of return and obtain commissions. However, in this process, the risk of the financial system increased significantly.

3 Bank Outsourcing Scale Measurement

Bank outsourcing means that the bank entrusts self-operated or on- and off-balance-sheet wealth management funds to non-bank financial institutions for active or passive management, which can be divided into two types: "channel services" and "outsourcing investments." Among them, the "channel business" refers to the financial institutions commissioned by the bank as a channel to establish one or more layers of asset management plans or trust plans and other investment products, in order to finance the bank's target customers or invest in other assets; "Outsourcing investment" refers to the investment business that the bank entrusts the funds to an external financial institution to actively manage and obtain a fixed income. After 2015, the vigorous development of outsourcing business has become a typical feature of banks' interbank business. While enriching the asset allocation structure of banks, it has led to an extension of the interbank chain, ambiguous underlying assets and raised the level of fund risk due to the flexibility of operations and the multi-nesting of outsourcing investment. In this section, we will make a general assessment of the size of the bank's outsourcing and analyze the flow of funds.

Our estimation of the size of the bank outsourcing is mainly conducted from three aspects. First, the bank outsourcing managers include trusts, securities asset management, insurance asset management, fund and fund subsidiaries and private equity funds, etc., among which, securities management and funds specialized account, fund subsidiary account and trust plan are the main subcontractors, and their data is more available and accurate. We take fund source of these four types of asset management products as the size of the bank, thus the total scale of bank outsourcing; second, the outsourcing size of the bank's on-sheet funds is estimated based on the "equity of the structured entities initiated by third-party organizations" published in the 37 banks' annual reports. Taking into account the bank's purchases of interbank wealth management products may also have subcontracted situations, to avoid double counting, the scale of interbank wealth management and asset securitization is excluded from the "equity of the structured entities that the third-party institutions initiated; Third, we measure the direction of the bank's outsourcing investment and the bank's self-managed investment direction of the off-sheet non-principal-guaranteed wealth management based on the asset allocation of the outsourcing managers and wealth management.

3.1 To Measure the Outsourcing Size of the Bank from the Perspective of the Outsourcing Manager

Outsourcing business of banks is mainly distributed in various asset management businesses such as securities companies, trust companies, funds and fund subsidiaries. Therefore, it is possible to roughly estimate the size of bank outsourcing based on the sum of bank funds in these asset management operations.

According to the "2016 Statistics Annual Report of the Private Equity Assets Management Business of the Securities and Futures Trading Institutions", as of the end of 2016, the bank's entrusted funds in fund companies' were 6.42 trillion yuan; in the fund company's specialized account, the entrusted funds by bank were 2.73 trillion yuan; among the investors of the directional asset management program of securities firms, banks and trust companies have a total entrusted scale of 12.68 trillion yuan. Assuming that the proportion of the entrusting scale of the trust company in the broker's directional asset management plan is equivalent to that in specialized accounts in the fund subsidiary as 7%, then in the broker's directional asset management plan, the bank's commissioning size is about 11.65 trillion yuan.

On the trust side, according to the data released by the Trust Industry Association, as of the end of the fourth quarter of 2016, the scale of funds from banks in securities investment trusts was 2.26 trillion yuan, which could be deemed as active management trusts; we estimated that bank's equity in trust plan is 2.69 trillion yuan based on the bank's annual report. This part of funds is counted in "investment in receivables" and can be regarded as a passive trust invested in non-standard assets. As a result, in the trust plan, the amount of bank entrusted funds was 4.95 trillion yuan.

In summary, the scale of bank outsourcing measured from the perspective of the outsourcing managers was 25.75 trillion yuan, of which 11.65 trillion yuan was in broker's directional asset management plan, 6.42 trillion yuan in specialized funds of fund subsidiaries, and 4.95 trillion yuan in trust plans, 2.73 trillion yuan in fund specialized account. It should be noted that the outsourcing scale we measured here includes the wide-caliber outsourcing scale with both the actively managed "outsourcing investment" and passively managed "channeling business".

3.2 Outsourcing Scale of Bank's On-Sheet Funds

After 2014, "equity in structured entities that are not included in the scope of the consolidated financial statements" was added to the notes to the bank's financial statements, in which "equity in the structured entities initiated by third-party agencies" mainly recorded the equity rights enjoyed by the group through direct investment in structured entities initiated by third-party agencies including trust plans, fund management plans, fund investments, wealth management products, and asset-backed securities. We believe that the bank's interest in holding trust plans, fund management plans and fund investments through direct investment can be deemed as bank's outsourcing size of on-sheet funds. In view of this, we compiled the annual reports of 40 banks, including 5 state-owned banks, 12 joint-stock banks, 18 city commercial banks and 5 rural commercial banks. Among them, two joint-stock banks and one city commercial bank only disclosed the summary of the bank's annual report, which did not include information on the bank's "equity in the structured entity initiated by the third-party organization," therefore, the total outsourcing scale of bank's on-sheet fund is estimated based on the information of 37 banks annual reports.

By sorting out the bank's annual report data, the outsourcing scale of the 37 banks was approximately 10.35 trillion yuan, and the purchase of wealth management products of other banks was 2.84 trillion yuan. By bank's types, the joint-stock banks are the main force of outsourcing, accounting for 64.4% of the total size of the 37 banks; city commercial banks followed after, accounting for 24.2%. In respect of the type of asset management products, asset management and trust plans are the major choices for large and medium-sized banks. In addition, compared with state-owned banks and joint-stock banks, city commercial banks and rural commercial banks are more inclined to invest in wealth management products issued by other banks. For city commercial banks, the scale of inter-bank wealth management was 1.05 trillion yuan, accounting for 29.5% of its investment in asset management products, 19.7% higher than that of joint-stock banks (see Fig. 8). This also confirms that small and medium-sized banks will invest in interbank wealth management to earn interest margins after obtaining funds through the issuance of interbank deposit certificates.

In order to estimate the outsourcing size and interbank wealth management scale of all banks' on-balance funds, we first calculated that the proportions of the corresponding scale in total investments of joint-stock banks, city commercial banks, and rural commercial banks that have published their annual reports, and the ratio is 52%, 54% and 38% respectively. Based on that, we assume that the proportion of

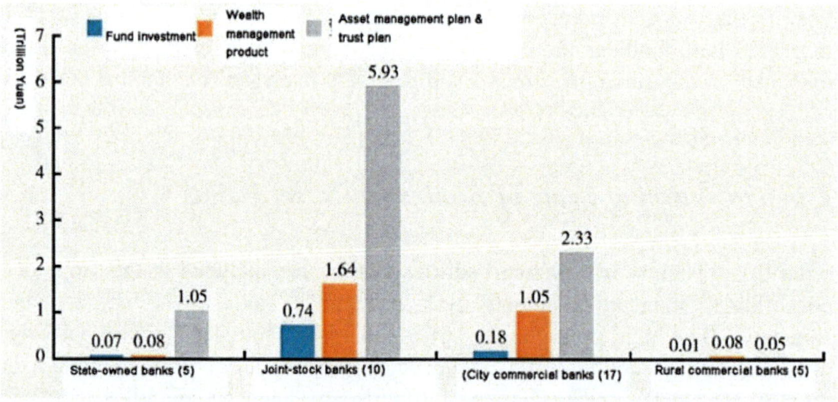

Fig. 8 Off-balance sheet fund outsourced scale and inter-bank wealth management scale of 37 banks (by bank type, 2016). *Sources* The authors compiled according to 37 bank annual reports

outsourcing and interbank wealth management of other banks in the their total investment is 45%; secondly, use the sum of the bond, equity and other investment scale of bank funds in Fig. 1 minus the 37 banks' investment, the scale of other banks is derived; finally, the total scale of other banks' on-sheet and interbank wealth management is calculated by multiplying the investment scale of other banks by 45%, and by referring to the proportion of interbank wealth management in annual reports issued by city commercial banks and rural commercial banks, we estimated the scale of interbank wealth management by 50%. Through calculations, we have obtained a total outsourcing scale of bank's on-sheet funds of approximately 12.14 trillion yuan for all banks, and an interbank wealth management scale of approximately 5.99 trillion yuan.[3] Specifically, among the outsourced on-sheet fund, 1.38 trillion yuan was invested in fund, 5.19 trillion yuan in asset management program of the securities companies, 2.88 billion yuan in the specialized accounts of the fund's subsidiaries, and the scale of investment in the trust plan was 2.69 trillion yuan.

It should be noted that, when analyzing the specific direction of bank's outsourced on-sheet, based on the importance of non-bank institutions in bank's outsourced and the availability of data, we first assume that the outsourcing managers only include investment funds, broker's asset management plan, fund subsidiary accounts and trust plans, ignoring the size of bank-entrusted insurance asset management plans and private equity funds, this assumption does not affect the calculation of the bank's outsourcing scale of on-sheet funds, but it will impact the estimates of specific investment direction and its scale. In the "equity rights in the structured entities imitated by the third-party organizations" announced by the bank's financial statements, it generally lists "fund investments" separately, but most banks will list "asset management plans and trust plans" together, as shown in Fig. 9a; out of the 37 banks, 13 banks have listed the "asset management plan" and the "trust plan" separately, as shown in Fig. 9b, the 13 banks' ratio of equity rights in "asset management plan" to that of "trust Plan" is roughly 3:1. Based on this, the estimated outsourcing scale of bank's on-balance-sheet fund invested in asset management plans and trust plans is approximately 8.07 trillion yuan and 2.69 trillion yuan respectively. In the asset management plan, based on the ratio of bank's fund invested in broker's asset management plan and fund subsidiaries' account, we also estimated that approximately 5.19 trillion yuan were invested in the broker's asset management plan and 2.88 trillion in fund subsidiaries' account for bank's outsourced on-sheet funds.

Considering the bank's total outsourcing size of 25.75 trillion yuan, the outsourcing scale of out-of-balance sheet non-principal-guaranteed wealth management funds is 13.61 trillion yuan, of which the scale of investment in funds, broker's asset management plans, fund subsidiaries account and trust plans were 1.35 trillion yuan, 6.46 trillion yuan, 3.54 trillion yuan, and 2.26 trillion yuan respectively.

[3] We estimate the size of inter-bank wealth management to be 5.37 trillion yuan, which is similar to the 5.99 trillion yuan of interbank wealth management announced in the annual financial report. We decided to use the official data to replace the estimated data, that is to say, the funds that bank used to purchase other bank's wealth management products are on-balance sheet funds.

December 31, 2016 Unit: Million yuan						
	Transactional financial asset	Hold to maturity investment	Available for sale financial asset	Account receivable investment	Total book value	Maximum exposure to loss
Asset backed securities	1,288	1,414	3,298	—	6,000	6,000
Private offerings asset backed securities	–	–	–	902	902	902
Asset management plan & trust plan	–	–	–	225,755	225,755	225,755
Inter bank wealth management product and others	–	–	45,406	7,512	52,918	52,918

(a)

	2016						
	Book value						Maximum exposure to loss
	Reverse purchase financial asset	Transactional financial asset	Available for sale financial asset	Hold to maturity investment	Account receivable investment	Total	
Wealth mgt.product	-	-	-	-	55,216	55,216	55,216
Asset mgt.product	1,050	-	-	-	369,168	37,218	370,218
Reliance beneficiary right	52	-	-	-	83,548	83,600	83,600
Asset backed securities	-	224	3,847	2,187	118	6,376	6,376
Fund	-	109	43,209	-	-	43,318	43,318
Total	1,102	333	47,056	2,187	508,050	558,728	558,728

(b)

Fig. 9 Two types of presentation of "equities in structured entities initiated by third-party organizations". *Source* From the bank's annual report

3.3 *Outflow of Funds from the Bank*

According to the asset allocation ratios of broker's directional asset management plans, fund accounts, fund subsidiaries and trust plans announced by the Securities Industry Association and the Trust Industry Association, we have calculated the flow of banks' funds. Among the bank outsourcing funds, 8.35 trillion yuan was ultimately invested in standardized securities, of which 6.18 trillion yuan was invested in bonds; 11.15 trillion yuan was invested in non-standard assets; 4.76 trillion yuan was continued to be invested in various asset management and trust plans; 0.88 trillion yuan were cash and interbank deposits, and 0.61 trillion yuan was invested in equity and other assets. The main investing directions of the bank's outsourcing managers are detailed in Table 1.

Table 1 The main investment destinations of the banks outsourcing Unit: Trillion yuan

On-balance sheet outsourcing		Off-balance sheet outsourcing	
Investment fund (1.38)	Securities: 1.19	Investment fund (1.35)	Securities: 1.17
	Include Bonds: 0.88		Include: Bonds: 0.86
	Cash and interbank deposit: 0.11		Cash and interbank deposit: 0.12
	Others: 0.08		Others: 0.06
Broker's asset mgt. plan (5.19)	Securities 1.30	Brokers asset mgt. plan (6.46)	Securities: 1.61
	Include: Bonds 1.13		Include: Bonds: 1.41
	Non-standard asset: 2.49		Non-standard asset: 3.09
	Various asset mgt. product: 1.19		Various asset mgt. product: 1.50
	Inter bank deposit: 0.21		Inter bank deposit: 0.26
Fund subsidiary special account (2.88)	Securities: 0.37	Fund subsidiary special account (2.88)	Securities: 0.45
	Include: Bonds: 0.17		Include: Bonds: 0.20
	Non-standard asset: 1.29		Non-standard asset: 1.59
	Various asset mgt products: 0.93		Various asset mgt. product: 1.14
	Cash and inter bank deposit: 0.08		Cash and interbank deposit: 0.10
	Equity: 0.11		Equity: 0.13
	Others: 0.1		Others: 0.13
Trust plan (2.96)	Non-standard asset: 2.69	Trust plan (2.26)	Securities: 2.26
			include: Bonds: 1.53

Source The authors make estimates based on the asset allocation ratio of the broker's directional asset management plans, fund special accounts, fund subsidiary special accounts, and trust plans announced by the Securities Industry Association and Trust Industry Association

4 Risk Analysis of Bank Outsourcing and Suggestions

The rapid expansion of the bank's outsourcing scale is accompanied by the central bank's offering of low-interest funds to the market and the issuance of interbank certificates of deposit. On the one hand, in 2016, the central bank provided a large amount of cheap funds to banks through a variety of monetary facility policy tools. According to statistics, by the end of 2015, the central bank's balance of loans to nation-wide bank's was 1.26 trillion yuan. By the end of 2016, this scale had soared to 6.21 trillion yuan, of which large banks have easier access to funds of the central bank because of their large number of collaterals and pledges. On the other hand, CDs have become an important channel of financing for small and medium-sized banks.

Since interbank deposits are not included in interbank liabilities and are not subject to the limit that "the balance of interbank financed funds cannot exceed one-third of the bank's total liabilities", joint-stock banks and city commercial banks have a strong need to expand their balance sheets by issuing interbank deposit certificates. Therefore, low-cost, unrestricted sources of funds provide the basis for the rapid expansion of bank outsourcing.

Large banks have a stable source of funds. Under the background of "asset shortage", because of their low risk preference, big banks are more willing to invest in interbank certificates of deposit with higher safety, earning risk-free spreads, and shifting liquidity to small and medium banks. After receiving funds, small and medium-sized banks generally have two types of outsourcing channels. The first channel is to purchase interbank wealth management. According to data from 37 banks' annual reports, the state-owned banks' purchase small amount of wealth management products issued by other banks, only 7.61 billion yuan, accounting for 0.34% of the state-owned bank's investment scale; the joint-stock banks' wealth management scale exceeds 16 trillion yuan, accounting 10.28% of their investment scale; for the 17 city commercial banks and 5 rural commercial banks, the proportion of interbank wealth management scale to their total scale is 19.38 and 22.08%, respectively. It can be seen that large banks with strong investment ability also play the role of the investment manager for small and medium-sized banks. Small and medium-sized banks obtain funds through the issuance of interbank deposit certificates and then invest in wealth management products issued by large banks to earn interest margins. The data shows that in 2016, the price of 1-year interbank certificates was less than 3%, and the average return of bank wealth management services was about 4%. The second type of outsourcing channel is for small and medium-sized banks to entrust funds out to non-bank financial institutions. In the case that asset income is difficult to cover the cost of capital, non-bank financial institutions will borrow funds from the money market, amplify leverage, and increase duration to create high returns.

The above process can be summarized as follows: the central bank issues currency to large banks through monetary policy instruments, large banks transfers liquidity to small and medium-sized banks through the purchase of interbank deposit certificates, small and medium-sized banks purchase interbank wealth management or commissions funds to non-bank financial institutions, non-bank institutions increase leverage, risk and duration to create high return, or outsource again to format the multi-level nesting of subcontractors, results in the long chain of "borrowing from the central bank—purchasing the bank deposit certificates—purchasing the bank's wealth management products—outsourcing". Large amount of funds are self-recycling within the financial system, the risk gradually accumulates. On the one hand, bank outsourcing investment often involves different regulatory agencies, which results in the inability of underlying assets to "penetrate". While non-banking financial institutions manage the bank's entrusted funds, in order to achieve the bank's expected return rate, they tend to sink risk preferences, and therefore increase credit risk rose sharply. On the other hand, in the investment process, non-banking financial institutions try to "dig" room for maturity mismatches to obtain maximum benefits. However, if the cost of financing rises or funds supply in the market become tight, there will be a break in the capital chain. Once a credit default or capital chain breaks, the risk will be transmitted upwards along with the chain, which will cause great impact on the financial market.

Starting from the second half of 2016, the central bank began to take the initiative to decrease leverage to increase the cost of capital. From the first quarter of 2017, the central bank included off-balance sheet wealth management in the general credit assessment of MPA. At the end of March 2017, the regulatory authorities issued multiple supervision documents and deployed special governance in "three violations" ("No.45 Document", "violation of financial laws, violation of regulatory rules, violation of internal regulations"), "three types of arbitrages" ("No. 46 Document", "regulatory arbitrage, idle arbitrage, linked arbitrage"), "four improper" ("No. 53 Document", "improper innovation, inappropriate transactions, improper incentives, and improper charges")—the so-called "three-three-fourth" special rectification work, and issuing research letters to banks to find out the scale and penetration directions about wealth management and outsourcing business. The central bank also requires banks to self-check whether the interbank liabilities joined in the interbank deposit certificates exceed 1/3 of the total liabilities. It is a high probability event to include interbank certificates of deposit in the interbank liability statistics. As a result, the central bank and regulatory authorities have basically controlled the bank's incremental expansion channels.

In reviewing the development of interbank business, we believe that we need to use dialectical and unified thinking for the innovation of the interbank business. On the one hand, continuous innovation in the inter-bank business is a natural result of breaking down financial repression and promoting financial development. It reflects the demand of investors for diverse financial products and financiers for diversified sources of funds, and also reflects the cooperation between financial institutions of different types and sizes according to their respective comparative advantages in competition; on the other hand, interbank business also leads to an unreasonable elongation of the financing chain, raising capital costs and risks. In this regard, the supervisory authorities must not only avoid indiscriminate suppressing measures blindly, but also must avoid the lack of coordination and apathetic attitude. Obviously, under the principle of the market determining the allocation of financial resources, it is the right thing to do to strengthen supervisory cooperation and establishing a macro and micro-prudential supervision system.

Chapter 3
Analysis of Fund Flow and Mechanism in Trust Market

From 2013 to 2016, the trust industry entered a period of transitional development. Under the background of economic transition and the restructuring of the supervision of grand asset management industry, the growth rate of the scale of trust assets has significantly slowed until the second half of 2016, when the growth rate rebounded. Judging from the sources and flow of funds, there is a structural imbalance in the trust industry. On the one hand, in the source of funds for trust assets, the fund trust still occupies an absolutely dominant position. Among them, bank financing is an important source of fund trusts; on the other hand, there is an obvious trend of trust funds flowing to FIRE[1] industry. The phenomenon of "shifting from real economy to virtual economy" is remarkable. In recent years, the implementation of regulatory arbitrage through cooperation between financial institutions or their own professional subsidiaries to issue financial cross-products remains an important business model for trust companies. From the transaction structure, "trust + limited partnership" is one of the structures widely adopted. At the same time, the trust companies also actively participated in new areas such as investment and loan linkages, debt-to-equity conversions, mergers and acquisitions financing and PPP. Under the macro policy ground of "risk prevention and deleveraging", the unified supervision of the asset management industry will impact the trust company's existing business model and profit model. In 2016, the recovery of the trust industry's growth rate may be a flash in the pan. In the long run, under the unified supervision framework, it will be an inevitable choice for the trust industry to explore the path of differentiated development based on the advantages of the trust system.

[1] Finance, insurance and real estate industry.

Written by Boying Wang and Qi Wang.

J. Yin et al., *Whither has the Money Gone*,
https://doi.org/10.1007/978-981-16-4931-8_3

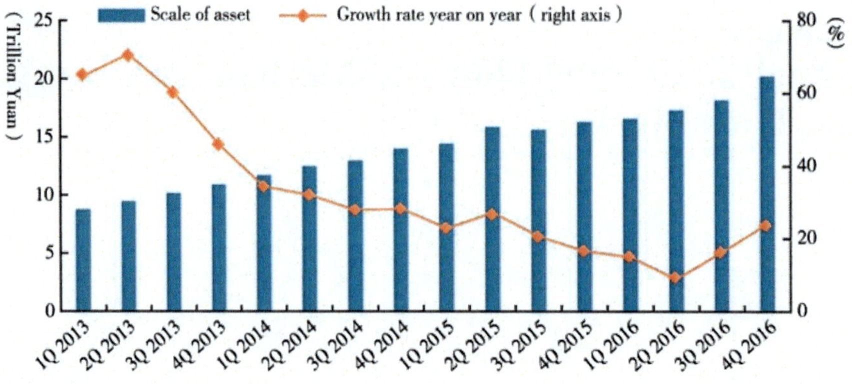

Fig. 1 Asset Management Scale and Growth Rate of China's Trust Industry. *Source* China Trust Industry Association

1 Source and Destination of Trust Funds

As of the end of 2016, the asset management scale of China's trust industry reached 20.22 trillion yuan, an increase of 24.01% compared to the year before, and an increase of 11.29% from the third quarter to the fourth quarter. Since the second quarter of 2015, the year-on-year growth of trust assets has declined quarter by quarter, and the trust industry has taken the lead in entering the transitional asset-management industry (see Fig. 1). There are three main reasons for this trend change First of all; economic development has entered a period of growth shifting. The overall rate of return of the real economy and the "labor pain" brought about by structural reforms on the supply side are the reasons at the macro level. Second, from the perspective of the meso-level, the competition in the asset management industry has intensified and the advantages of the trust system have been squeezed, resulting in the shrinkage of the traditional channel business in the trust industry. Finally, at a micro level, the trust industry has long history of relying on basic industries and the real estate industry, plus its extensive exposure to cumulative industry risks through channel-based business. Under multiple pressures, the trust industry is eager to seek transformation and development.

In 2016, the trust industry ushered in a transition speed-up. From the third quarter of 2016, the year-on-year growth of the trust asset scale recovered. As the economy has become steady and slow, the supply-side reform has achieved certain results. At the regulatory level, the related businesses of fund subsidiaries and brokerage assets management are strictly regulated. In July 2016, the China Banking Regulatory Commission issued the "Measures for the Supervision and Administration of Commercial Banking Wealth Management Services (Draft for Solicitation of Comments)", stating all special purpose carriers[2] other than trusts may not directly

[2] Bank wealth management, trust plans, asset management of securities company, fund asset management, futures asset management and insurance asset management.

or indirectly invest in non-standard debts, causing a large number of channel businesses to revert back to trust channels. This is the direct cause of the rise in trust growth. In addition, the trust companies actively explored business innovations such as debt-equity conversions, merger and acquisition funds, asset securitization, land circulation trusts, consumer trusts, charitable trusts, etc., which helped the transformation and development of the economic structure, and made certain achievements in the transformation and upgrading of the trust industry. However, from the perspective of sources and flows of trust funds, the structural problems of the entire industry still exist, and there is still a long way to go for trust to return to its origin.

From the sources of trust funds, fund trusts still are in absolutely dominant position. Since 2013, the proportion of single-fund trusts has continued to decline, from 69.62% at the end of 2013 to 50.07% at the end of 2016. The proportion of collective fund trusts and managed property trusts continued to rise, reflecting the fact that the trust companies' proactive management capabilities have improved. From 2013 to 2016, the proportion of collective fund trusts rose from 24.90 to 36.28%, and the proportion of managed property trusts increased from 5.49% to 13.65%. The proportion of balances of collective fund and management assets trust is close to 50%, indicating that the source of trust assets is diversified and the business structure is constantly optimized. However, compared with the fund trust in its dominant position, the balance of the managed property trusts is only 2.76 trillion yuan, accounting for 13.65%. In addition, bank wealth management is still an important source of trust funds. Here, we use the scale of the bank-trust cooperation business and the scale of single-fund trust announced by the Trust Industry Association as the lower and the upper limit respectively, and estimate the size of the bank's wealth management fund flowing to fund trust, as shown in Fig. 2, as of the end of 2016, the scale of investment by bank wealth management funds directly or indirectly through the trust channel is expected to be between 4.75 trillion yuan and 10.12 trillion yuan.

Looking into the investment direction of the funds trust, the trend of investing in the FIRE industry is obvious, and the phenomenon of "shifting from real economy to virtual economy" is significant. From the perspective of stock funds, at the end

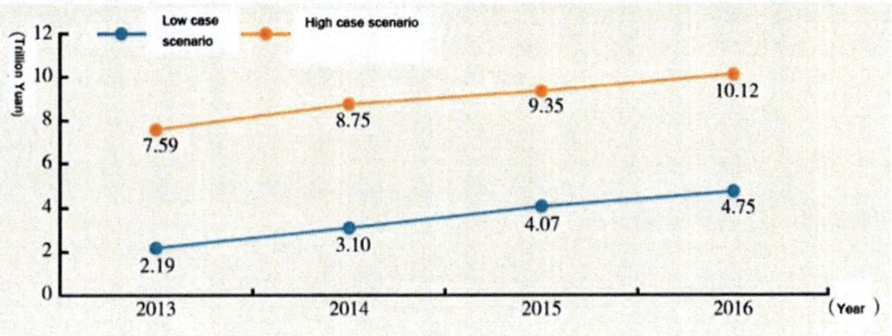

Fig. 2 Estimates of bank financing funds in fund trusts. *Source* Estimated based on data from the China Trust Industry Association

of 2016, the investment of the trust was concentrated in the five major areas such as industrial and commercial enterprises, financial institutions, securities investment (bonds, stocks, funds), fundamental industries and real estate (see Table 1). From 2013 to 2016, the proportion of trust funds flowing to financial institutions and securities investment increased significantly. The balance as of the end of 2016 was 6.45 trillion yuan, the proportion increased from 22.35% at the end of 2013 to 36.91% in 2016, of which the proportion of securities investment rose from 12 to 16.21%, the proportion of financial institutions rose from 10.35 to 20.71% (see Fig. 3). The proportion of the fundamental industry has dropped significantly, from 25.25% at the end of 2013 to 15.64% at the end of 2016. This is mainly due to the emergence of local debt risks and the issuance of State Council's "Opinions on Strengthening the Management of Local Government Debts" ("No. 43 Document"). The proportion of trust funds flowing into the real estate decreased steadily from 10.03% at the end

Table 1 List of Fund Trust Stock (as of the end of 2016)

Source of fund 17.46 (Trillion yuan)		Flow direction of fund 17.46 (Trillion yuan)			
Single fund 10.12	Collective fund 7.34	Industrial and commercial enterprises	4.33	Bond	1.92
		Financial institution	3.62		
		Securities investment	2.83	Stock	0.63
		Fundamental industry	2.73		
		Others	2.52	Fund	0.28
		Real estate	1.43		

Source China Trust Industry Association

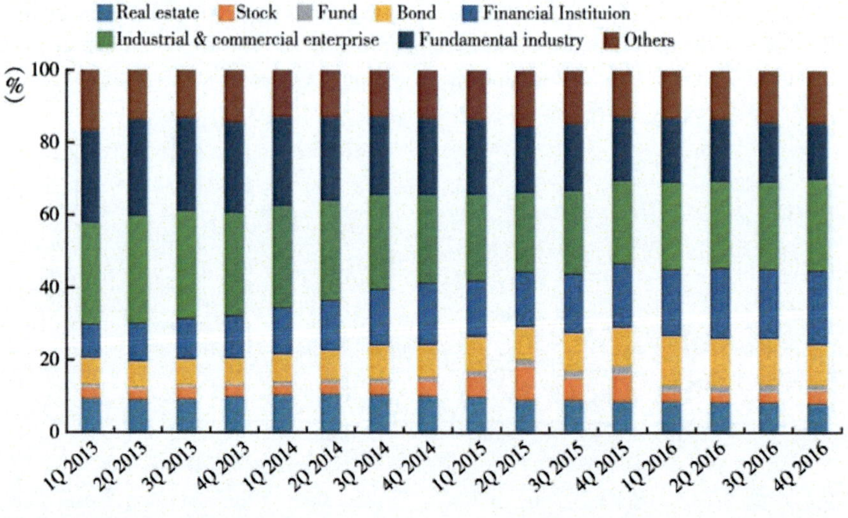

Fig. 3 Distribution of fund trust stock investment. *Source* China Trust Industry Association

of 2013 to 8.19% at the end of 2016, indicating that the trust has a more cautious approach to the real estate sector.

In terms of specific industry distribution, the top five industries that have fund inflows are: finance, leasing and business services, public facilities management of water conservancy environment, real estate and construction (see Fig. 4). Since 2013, large-scale trust funds have flowed into the financial industry. As of the end of 2016, the balance of trust funds in the financial industry was 7.36 trillion yuan, an increase of 38.50% year-on-year and an 81.72% increase from the end of 2014. Downward pressure on the real economy and rigid payment on the liability side have prompted financial institutions to raise their earnings through maturity mismatches, leveraging, and regulatory arbitrage. The fund idling within the financial system has been intensified, and trust is a key link in this chain. Overall, as of the end of 2016, a total of 8.89 trillion yuan in trust funds had flowed into the FIRE industry (finance,

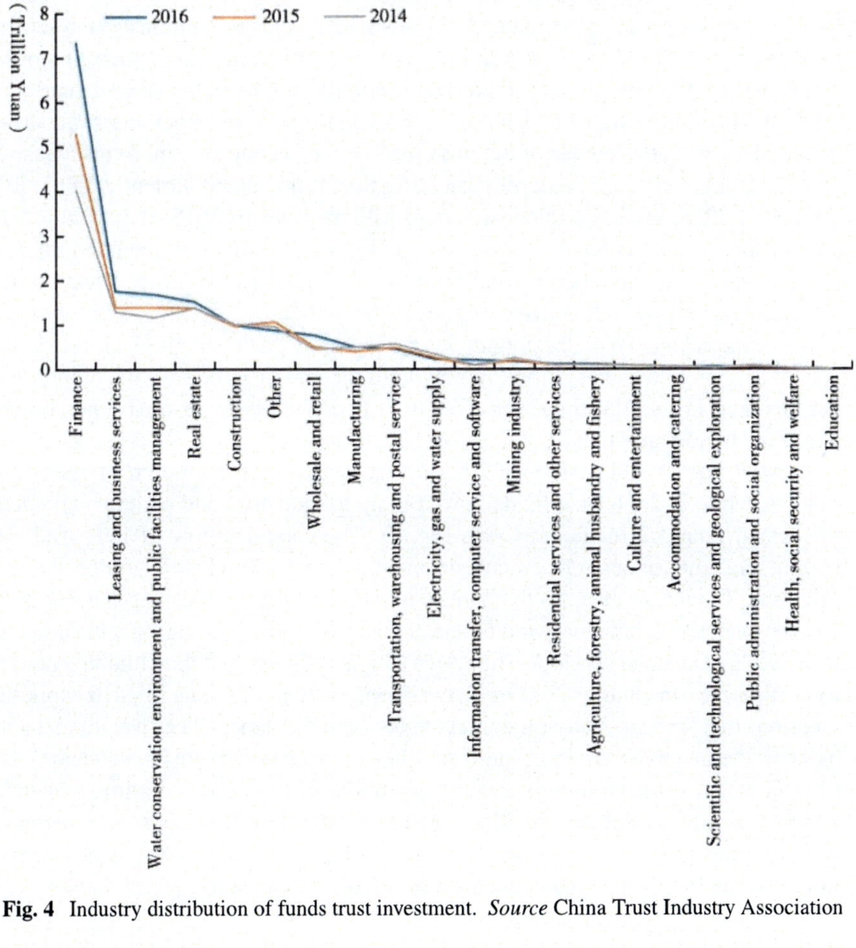

Fig. 4 Industry distribution of funds trust investment. *Source* China Trust Industry Association

insurance, real estate), accounting for 50.80% of the total. The balance of funds flowing into ICE[3] industry A was only 0.39 trillion yuan.

Through analysis of the flow of trust funds, it can be seen that it is closely related to changes in financial markets and regulatory policies. Look at table of the annual trust fund flow (see Table 2), in 2014, trust funds mainly flowed into financial institutions, bond markets and real estate. In 2015, trust funds flowed out of the fundamental industry and real estate with net inflows into the stock market, bond markets and financial institutions. In 2016, trust funds mainly flowed into industrial and commercial enterprises, financial institutions and bond markets (ignoring "others"), and there was a net outflow of trust funds in the stock and fund markets. Figure 5 shows the quarterly changes in trust fund flows. Since 2013, with the highlighted emergence of local debt problems and the escalation of adjustment and control of real estate, there have been some changes in the flow of trust funds. It flows out of real estate and fundamental industries, entering the capital market and financial institutions. The fund flow in the financial market fluctuates most violently. Since the second half of 2014, a series of systematic dividends such as the registration system reform have driven a bull market, and a large amount of trust funds have poured into the stock market. The net inflow of funds has continued to rise, in the second quarter of 2015, the net inflow was 0.65 trillion yuan. In June 2015, the stock market disaster occurred, trust funds flew out of the stock market, the net outflows in the third quarter of 2015 amounted to 0.51 trillion yuan, after that, it fluctuated violently. In the first quarter of 2016, the net outflow was 0.70 trillion yuan. In 2015, the "double bull market for stocks and bonds" also drove the inflow of funds into the bond market. In particular, after the stock market turmoil, the capital inflow in the bond market increased significantly. It reached its peak in the first quarter of 2016, with an inflow of 0.45 trillion yuan. With the continuous escalation of "deleveraging" measures, the size of capital inflows has shrunk rapidly until the end of 2016 with the outbreak in debt market. In the fourth quarter of 2016, 0.11 trillion yuan of trust funds flowed out of the bond market.

Overall, the capital market in 2015 has attracted a large amount of trust fund inflows, while in 2016 trust funds flowed more to industrial and commercial enterprises and financial institutions (see Fig. 6). The capital inflow of industrial and commercial enterprises reflects enhancement of the trust industry serving the real economy. The inflow of funds to financial institutions reflects the interbank cooperation between trust companies and financial institutions, which is mainly the increase in the scale of channel services. The "2016 China's Monetary Policy Implementation Report for the 4th Quarter" issued by the People's Bank of China in 2016 explicitly mentions that "we are studying to include the out-of-balance-sheet wealth management in the generalized credit indicators in the macro-prudential assessment". At the end of 2016, the strong US dollar triggered a serious capital outflow. Financial institutions increased their liquidity reserves for "two-holidays" and the assessment of MPA, and the shortening and prolonging monetary policy led to a shortage of liquidity, the fragile leveraged market was severely. Bank self-operation and wealth

[3] Information, culture and education industry.

Table 2 Fund trust flow (2014–2016)

Source of Fund (Trillion yuan)						Direction of fund flow (Trillion yuan)			
2014		2015		2016		3000	2014	2015	2016
Single 1.16	Collective 1.58	Single 0.60	Collective 1.05	Single 0.77	Collective 1.99	Industrial and commercial enterprises	0.23	0.17	1.03
						Financial institution	1.03	0.37	0.98
						Others	0.24	0.13	0.68
						Bond	0.47	0.40	0.37
						Real estate	0.28	− 0.02	0.14
						Fundamental Industry	0.17	− 0.14	0.10
						Fund	0.07	0.19	− 0.05
						Stock	0.25	0.56	− 0.48
2.73		1.65		2.76		3000	2.73	1.65	2.76

Source China Trust Industry Association

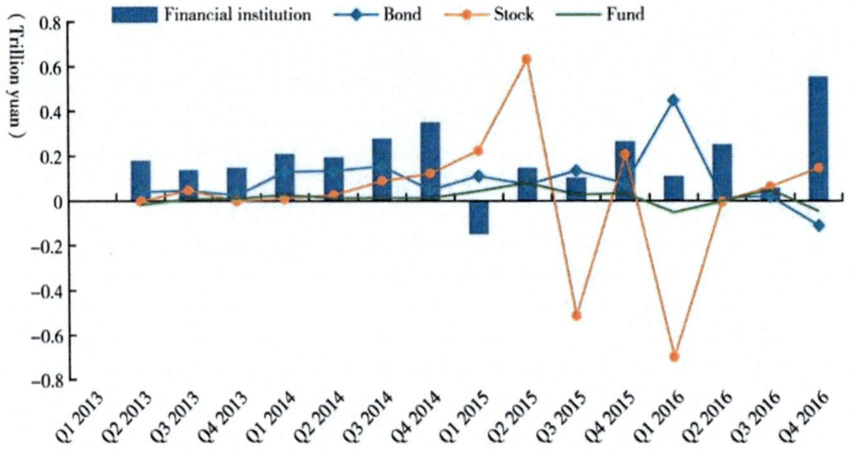

Fig. 5 Investment Direction of Fund Trust's Incremental Capital (Financial Industry). *Source* China Trust Industry Association

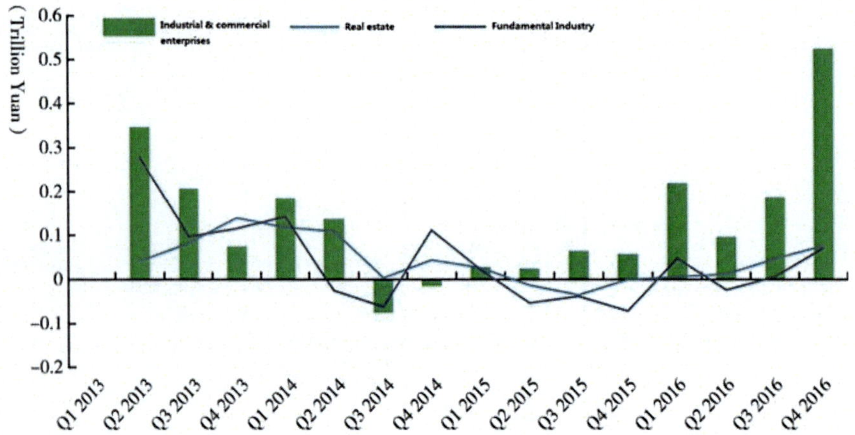

Fig. 6 Investment Direction of Incremental Capital Trust Funds (Non-financial Industry). *Source* China Trust Industry Association

management funds sold off their interbank certificates of deposit, redeemed money funds, and suspended interbank lending. As a result, interbank deposit rates soared and triggered a series of chain reactions: soaring bond interest rates, collapse of 10-year period government bond future and outbreak of breach of contract, the bond market suffered a crisis of confidence. In this context, a large amount of money flowed back to financial institutions. In the fourth quarter of 2016, 0.56 trillion yuan of net trust funds had flowed into financial institutions.

From the perspective of trust assets function, the structure of trust assets has changed significantly since 2014. The proportion of transaction management trusts

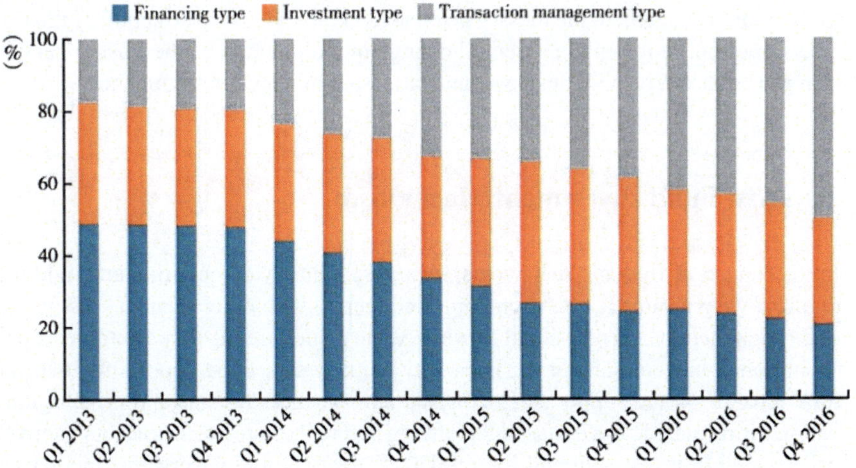

Fig. 7 Functional distributions of trust assets. *Source* China Trust Industry Association

continued to increase, while the proportion of financing trusts showed a declining trend, and the proportion of investment trusts remained relatively stable. At the end of 2016, the balance of transaction management trust was 10.07 trillion yuan, which represented an increase in the proportion of trust assets from 17.46% at the end of 2013 to 49.79% (see Fig. 7). The transaction management trusts are mainly driven by the trustees. The trust companies generally do not actively manage and use the trust assets. They mainly take the advantages of equity restructuring and risk isolation systems in trust to provide trustees with trust affairs management services and thus gain profits. Therefore, the transaction management trust business was taken as an important direction for the transformation and development of the trust industry and its return to its origin. The trust companies have made certain breakthroughs in exploring innovative businesses such as consumer trusts, land circulation trusts and family trusts. However, in recent years, the main reason for the rapid expansion of transaction management trusts was that the "channel" business was classified as a transaction management trust. In 2014, the China Banking Regulatory Commission strengthened trust risk management and issued the "Guiding Opinions on Risk Supervision of Trust Companies" (referred to in the industry as "Document No. 99") and the "Notice on Adjusting the Calculation Standard of Net Capital of Trust Companies" (Draft for opinions), requiring the trust company to define the risk-taking entity of the channel business; and the financial cross-product to which the trust company participate should be clarified the risk-bearing entity and the channel entity; the trust company should calculate the risk capital for transaction management business when acting as the channel entity. Compared with financing and investment businesses, transaction management businesses face lower risk capital constraints. It can be seen that the direct driver of the surge in the scale of transaction management trusts is that the China Banking Regulatory Commission (CBRC) has identified the risk-taking entities in the trust business and incorporated traditional "channel" services into the transaction management business. The change in the functional structure of the trust assets does not represent an essential change in the function of the trust. Structural changes are not driven by business innovation but by regulatory guidance.

2 Trust Fund Investment Mechanism

In the context of frequent risk events, increased industry competition and tightened regulatory environment, trust companies cooperate with other financial institutions or through their own professional subsidiaries to achieve regulatory arbitrage, capital savings and thickening revenue. The trust company seized the opportunity of structural reforms on the supply side, explored new business models and product innovation forms outside the traditional platform and real estate businesses, and actively participated in investment and loan linkages, debt-equity conversions, merger and acquisition financing and government and social capital cooperation (PPP), asset securitization, consumer trust and other new areas. The transaction structure of "Trust + Limited Partnership" combines the advantages of "trust" and "limited partnership funds". It has the characteristics of low supervision threshold and tax saving, and has become a widely adopted transaction structure. Next, it focuses on the investment mechanisms of several innovative trust businesses.

2.1 Securities Investment Trusts: Targeted Additional Offering Trusts and Umbrella Trusts

The investment targets for the securities investment trust business include stocks, bonds, funds and financial derivatives (such as stock index futures). Managed securities investment trusts are the most basic form of securities investment trust business. They can be further divided into active management, investment advisory and limited partnership based on whether external investment consultants are introduced and the management responsibility of the trust company.

Active management and investment consultants are mainly used for bond investment and secondary market investment. Since securities regulators do not allow trust companies or trust plans to directly invest in the primary stock market investments or targeted additional offerings, trust companies usually make indirect investment through limited partnership models or through fund and broker asset management plans. In the limited partnership model, the trust plan generally holds LP[4] share of the

[4] LP and GP are two forms of parties involved in a limited partnership of a private equity fund, with the sponsor acting as a general partner (GP) and the investor as a limited partner (LP). The general partner assumes unlimited legal liability, and the limited partner assumes legal liability limited by the amount of investment. The general partner plays the role of the fund manager, and in addition to

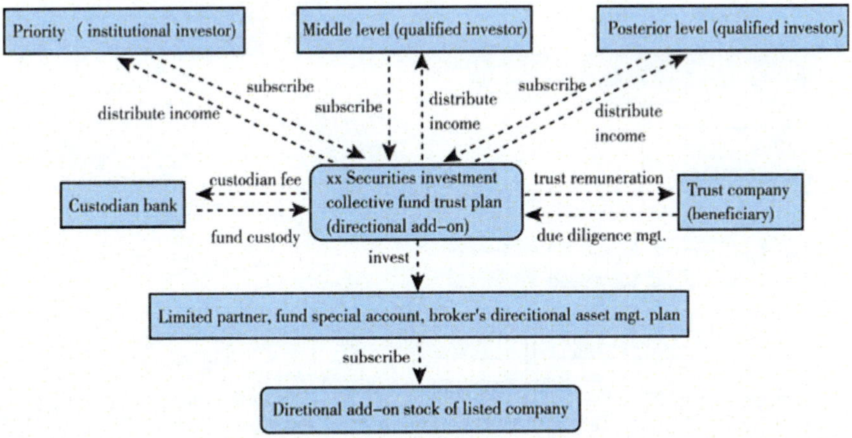

Fig. 8 Directional Offerings for Collective Funds Trust Transactions. *Source* Huaxin Trust

limited partnership; the investment adviser holds the GP share of the limited partnership and assumes the management responsibility to invest in the name of the limited partnership. In a certain sense, the limited partnership model can be understood as a variant of investment consultant, but its transaction structure and legal relationship have changed significantly. Figure 8 shows a typical model for a collective trust plan participating in targeted additional offerings.

In order to meet the needs of investors with different risk preferences, risk bearing capacity and income requirements, the trust company has developed a structured securities investment trust based on the initial managed securities investment trust and introduced priority and posterior level in the trust plan. Investors, posterior investors are usually also the investment advisers. Subsequently, umbrella trusts were developed on the basis of structured securities investment trusts. Umbrella trusts provide multiple posterior beneficiaries with structured securities investment financing services through the establishment of secondary virtual sub accounts under the unified shareholder accounts and trust accounts (primary parent accounts) (see Fig. 9).

It can be seen from Fig. 9 that in the entire transaction structure, several sub-trust units are nested under the parent trust, and a number of priority and posterior investors are nested under the sub-trust unit just like an umbrella. Each sub-trust unit under the parent trust is actually a structured securities investment trust. The priority investors under each sub-trust provide capital financing, which is mainly connected to the bank's wealth management fund pool; the posterior investors are financed party, which is the actual investor. Priority investors obtain stable income, and posterior investors gain risk income.

charge management fees, he enjoys a certain percentage of profits based on the limited partnership contract.

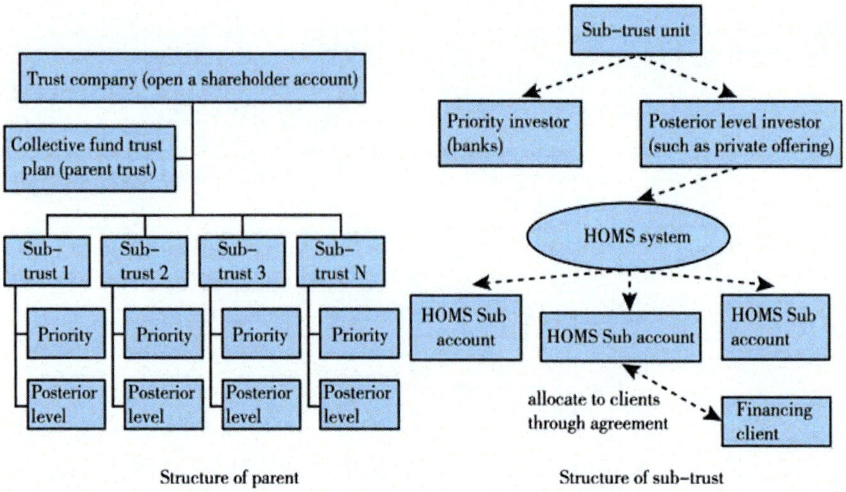

Fig. 9 Umbrella trust transaction structure. *Source of data* Authors'drawing

From 2014 to the first half of 2015, umbrella trusts evolved into an important tool for off-site fund allocation in the stock market by virtue of their convenient setup and wide-ranging investment scope. They have the "convenience" of magnifying leverage. Umbrella trusts have more leverage than margin financing. The leverage ratio is generally 1:1 for margin financing, while the common umbrella trust ratio is 1:2 or 1:3. The priority funds of umbrella trusts are mostly bank wealth management funds with lower cost of capital allocation than margin financing. With umbrella trusts, posterior investors can often conduct market transactions with amplified low-cost bank funds by 3 times. To enlarge the scale, some umbrella trusts allow private fund-raising companies to use their own funds as the posterior level of the sub-trust under the umbrella trust, and then connect the sub-trusts with the Hang Seng Electronics' HOMS system to create multiple structured entities under the sub-trusts. This new structure then is packaged to form another umbrella-type trust, and the sub-trust funds are used as the priority of the "new umbrella", other posterior assets are introduced later to form an "umbrella in umbrella" structure, which is sold through spin-off to investors. The threshold for investment can then be decreased as low as 1,000 yuan, and a 1:5 or even higher leverage ratio can be formed. In addition, the scope of the investment target of the umbrella trust greatly exceeds the margin financing, besides the main board, small board and GEM stocks, there are even umbrella trusts can participate in ST blocks that cannot be touched by margin trading, and it can also participate in trading of closed-end funds, bonds and other investment products. Since June 2015, the stock market has fluctuated sharply, and the supervision authorities continued to advance the oversight of the over-the-counter allocations, umbrella trusts have been suspended.

2.2 *Channel Trusts: Stock Orientation Trust (SOT) Directional Channel Services*

SOT directional services refer to the broker's asset management plans entrusted by bank wealth management funds to invest in the bank's designated trust plan. In this business model, the trust company is appointed by the bank, the object of financing is the bank's credit client, and the bank's wealth management fund is used to grant credit to the customer through the two-tiered channel of the brokerage asset management and trust, thereby avoiding the regulatory limitation set by 2011 ("No. 14" Document) of bank-trust cooperative financing. The entire business process can be divided into five steps: In the first step, the principal and the securities company sign a directional asset management contract and entrust the securities company to invest their own funds or wealth management funds; in the second step, the custodian bank opens a trusteeship account fund for the entrusted funds, transfer the fund in accordance with the securities company's instructions; the third step, the securities company use trust funds to purchase a trust plan and makes payment to the trust plan; the fourth step, the trust company transfers the funds received through the trust plan to the specifically designated borrower of specific credit project; step5, at the end of the period, the borrower returns the loaned funds, and the trust company will pass the received proceeds and income to the directional asset management plan of the securities company, and the principal and income of the directional asset management plan shall be transferred to the client's account, the oriented asset management plan then is terminated.

Take the "Three Gorges No. 1 Fengjie Project" as an example (see Fig. 10). Three Gorges Bank signed "Three Gorges No. 1 Oriented Assets Management Contract"

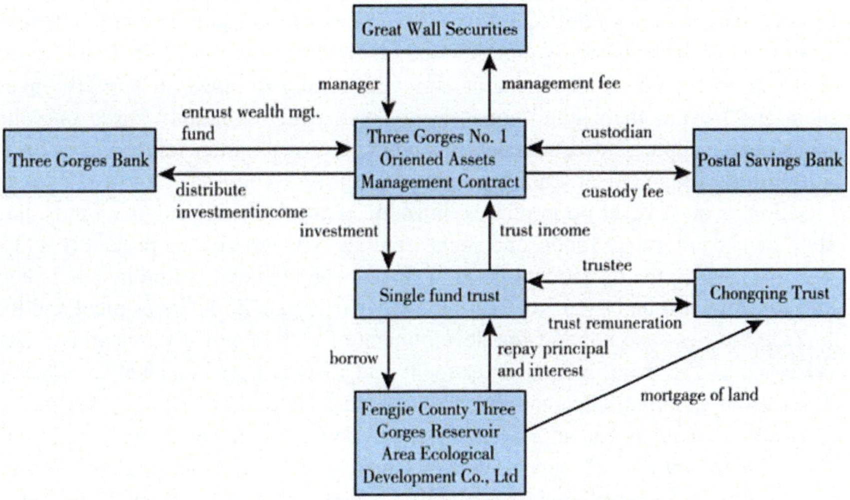

Fig. 10 Three Gorges No. 1 Fengjie Project Trading Structure. *Source of data* Authors' drawing

with Great Wall Securities and Postal Savings Bank, after receiving the investment income, this orientation plan pays the management fee to the manager, pays the trustee fee to the custodian, and distributes the investment net income to the client. Great Wall Securities signed a trust contract with Chongqing Trust in its own name per the requirements of the principal, Three Gorges Bank, with commissioned funds to invest in the corresponding trust plan and obtain proceeds in accordance with the trust contract. As the trustee of the trust plan, Chongqing Trust signed a trust loan contract with the borrower Fengjie County Three Gorges Reservoir Area Ecological Development Co., Ltd., and issued trust loans and conduct post-lending management based on this. The borrower signed a mortgage guarantee contract with Chongqing Trust, secured the mortgage with its own state-owned land use rights, and at the same time handled the relevant procedures in the State Land Bureau and obtained the mortgage certificate.

2.3 Industrial and Commercial Enterprise Trust: Investment and Loan Linkages and Debt-to-Equity Conversion Model

Industrial and commercial enterprises have always been the primary investment target for trust funds. Traditional industrial and commercial enterprise trusts mainly adopt models such as "one-on-one" "packaged bonds", "outright purchase of creditor's rights" and "fund pool". On the basis of the traditional creditor's rights model, in recent years, trust companies have actively explored the PE business, and some innovative models have emerged in the investment and financing businesses for industrial and commercial enterprises, such as the "PE fund model" and the "trust + limited partnership" model, adopting the combination of equity and creditor rights. Compared with the business model based on creditor rights, the "PE Fund Model" exerts more of its trust management capabilities. For example, the "Gazelle Investment and Development Fund" of Beijing Trust, which is mainly based on equity investment, supplemented with debt financing to provide financial resources for the long-run development of Zhongguancun enterprises. The total size of the fund is 5 billion yuan. It is set up in phases, introduced government guidance funds, large state-owned enterprise funds, and social capitals. The term of the project is set to 3 + 2 + 2, that is, the investment period is 3 years and the exit period is 2 + 2 years.

Ping An Trust and Changan Trust actively participate in the investment and loan linkage business and support the development of technologically innovative enterprises. Take the experimental investment and loan project launched by Changan Trust as an example. Changan Trust issued trust plans for qualified investors and provided trust loans for an e-commerce company. At the same time, the loan is accompanied by a stock option, that is, Changan Trust has the right to choose at any time after the establishment of the first phase of the trust, but before the investment e-commerce company is listed (before the material is officially submitted to the competent authority), to purchase 5% equity from the actual controller (or designated affiliate) of the e-commerce company for 20 million yuan (newly raised trust funds).

From the sequence of the implementation of equity and debt investment, the investment and loan linkage model mainly includes the following types: “Lending first and then investing”, investing first and lending later”, “investing and lending at the same time” and “converting investment and loans”. “Lending first and then investing” refers to the fact that after a trust company grants loans to technical innovative enterprises, and after fully understanding the current status and prospects of the company, it will invest in shares by either accepting equity or raise new fund to expand the capitalization. “Investing first and lending later” is that a trust company invests in the technical innovative company’s equity first, and in order to support the development of the enterprise, the trust company shall issue a certain amount of loans for the enterprise. “Investing and lending at the same time “ means that the trust company adopts the “share + debt” approach to invest in equity of the company and grant loans simultaneously. “converting investment and loans” is mainly a debt-to-equity conversion, that is, after a trust company grants loans to a technical innovative company, when the growth of the company meets certain conditions, the trust company can convert the loans to company’s equity at a pre-agreed price through capital increase and stock enlargement.

In addition, the trust company’s active participation in debt-to-equity conversions has also become one of its specialty businesses. At present, Wuhan Iron and Steel Group, Yunnan Tin Industry and China’s Heavyweights have successively disclosed debt-to-equity conversions. The operation mode of Wuhan Steel’s debt-to-equity program is through the establishment of funds to hold equity in debt-to-equity conversion. Wuhan Iron & Steel Group (WISCO) and CCB (China Construction Bank) Trust jointly established Wuhan Wugang Transformation Development Fund Partnership Enterprise (limited partnership). CCCB, through CCB International and affiliated fund companies of WISCO, jointly serve as GP (General Partner), and LP (Limited Partner) will be the CCB wealth management fund and WISCO Group’s own funds. GP’s contribution ratio is approximately 2:1, Wuhan Iron & Steel contributes one million yuan, and CCB contributes 490,000 yuan. LP’s contribution ratio is 1:5, WISCO invests two billion yuan, and CCB invests 10 billion yuan.

The purpose of WISCO’s transformation and development fund is mainly to help Wuhan Iron and Steel Group to reduce the leverage ratio, the asset-liability ratio, and at the same time reduce the financing costs. It holds some of the direct investment in the shares of the Wuhan Iron and Steel Group’s subsidiaries, and will also honor the due debt of Wuhan Iron and Steel Group. The partnership undertakes the equity generated by debt-to-equity conversion. The managers of the limited partnership fund are CCB International and CCB Capital. According to the conversion agreement, CCB sold its held claims to the partnership fund, who undertook the liabilities at a 1:1 ratio of the corporate book value. The conditions for the implementation of the debt-for-equity conversion and the specific transfer of shares have not been disclosed in WISCO’s conversion program. In general, the equity of the non-listed company was evaluated and converted into shares at the market price, and the equity of the listed company was arranged with reference to the secondary market

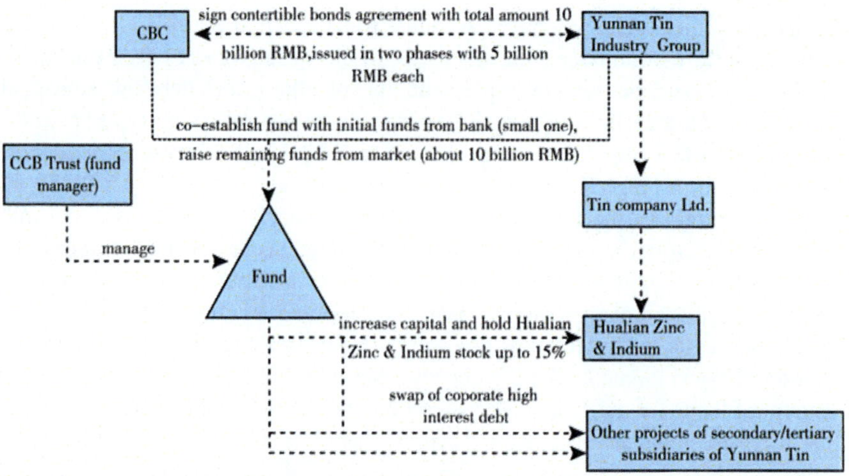

Fig. 11 Yunnan Tin debt-to-equity conversion transaction structure. *Source* CCB Trust

price. After the partnership enterprise converts the creditor's rights into equity of the debt unit and becomes a shareholder, the partnership fund can then participate in the management of Wuhan Iron and Steel Group and enjoy the right of shareholder dividends. According to related disclosures, the converted equity of Wuhan Iron and Steel Group may exit through secondary markets, corporate repurchases, new three boards, or regional equity transactions.

Different from Wuhan Iron and Steel's conversion model, Yunnan Tin's debt-to-equity conversion did not adopt a partnership fund model. Instead, CCB's subsidiaries independently set up funds to undertake the equity. CCB Trust serves as fund management. Specific transactions structure is shown in Fig. 11.

2.4 *Fundamental Industry Trust: Trust Model of PPP Business*

In order to reduce the capital cost of infrastructure investment and local government's debt repayment pressure, the State Council has issued the "Guiding Opinions of the State Council on Local Debt Management" to promote the use of PPP model.[5] The

[5] The PPP (Public-Private-Partnership) model refers to a partnership between the government and private organizations. It is a cooperative partnership relationship formed to provide certain public goods and services and is based on the franchise agreement. All rights and obligations of both parties are clarified through contract to ensure the success of the cooperation and ultimately achieve a more favorable expected outcome than that by individual actions.

introduction of the PPP model has challenged the traditional mode of government-trust cooperation; the fundamental industry trust is facing innovation and adjustment. At present, through the issuance of trust products, social funds are collected to participate in PPP projects and become an emerging business in the trust industry. CITIC Trust raised 608 million yuan of social funds through a collective trust plan and invested it in the Tangshan World Horticultural Exposition. The proportion of project equity was 60%, making it the first PPP project participated by the domestic trust industry. Although more and more trust companies are exploring PPP business, the proportion of PPP models is still at a relatively low level. Compared with the traditional government-trust model, trust companies have three constraints when undertaking PPP projects. First, the gains are mismatched. Trust companies raise funds for PPP projects, while trust plans often require higher returns, PPP project usually has the feature of long-term and low rate of return due to its public welfare nature. Second, the duration is mismatched. The cycle of PPP projects is relatively longer, ranging from 5 years to 10 years, while the duration of traditional government-and-trust cooperative trusts is generally 1 to 3 years. Investors may find it difficult to accept long-term PPP products. Thirdly, by PPP model, trust funds investments are mostly in the form of equity, the return on investment is floating income. In the traditional government-trust business, trusts are often involved in debt, and the return on investment is fixed income. Investors who prefer fixed-income trusts are less likely to accept PPP trust plans.

In general, the trust companies' participation model of PPP projects mainly includes the following: directly investing in the project company in the form of equity, participating in the financing of government guidance funds, participating in the financing of social capital, and participating in the establishment of the project company as fund and provide direct loans for PPP project companies. The specific transaction structure is shown in Fig. 12. Taking model a (directly investing in the project company in the form of equity) for example, the general operation flow is: the trust company raises funds and invests in PPP project companies in the form of equity investment. The project company obtains income through franchising or other commercial operations. At the same time, the government usually provides a certain subsidy to the project company in the form of "feasible gap subsidy". The trust plan will recover the investment through the dividend of the project company.

2.5 *Real Estate Trusts: Property Beneficial Rights Model and Equity Financing Hybrid Financing Model*

Traditional real estate financing trusts are divided into two modes: loan and equity. Under the loan financing model, the trust company raises funds through the issuance of a trust plan, and then finances the developer in the form of a trust loan. The developer pays interest regularly and repays the principal when the trust expires. Under the equity financing model, the trust company will invest in the equity (purchase of

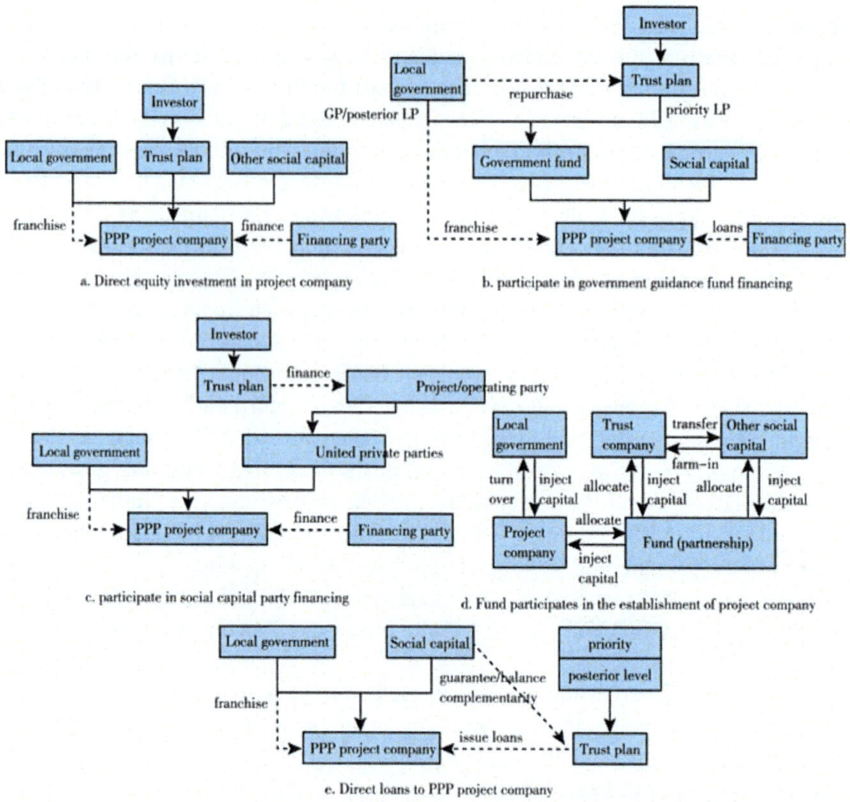

Fig. 12 Transaction Structure of Participation of the Trust Plan in the PPP Project. *Source* authors' drawing

equity or capital increase) to inject funds into the project company, while the project company or associated third party promises to repurchase the equity from the trust company with premium after a certain period of time.

In recent years, in addition to traditional model, trust companies have explored property beneficiary rights financing models and equity-bond combined mezzanine financing model. Under the property beneficiary rights financing model, it utilizes the characteristics of separate ownership of trust property and beneficiary rights. The real estate developer entrusts the trust company to establish a property trust plan based on the property held by the developer. The beneficiary is the developer himself. The priority beneficiary right and the posterior beneficiary right thus will be formed. and the developer will entrusts the trust company to sell its priority beneficiary rights. This model is generally completed by a trust company and a bank and the bank is generally in a dominant position for recommendation of financing projects. The bank directly purchases the priority beneficiary right with wealth management funds, or the trust company issues fund trust plan to buy the priority beneficiary right first, and the bank then subscribes for the fund trust plan with the wealth management fund. For the business model, please refer to the "property beneficiary rights transfer model" in bank-trust cooperation mentioned in the first chapter. Enterprises use pledged financing to obtain funds from commercial banks through the channel of trust companies. The essence of the entire business is the implementation of credit in the name of managing a property trust.

The hybrid financing model of equity and creditor's rights mainly meets the needs of developers for project funds through the combination of equity and creditor rights. It has the characteristics of flexible design and complex transaction structure. Figure 13 shows the project of an equity-creditor's rights-combined real estate financing model. This project not only introduces equity and creditor's rights financing but also the "trust + limited partnership" model. Specifically, C Co., Ltd. as a general partner establishes a B limited partnership real estate investment fund, in which the priority LP shares are subscribed by A trust company with the raised funds of the "XX project collective fund trust plan" established by A, and the posterior LP shares are subscribed by D fund management company. and E Co., Ltd., as the parent company of C limited and D fund management, promised to purchase the priority LP shares held by the trust plan at the agreed prices. B fund indirectly hold the 24.5% equity and debt of the project company by acquiring 100% of the shares and debts of one of the shareholders of the project company to realize the investment in the target project.

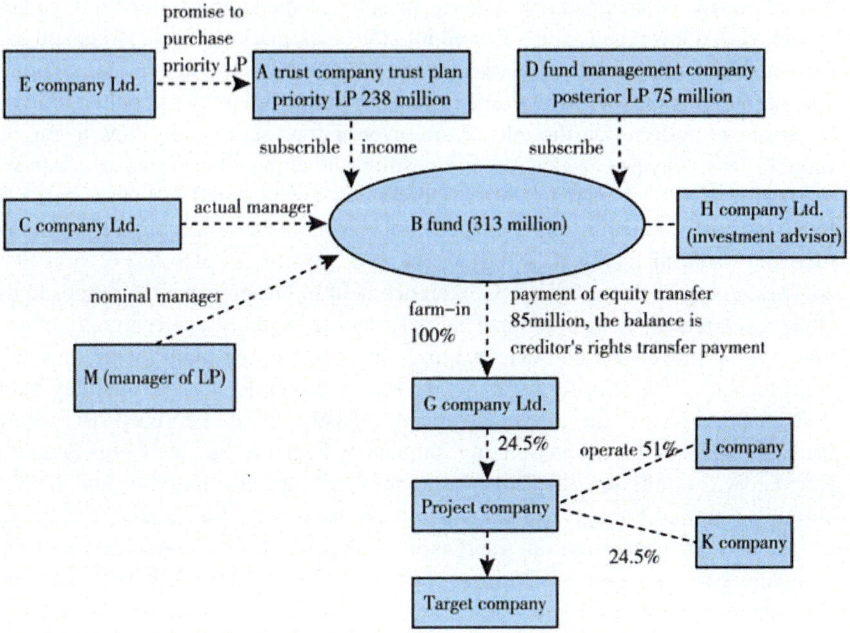

Fig. 13 Real Estate Collective Fund Trust Trading Structure. *Source* author compiled

3 Conclusion and Outlook

In recent years, China's asset management business has developed rapidly. Commercial banks, trust companies, securities companies, fund companies, and insurance companies have established various types of asset management products. In a positive sense, this type of "shadow banking" businesses, as financial innovation activities, has broken through financial repression, promoted the diversification of the financing mechanism in China, facilitated better connection of surplus funds and shortages, and improved the efficiency of allocation of funds. However, this positive feedback mechanism presupposes that finance serves the real economy and that funds are actually used in the real economy sectors that increase productivity, rather than circulating within the financial system or investing in stock assets (such as real estate) and industries with excessive.

Under the current separate industry supervision system, different supervisory departments oversee the asset management business by institution types. The same product with different issuing institutions, they will be different in investment threshold, scopes and capital risk accruals. At present, the asset management industry has inconsistent regulatory standards, it is lack of unified monitoring, implicit rigid payment exists, creating multi-nesting of asset management products, leveraging on levers and so on, triggering many problems such as regulatory arbitrage and capital shifting from real economy to virtual economy. On the one hand, rigid payment on the fund side and interbank cooperation among agencies has aggravated the accumulation and spread of financial risks among different products, institutions and markets. The disguised leveraged capital flowed into the stock market, bond market and even the housing market, driving up asset prices, leading to continuous accumulation of risks in the financial cross-sections, increasing the complexity and vulnerability of the financial system. On the other hand, even if funds eventually flow to the real economy after layered packaging and nesting, the elongation of capital chain will inevitably lead to an increase in transaction costs, which will further increase the financing costs of the real entity and will not be conducive to solving the problem of hard and costly financing.

The Central Economic Work Conference held in December 2016 proposed that "the prevention and control of financial risks should be put to a more important position." "Risk prevention and deleveraging" has become the main theme of macro-control, "substance over form" and "penetration principle" has become key words in the supervision of the asset management industry. In late February 2017, led by the Central Bank, the China Banking Regulatory Commission, the China Securities Regulatory Commission, the China Insurance Regulatory Commission and the State Administration of Foreign Exchange jointly sponsored the drafting of the document for the unified supervision on grand asset management, the "Guidelines on Regulating the Asset Management Business of Financial Institutions (Draft for Comment)" (hereinafter referred to as "new regulations"). The "new regulations" have not yet been officially released, but they have far-reaching implications, implying that the entire asset management industry, including banks, securities firms, private equity, insurance, public offerings and other institutions, will usher in unified regulatory standards. Its practical significance will surpass the asset management industry itself, and it will mark the transition from separate supervision to classified supervision in China, from single institutional supervision to functional supervision and institutional supervision. While reducing systemic financial risks, it also reflects the direction of China's financial regulatory system reform. The "new regulations" combine the supervision of institutions and functions, and based on principles of penetration supervision, macro-prudential management and real-time supervision, it applies the same regulatory standards to the same type of asset management products, reducing regulatory vacuums and arbitrage, and regulating microscopic products in combination with macro-prudential supervision. It establishes a macro-prudential policy framework for shadow banking activities such as asset management business, improves policy tools, and strengthens monitoring, evaluation and adjustment from a macroscopic, countercyclical and cross-market perspective.

Specific to the trust industry, the impact of the "new regulations" is mainly reflected in the following aspects. First, to unify the investment scope and leverage level of various asset management products, eliminating the advantages of trust institutions' cross-market asset allocation and leveraged investment. Second, the prohibition of multi-level nesting, the restrictions on channel business will impact the trust company's existing business model. Trust has always been the major carrier of all types of channel business, and the "new regulations" will cause hard shocks for trust institutions on channel businesses. Third, strengthening the supervision of non-standardized debt assets will further reduce the size of traditional trust business where they are best at. To strengthen the non-standard investment management of financial institutions will narrow the source of interbank funds and interbank asset at the same time. Fourth, the requirements for accrual of risk reserves and concentration control have made it more difficult to allocate assets. The "New Regulations" require stronger capital constraints. Financial institutions must raise the risk reserve accordingly to 10% of the income from asset management, which is higher than the current provision for trust claim reserves.[6] In terms of concentration control, the "double 10%"[7] rule requires higher capability of asset allocation for securities companies investing in securities. Fifth, breaking the rigid payment will help the long-term development of the asset management industry and prevention of short-term risks with the education upgrade of investors. Rigidity redemption is more common among bank wealth management and trust products, it will need fine design to break it and investor panic and financial market instability at the same time.

It can be seen that the unified supervision of the asset management industry will impact the trust company's existing business model and profit model. Trust companies need to get rid of the traditional path of excessive dependence on channel services

[6] According to Article 49 of the "Administrative Measures for Trust Companies", the reserve for trust compensation shall be drawn at 5% of the net profit. However, if the compensation reserve totals more than 20% of the registered capital of the company, it may stop drawing.

[7] The market value of a single asset management product investment in a single security or a securities investment fund may not exceed 10% of the net assets of the asset management product.

and non-standard debt services. At present, domestic asset management agencies vary greatly in essence endowments and business advantages. Commercial banks have natural advantages in terms of funding sources and customer resources. Securities companies and fund companies have significant advantages in capital market investment and asset allocation. Insurance companies have long-term, stable and low-cost sources of funding. What is strikingly different from other institutions for trust is that trust companies have the advantage of the trust system. The trust system gives trust products unique advantages in bankruptcy segregation and equity restructuring. However, the current trust industry is subject to factors such as imperfect trust registration system, ambiguous taxation system and lack of precedents, etc. Trust assets mainly consist of monetary assets. The architecture design service is mainly limited to payment management of currency trust assets, asset management service is mainly about monetary trust assets investment, which is usually accomplished by cooperation between financial institutions.

In the long run, under the framework of unified supervision, exploring the path of differentiated development is an inevitable choice for asset management agencies including trust companies. Various types of asset management agencies shall form a sound cooperative and competitive relationship based on their respective. The core competitiveness of the trust company is to give full play to the advantages of the trust system. At the same time, it is necessary to enhance the active asset management capabilities, train comprehensive financial talents, improve customer segmentation and demand management, provide standardized products and services for ordinary customers, and provide comprehensive financial and non-financial service solutions for high-end customers through customer-oriented integrated products service platform based on financial institutions' cooperation.

Chapter 4
Analysis of Insurance Funds Utilization Channels and Mechanisms

From 2013 to March 2017, the scale of insurance funds increased from 7.67 trillion yuan to 14.07 trillion yuan. In terms of insurance funds utilization, "other items" have increased from 2.21 trillion yuan to 5.28 trillion yuan. At present, the "other items" account for 37.5% of the total inventories of insurance funds, and they also accounted for 47.97% for the incremental insurance fund, nearly half of it. What exactly is the "other item"? Why is the growth rate so high? To answer these two questions, this article focuses on the "other items" of insurance fund utilization and its operating mechanism. The conclusion is that "other items" are mainly "alternative investments" and consist of non-standard investments such as creditor's rights plans, equity plans, project asset plans and real estate plans, plus cooperative businesses between insurance and commercial banks, trust companies and securities companies. The business models include creditor's rights, equity and project asset plan and guarantee, repurchase and other credit enhancement measures, as well as the agreement deposit channel of insurance-bank cooperation, the insurance trust of insurance-trust cooperation, and the income beneficiary rights of margin financing of insurance-securities cooperation. As for the problems existing in alternative investments and the future direction of development, we believe that the normal credit placement function should be given to insurance companies so that alternative investments can become rational and legal loans.

Written by Zengwu Wang and Yali Duan.

J. Yin et al., *Whither has the Money Gone*,
https://doi.org/10.1007/978-981-16-4931-8_4

1 Utilization of Insurance Funds: Dismantling "Other Items"

China's insurance industry began in 1805 when the British established Yu Ren Insurance Co., Ltd. in Guangzhou. It was interrupted by the "de-insurance" movement of the People's Commune in October 1958 and resumed in the reform and opening up in 1978, and developed by segregated supervision in 1998, i.e. the establishment of the China Insurance Regulatory Commission (CIRC). The current regulatory framework was then formed as "led by CIRCF and assisted by industry associations". In 1984, with the approval of the People's Bank of China, the People's Insurance Company of China could use part of the insurance reserves to invest and set up insurance company. Subsequently, the State Council approved the "Report on Accelerating the Development of China's Insurance Business" of the People's Insurance Company of China, stating that "the remaining insurance premiums of parent and branches after deducting the claims, compensation reserves, expenses and taxes from the total, could be used by themselves," therefore opened the prelude of the insurance fund utilization.

Since 1984, the regulatory system related to the use of insurance funds evolved in three phases: first, from 1984 to 1995, the phase of disordered credit allocation under quota control; second, from 1996 to 2013, the era of strict control where both direction and investment ratios are strictly constrained; third, deregulation after 2014. Adhering to the three principles of "safety, profitability and liquidity", and under the premise of controllable risk, in 2014, insurance funds could be gradually invested in bonds, stocks, financial derivatives, financial products, infrastructure debt investment plans, real estate, alternative investments and overseas investments. Under the guiding ideology of "opening the front and managing the back", on April 4, 2014, China Insurance Regulatory Commission issued the "Decision on Amending the Provisional Measures for the Administration of Insurance Funds" to revise the previous constraint to investment proportions of different types of assets in Article 16. The adjustment was that "insurance group (holding) companies and insurance companies engaging in the use of insurance funds should meet the relevant requirements of the China Insurance Regulatory Commission, and specific regulations shall be separately stipulated by the CIRC. The CIRC may adjust the proportion of investment in the use of insurance funds according to the situation." The use of insurance funds has shifted from the strict control of the past to the third stage of deregulation.

With the changes in regulations, as the scale expanded, the use of insurance funds is altering. According to statistics (see Fig. 1), the balance of operational insurance funds increased from 1.08 trillion yuan in 2004 to 14.08 trillion yuan at the end of March 2017, an increase of 12.06 times over 10 years with an average annual increase of 23.68%. Regarding the growth rate of the use of insurance funds, 2012 was taken as the demarcation point, before it was the rapid growth phase followed by the steady development phase, in which a slight fall occurred in 2008 when the global financial crisis broke out. Behind the rapid growth in the use of insurance funds is the rapid growth of the sources of insurance funds, that is, the increase in premium

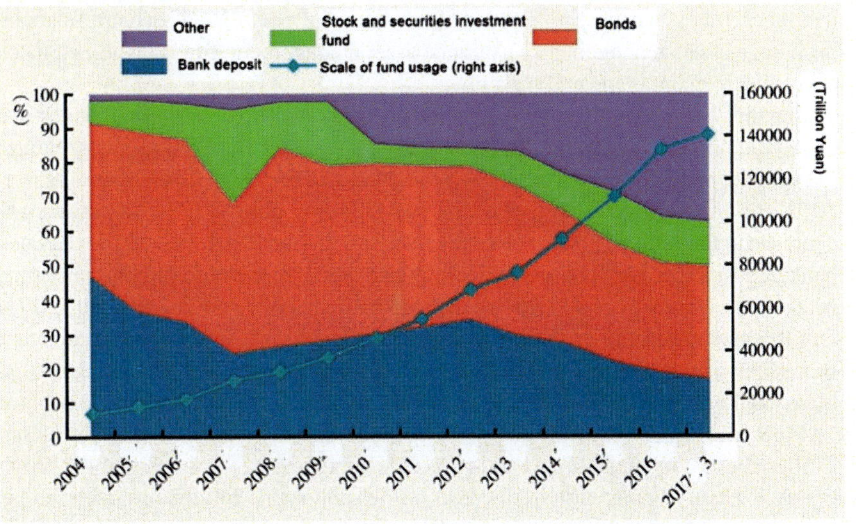

Fig. 1 Scale of insurance funds usages and their proportions. *Source* China Insurance Regulatory Commission

of the insurance industry, especially the premium from investment-linked insurance and universal insurance have increased significantly, indicating that insurance has become more important in the allocation of residential. With respect to the channel of the use of insurance funds, there are three characteristics.

First, the proportion of traditional investment channels has dropped sharply, and the proportion of "other items"[1] with alternative investment as the main component has soared. Traditional and alternative types have obvious substitution effects. In terms of the proportion of "other items" to the scale of the use of insurance funds, in 2004 it was only 1.95%, from 2009 onwards, this proportion did not exceed 5%. In 2010, "other items" jumped to 14.61% and then soared to 37.5% at the end of March 2017. The reason behind this change lies in the continuous maturation and innovation of alternative investment models, while the innovation is represented by the use of

[1] According to the industry's definition, the so-called alternative investment or other investment includes real estate and related financial products, infrastructure investment plans, unlisted companies equity and equity investment funds and other related financial products, in addition, commercial banks financial products, banking financial institutions credit asset-backed securities, trust company collective fund trust plans, insurance asset management company project asset backed plans, and securities company special asset management plans. Among them, the main direction of debt investment plans is infrastructure projects such as energy, transportation, municipal administration, environmental protection and telecommunications, housing protection projects based on shed change and public rental housing; and real estate creditor's rights investment plans such as commercial real estate and land reserve projects; equity investment plans are focused on corporate equities of financial, pension, medical, automotive services, agriculture, resources, trade and other industries, and office real estate equity investment; project assets backed plan refers to those assets, property rights or portfolio of assets and property rights that are in compliance with legal requirements, and can directly generate independent and sustainable cash flow.

insurance funds and nesting services with financial peers such as bank financing, brokerage assets management, insurance asset management, fund subsidiary special asset management plans and trust plans.

Second, the percentage of fixed-income investments in traditional investment channels continues to decline, and equity investments are stabilizing. The proportion of bank deposits dropped from 47.05% in 2004 to 16.77% in 2017. Even just from 2013, the proportion of bank deposits has fallen by almost 13%. In contrast, the decrease in the ratio of insurance funds investing in bonds is less than the decline in bank deposits, but it still has been declining since 2013: the ratio of bond investment in insurance funds in 2004 was 44.78%. 43.52% in 2013c and 32.99% in 2017. In fact, the decline in the proportion of fixed-income assets investment by insurance funds lies in the continuous relaxation of insurance investment channels and the high-yield pressure on the debt side such as the rising yield of universal insurance.

Further, if we observe the temporal changes in the proportion of investment in Chinese bonds, financial bonds and corporate bonds, we can also see that the proportion of Treasury bonds with high credit ratings and stable returns has declined year by year, from 61% in 2004 to 15% in 2015. Financial bonds showed an inverted "V" trend as it rises first and goes downward later. Corporate bonds investment shows a rapid increase (see Fig. 2). This indicates that we can subdivide the use of insurance funds into bank deposits, government bonds, financial bonds, corporate bonds, stock and securities investment funds and others.

Third, alternative investments can be further divided into two categories. One is the "investment banking business" represented by infrastructure debt investment plans, real estate claims investment plans, equity investment plans and project support plans. The other is related to the cooperative business between commercial banks

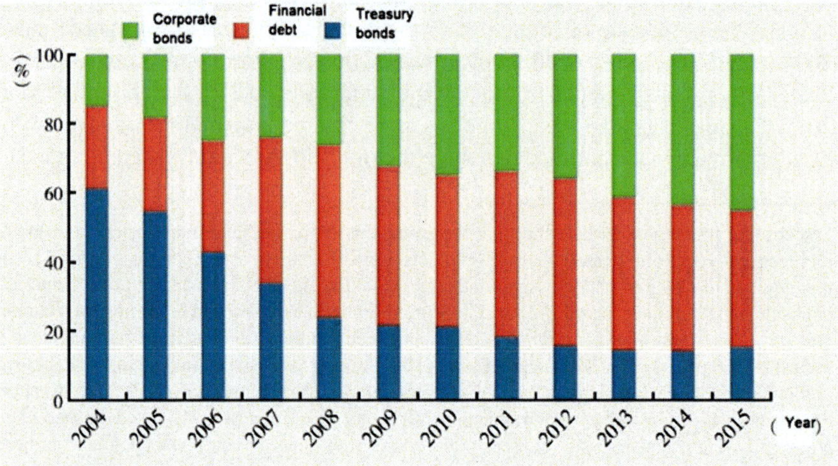

Fig. 2 The proportion of bond classification in the application of insurance funds. *Source* China Financial Statistics Yearbook

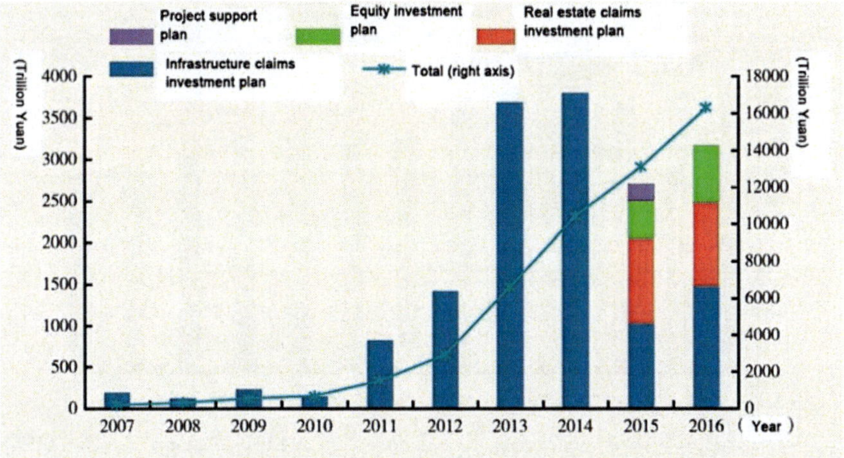

Fig. 3 Time series of investment banking scale and classification performance. *Source* Jiang Shunqi: "Compensatory second generation and alternative investment in insurance funds", "Shanghai Insurance" December 2016

and securities companies, insurance companies, fund companies and trust companies cooperate, the "inter-bank business"[2] (i.e., other items in the alternative investment except investment banking business). According to statistics,[3] the stock size of "investment banking business" from 2007 to 2016 was approximately 1.63 trillion yuan. The fund flow and classifications by the calendar year are shown in Fig. 3. In addition, since 2011, the proportion of alternative investments in the scale of insurance fund utilization (annual data) has been 8.83%, 9.41%, 16.90%, 23.67%, and 28.65%, respectively, and 33.41% of May 2016.[4]

In summary, bonds investment of bank deposits, bonds, stocks and securities investment funds and other items in the use of insurance funds can be further subdivided into treasury debts, financial bonds and corporate bonds, investment banking business and interbank investment can be further spin off from other investment items. In fact, the "investment bank business" in the use of insurance funds is actually "non-standard investment" in bank wealth management. For the sake of uniformity, we also call it non-standard investment here. As a result, insurance funds can be subdivided into bank deposits, treasury bonds, financial bonds, corporate bonds,

[2] China Insurance Asset Management Association, China Insurance Asset Management Development Report, "China Finance", Issue 6, 2016.

[3] Changchun Du and Zhidong Zhang: "How can insurance funds better serve the real economy in terms of financial resource composition?" China Insurance Asset Management, issue 1, 2017; Fangbin Xing: "China's insurance bond plan development strategy recommendations", "Journal of Insurance Vocational College", issue 5, 2015.

[4] Shunqi Jiang: "Compensatory Secondary Generation and Alternative Investment of Insurance Funds", "Shanghai Insurance", December 2016.

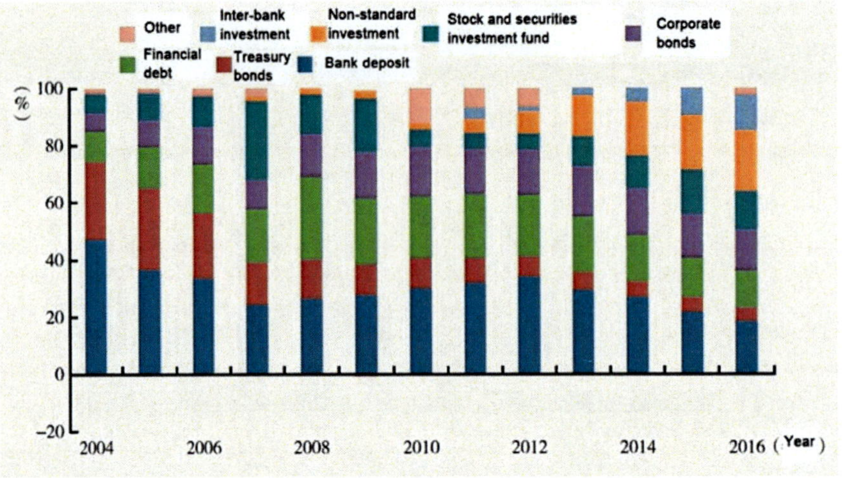

Fig. 4 The use of insurance funds after splitting "other items". *Source* Authors' calculations

stock and securities investment funds, non-standard investments, interbank investment, and others. In order to give the scale and proportions of the above subdivided investment channels, we make the following three points, which lead to Fig. 4.

First, since the classification data of bond investment is only until 2015, we use the proportion of the classified data for 2015 as the calculation base for 2016.

Secondly, from 2007 to 2010, the alternative investments only include non-standard investments; the proportion of their scale in the use of insurance funds is taken as the statistical measure. The proportion data of alternative investment from 2011 to 2016 is derived from the sournce in footnote 5.[5]

Third, the proportion of interbank investment is equal to the difference between the proportion of alternative investment and of non-standard investment. The proportion of inter-bank investment calculated based on the above calculation is increasing year by year. The proportion of inter-bank investment at the end of 2016 is 12.14%, which is higher than the scale of treasury bond investment and close to the total investment scale of stocks and securities investment funds. The cause behind this is nothing more than the so-called "shift from real economy to virtual economy" or "three arbitrages" and so on.

In particular, according to data from the China Insurance Asset Management Association, as of the end of November 2015, the proportion of fixed income assets in the insurance assets allocation was 58.12%, of which bond investment accounted for 34.3%, and equity investment 14.07%, of which the stock investment accounted for 7.26%; the alternative investment accounted for 22.6%, of which the project

[5] China Insurance Asset Management Association, China Insurance Asset Management Industry Trusteeship Management Capability Report, China Insurance Asset Management 2016 No. 2. China Insurance Asset Management Association, China Insurance Asset Management Development Report, China Finance, 2016, Issue 6.

debt investment accounted for 12.35%, the long-term equity investment accounted for 7.18%, the investment real estate 0.83%; the insurance asset management products accounted for 2.24%, remaining are for others. Through this description, we can draw the following three conclusions: First, stocks and equity investment funds equity investment can be further divided into stock investment and securities investment fund investment, each accounts for almost half of the total, the share of stock investment is slightly higher; Second, long-term equity investment and investment real estate can be spin off from alternative investments, in which the proportion of investment real estate is less than 1%. If the sum of long-term equity investment and stock investment (14.44% = 7.26% + 7.18%) is called equity investment, then equity investment ranks fourth (see Fig. 4). The top three are non-standard investment, bank deposits and corporate bonds; third, the investment in insurance assets management products can be spin off from the interbank investment. 22.6% of alternative investments minus 12.35% of project debt investment, we can calculate the interbank investment is 9.91%. Of the 9.91% interbank investment, 2.24% is insurance asset management products accounting for 22.61% of the interbank investment, therefore the insurance asset management products accounted for about 1/4 of the interbank investment. In short, investment in stocks and securities investment funds can be split into investment in stocks and investment in securities investment funds. Long-term equity investments and investment real estate can also be spinning off from alternative investments. The proportion of insurance asset management investment can be derived from the interbank investment. Since we only have the segmented data until the aforementioned time point and if we use this as a benchmark to measure the breakdown of the overall data (see Fig. 4), there will be a lot of error, and so only explanations are presented here. Interested readers can make their own calculations.

Finally, we use two samples to illustrate the splitting of interbank investment (see Fig. 5). Obviously, the alternative investment of Dongwu Life Insurance and Evergrande Life Insurance basically covers the above listed items. With respect to the size of alternative investments, both cases have experienced explosive growth in 2016, partly because the scale of unlisted equity investment in the interbank investment through nesting has soared. For example, Evergrande Life invested in unlisted equity through limited partnership, trust plans and insurance asset management products in 2006 and scale was aggregated to 25.374 billion yuan, accounting for 48.73% of Evergrande Life's alternative investment scale. Further, in the financial statements of insurance companies, alternative investments are generally recorded under investment items such as financial assets at fair value with profit or loss being included in the current period, available-for-sale financial assets and held-to-maturity investments, or are classified as loans and account receivables. Dongwu Life classified the trust plan and credit investment plan under loans and receivables, which means non-standard investments. This shows that there are also non-standard investments in the interbank investment. Since there is not much sample data available for this information, we will not do further detailed disaggregation, providing only brief explanation.

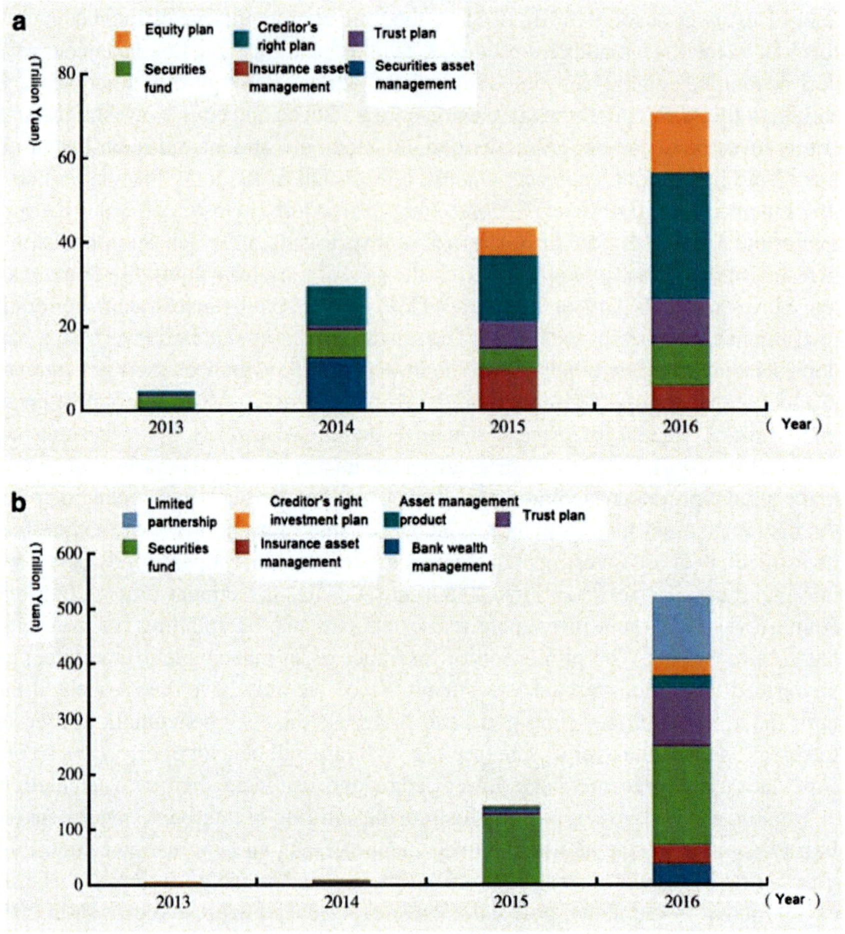

Fig. 5 Example of "alternative investment" in the use of insurance funds (Case of Dongwu Life Insurance). Example of "alternative investment" in the use of insurance funds (case of china evergrande life insurance). *Source* Annual report of the company

2 Alternative Investment Model: Non-standard and Interbank

The mechanism for the use of insurance funds is no more than direct investment and indirect investment. Among them, bank deposits, bond investments, and stock and securities investment funds are mainly direct investments, while the "alternative investment" with an increasing share focused on indirect investment such as trading structure and business innovation, and the two are in line with non-standard investment and interbank investment mechanisms respectively.

2.1 Non-standard Investment: Debt-Equity-Project-Debt Under Disguise of Equity

The non-standard asset debt investment is a type of fixed income product designed according to the principle of trust. Participating parties include the trustees who establishes investment plan and are responsible for the operation and management, namely the insurance asset management company; the principals who subscribes the beneficiary certificates and enjoy the investment income (such as insurance or banking institutions); debtors who receive funds and pay out the principals and interest, i.e. project financing parties; guarantors who provide credit enhancements; custodians who are responsible for investment project special account trusteeship and independent supervisors who provide supervision services. In short, the main participants of the basic structure of insurance debt investment plan are trustees, principals, debtors, guarantors, custodians and independent supervisors (see Fig. 6).

In actual operations, the guarantors, custodians, and independent supervisors, are all supplemented by changes in regulatory policies. Therefore, three types of businesses can be driven from the debt investment plans: credit guarantee-exempted model, third-party guarantee model and counter-guarantee model. In Fig. 7, they are showed in the above order, first model is in solid line, then the structure indication with the addition of link 1, followed by structure indication with the addition of link 1 and 2. In practice, from the perspective of the participating entities, a fund supervisor who is responsible for monitoring the use of funds and guaranteeing debt payments has been added.

In the transaction structure of the third-party guarantee model, the guarantor may be a commercial bank or other company. Among them, the commercial bank with the guaranty qualification is a bank on the "joint-stock commercial banks" list of the China Banking Regulatory Commission or a listed joint-stock commercial bank in domestic or overseas stock market; the requirements for the guarantee company are that the guarantor's credit rating is not lower than that of the repaying entity, and the total amount of the same guarantor's guarantee is not more than 50% of its

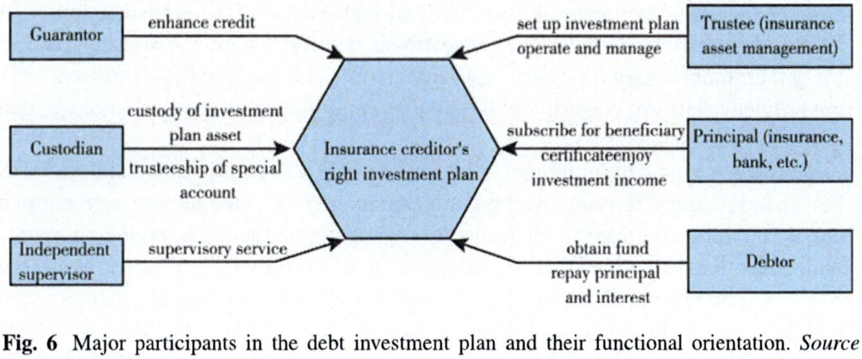

Fig. 6 Major participants in the debt investment plan and their functional orientation. *Source* Author's drawing

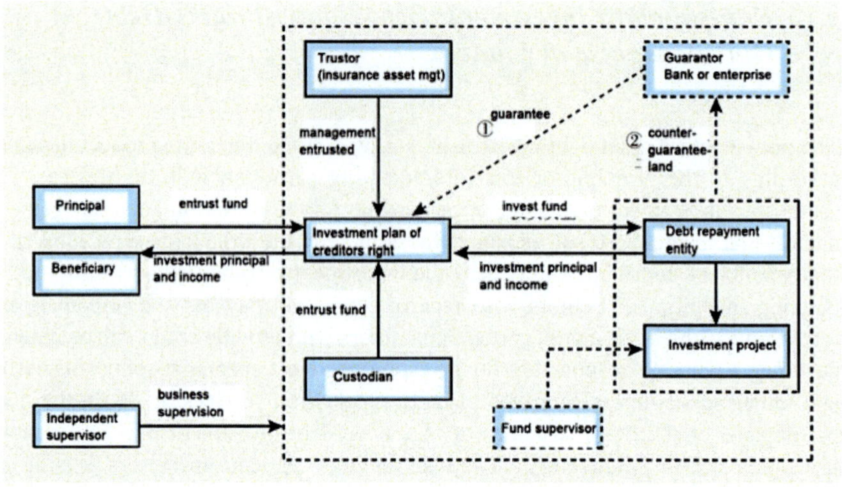

Fig. 7 The transaction structure of debt investment plan. *Source* Author's drawing

net assets. If the repayment' entity's parent company or actual controller provides for the guarantee, the net assets of the guarantee shall not be less than 1.5 times the net assets of the repaying entity. On June 1, 2015, the National Development and Reform Commission and other six departments including Ministry of Finance jointly issued the "Administrative Measures for Franchising of Infrastructure and Public Utilities", clearly requiring the government to purchase related projects from the government financing platform, the government and the financing platform signed a "franchise agreement". The government provides franchise subsidies to enterprises on an annual basis and the government financing platform completes the construction of the project in accordance with the contract and pledges the accounts receivable under the "franchise agreement", the pertaining funds are supervised by the bank. This is the origin of funds supervisor. Furthermore, to better ensure that the debt investment plan will be covered for principal and interest payments, the insurance assets will sign a "pledge agreement for receivables" with the government platform company. The government platform company guarantees for the responsibility for all the debt liabilities under the "investment contract" with the subsidy paid by the government under the "franchise agreement". In the "pledge agreement", the government platform company is the pledger, and the insurance asset management or bank is the pledgee.

Compared with similar financing instruments such as enterprise bonds, corporate bonds and medium-term notes, the main characteristics of the debt investment plan are as: First, the interest rate determination is negotiated with strong the autonomy, while the others are priced by the market; second, currently there is no net assets size ratio requirement, only linked to the project investment amount, while other financing methods require the accumulated balance not to exceed 40% of the net assets; third, the issuer of the creditor's rights plan is a corporate with legal person status, while the enterprise bonds have to be issued by state-owned enterprises, the corporate bonds by joint-stock companies and limited liability companies, and the medium-term note by a non-financial enterprise with legal person status; fourth, the creditor's rights plan basically has no requirements for the financial status of the issuer, while other financing methods such as corporate bonds require the issuer to make a profit for three consecutive years with sound profitability; fifth, the duration structure can be long-term or short-term, while other financing methods have durations either as short as 3 years or as long as 7 years. In view of this, many companies choose creditor's rights plan as their financing methods. The case with almost all the characteristics of Fig. 7 is the Pacific-Nanjing Youth Olympic Center debt investment plan, the trustee Pacific Asset Management Company is responsible for setting up the Pacific-Nanjing Youth Olympic Center debt investment plan (see Fig. 8), the principal and the beneficiary are responsible for entrusting funds and obtaining the investment principal and income respectively. Minsheng Bank takes the integrated role of three functions as the "custodian, guarantor and fund supervisor". At the same time, the repayment entity, Hexi State-owned Assets Group makes counter-guarantee for the guarantor, Minsheng Bank, to enhance the credit, Dacheng Law Firm acted as an independent supervisor to supervise the operation of the entire debt plan.

The essence of the non-standard assets equity investment model is to adjust the creditor-debtor relationship between the trustee and the borrower in Fig. 7 to the equity relationship, that is, the trustee obtains the equity of the financing party or

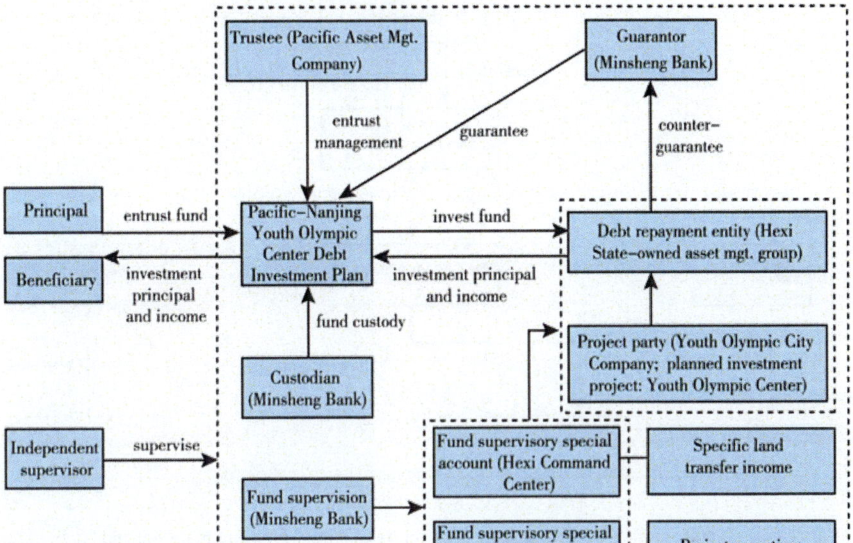

Fig. 8 Pacific-Nanjing Youth Olympic Center debt investment plan transaction structure. *Source* Author's drawing

its project company with the equivalent value of the funds that they provided with. The company's equity and basic transaction structure are detailed in the solid line in Fig. 9. The main process is as that the trustee such as insurance company or the insurance asset management company establishes an equity investment plan, and invests in the equity with the financing party of its project company to obtain equity income at the time of maturity. In practice, the financing part promises the trustee or the principal to repurchase of the equity or the financial instrument (share) that holds the equity (beneficiary rights) in the future, so as to protect the client's exit per schedule. In order to further enhance credibility, it is also feasible for entities with higher credit ratings guarantee to make up for the lack of funds for the repurchasing entity, or to enhance the credibility of financial instruments (shares) that hold equity (beneficiary rights). In Fig. 9, the schematic diagram in integrated solid line and dotted line shows this structure. The equity financing and repurchase and the related rights and obligations of different complement are all achieved through the dual-service contracts and are subject to the "Contract Law". In summary, although the equity financing model for the financing party and its stakeholders has the legal form of equity, it can be deemed as a debt financing instrument in risk essence when we take into account the repurchase and difference complement promise as well as other forms such as stipulations to guarantee the investment principal and interest, for example, the unconditional subscription to subordinated limited shares at the

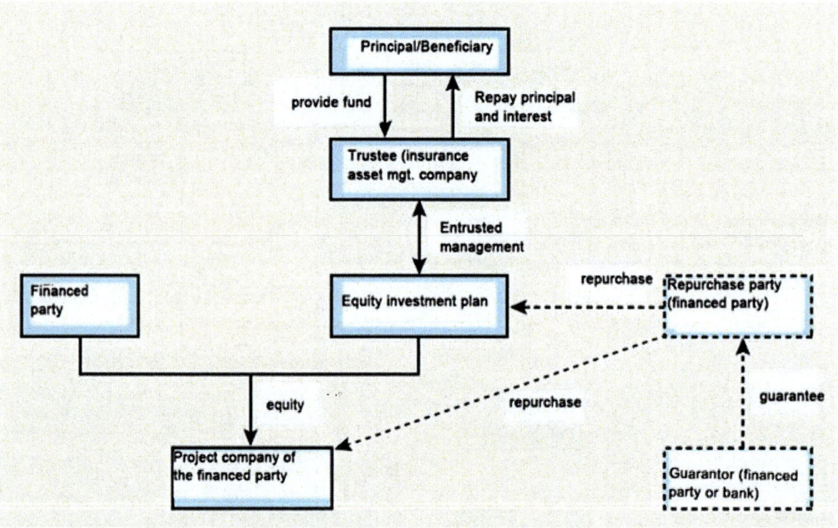

Fig. 9 Schematic diagram of the transaction structure of equity investment model and "debt under[6] disguise of equity" investment model. *Source* Author's drawing

[6] Kui Wu: "Definition and Risk Identification of "Debt under Disguise of Equity" Financing Instruments", China Insurance Asset Management, No. 4, 2016.

equity investment fund level in order to provide liquidity support for the exit of priority limited shares. In other words, the equity financing model with explicit or implicit repurchase terms has the dual nature of equity and creditor's rights. The commitment of financing the project company's equity made by the principal or trustee is conditioned on the effective exit and rigid payment of the agreed interest income in the future. This results in the co-existence of the equity nature at the project company level and the debtor nature of the financing party, so it is called "debt under the disguise of equity".

As a non-standard financing instrument for private placement, the "debt under disguise of equity" financing model satisfies the demands of investors and financing parties on the term design of the trading structure, and is implemented under the restraint and protection of the "Contract Law." It can be a special purpose vehicle that follows the entire process of fund raising and project equity investment for asset management plans such as equity investment plan and trust plan that has a strong regulatory constraint. It can also invest in equity indirectly through obtaining private equity fund share (priority LP share). Or it can superpose the asset management plan special purpose vehicle above the priority limited partnership share to better meet regulatory and asset allocation requirements. At the same time it enhances credit through repurchase of transferred equity in the future and supplementing the fund difference by the non-project-entity, in order to complete the structural design of "debt under disguise of equity". It shall be noted that the addition of private equity funds share or the superposition of asset management plan special purpose vehicle is simply to add corresponding links or participants to the basic transaction structure (see Fig. 9). No individual illustration will be presented here. The representative case of equity investment model is the equity investment plan of Beijing-Shanghai High-speed Railway, where Ping An Asset Management Corporation, Pacific Asset Management Corporation, Taikang Asset Management Corporation and Taiping Asset Management Corporation as trustees, Ping An Life Insurance and Taiping Life Insurance act as principals, China Reinsurance Group, China-Italy Life Insurance Company and China People's Property Insurance Company are participating subscribers and beneficiaries, China Construction Bank is the custodian, and China Development Bank is the independent supervisor.

Non-standard asset investment model for project assets support plan follows this process: Professional institutions such as insurance asset management companies establish a support plan as a trustee, repay with cash flows generated from fundamental assets as the support, and issue beneficiary certificates to qualified investments such as insurance institutions, i.e., the transfer of asset beneficiary rights or securitization of assets, among which fundamental assets are financial assets such as credit loans assets, small loan assets or financial lease assets that have their own cash flows. The basic transaction structure of the project asset support plan (see the solid line in Fig. 10) is that the trustee insurance company or insurance asset management company is entrusted with setting up the project asset support plan, and the funds raised from the principal will be paid to the original assets beneficiaries of the fundamental assets in order to meet the transfer financing requirement of the original equity

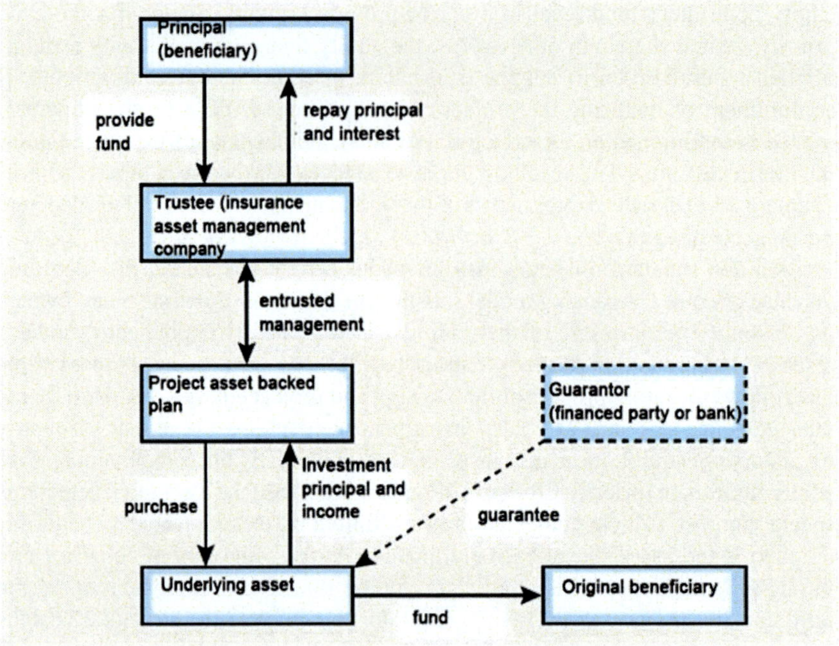

Fig. 10 Transaction structure project asset backed plan. *Source* Author's drawing

holders. At the end of the period, the trustee will pay the beneficiary's principal and interest by the income generated from the fundamental asset.

In practice, on the basic transaction structure of the project asset support plan, there are also additions of other participating entities or links such as guarantor (dotted line in Fig. 10). "Minsheng Tonghui - Ali Finance Project No. 1 Project Asset Support Plan" is a typical case of the project asset support plan. It was launched by Minsheng Tonghui and Ant Microfinance of Ant Financial Services Group. The only investment channel is Minsheng Life Insurance Universal Insurance, "Gold Ingot". It was sold through Taobao Minsheng Insurance's flagship store and Juhuasuan platform. The expected first-phase annualized rate of return will reach 6.2%. According to different risk and income characteristics, the project asset support plan will be divided into priority and posterior level certificates, in which the products of Minsheng Insurance's universal insurance "Golden Ingot" will be invested in the priority asset support securities of the plan, Ant Financial's affiliates Microloans hold all posterior level shares.

In the aforementioned equity investment plan, we said that it is possible to introduce private equity LP shares or other asset management plans special purpose vehicles to achieve indirect equity investment. In fact, this type of stock investment model is essentially a project asset support plan, that is, the "debt under disguise of equity" model, the transaction structure is shown in Fig. 11. Obviously, the transaction structure basically integrates multiple elements in debt and equity investment

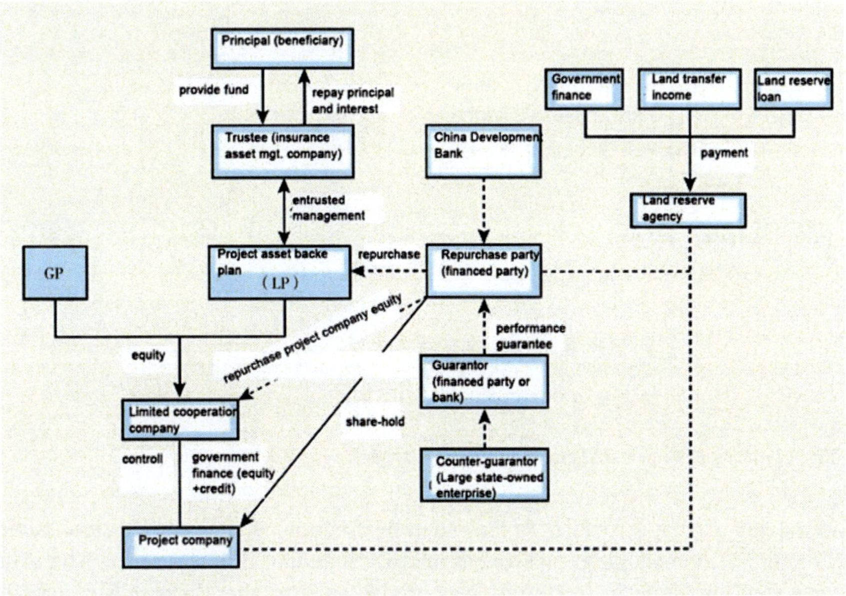

Fig. 11 Transaction structure of the "debt under disguise of equity" investment model. *Source* Author's drawing

models, such as guarantees, counter-guarantees and so on. From the policy level, the transaction structure is an innovative result after the "No. 43 Document", because such trading results do not require bottom line guarantee by fiscal department, or mortgages of government assets, or the need to increase the local government debt ratio. The investment of insurance funds provided capital for the project company and created the conditions for the project company or related upstream units to introduce commercial bank loans. The income generated by the project company can cover the "debt under disguise of equity" financing from insurance funds and the financing costs of commercial bank loans. In fact, in addition to the guarantee and counter-guarantee credit enhancement measures, the transaction structure has also made two kinds of credit enhancement programs: first, requiring the financiers to actually participate in the project company; second, it requires the land reserve agencies backed by fiscal and land sales revenue and land reserve to implicitly guarantee the repurchase and the project company. This is an innovation responding to "No. 43 Document".

In short, we mainly introduced above the six types of non-standard investment transaction structures with different combinations of creditor's rights, equity and project asset plans, and two credit enhancement measures such as guarantee and repurchase, as well as the derived transaction structures of "debt under disguise of equity" and "project under disguise of equity", a total of eight kinds of non-standard

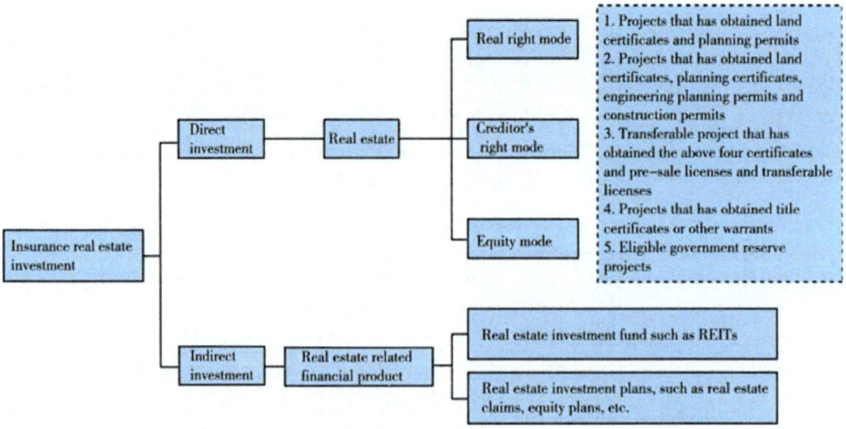

Fig. 12 Insurance funds real estate investment channel. *Source* Author's drawing

investment trading structure. At the end of this section, we introduce the transaction structure of non-standard investment in real estate and PPP insurance. The insurance fund investing in real estate was originated from the "Interim Measures for Real Estate Investment of Insurance Funds" promulgated by the China Insurance Regulatory Commission in 2010, and further developed by the overseas real estate investment practice according to "Detailed Interim Measures for the Administration of Overseas Investment Management of Insurance Funds" promulgated by China Insurance Regulatory Commission in 2012. Just like other investment directions, insurance fund investing in real estate is also through direct investment or indirect investment. Direct investment can be further divided into three ways: property rights, creditor rights and equity. Indirect investment mainly refers to investment in real estate financial products, such as real estate investment funds and real estate investment plans, details in Fig. 12. Take the London Canary Business District No. 10 project purchased by China Life Insurance as an example[7]; we briefly describe the transaction structure of offshore real estate purchases. First, we propose the adoption of an internationally preferred transaction structure. Based on considerations such as legally reducing tax burdens, isolating legal risks, and improving the flexibility of exit and transfer, cross-border investment will often have a multi-tiered structure, including setting up SPVs offshore, or conducting joint venture investments through limited partnerships. Second, we must consider the need for project management after investment. The 10th project requires the Canary Group to retain 10% of the shares during the equity structure design and be responsible for the asset management. This approach can ensure the consistent interests of both parties (Canary Group is the developer and operator of the entire area.) and can also reduce the difficulty of management since China Life has not established the professional management team overseas. In the course of the transaction, Qatar Investment Group, a shareholder of

[7] Hui Liu, "Analysis of Cases of Overseas Real Estate Investment with Insurance Funds", "China Insurance Asset Management", 2016(1).

the Canary Group, also showed great interest and hoped to invest together. Based on the consideration of risk reduction, China Life Insurance agreed to sell 20% of the shares, thus achieving a transaction framework in which the three parties jointly invest and China Life takes a dominant position.

In order to implement the decisions and deployment of the Party Central Committee and the State Council, the insurance industry has made great efforts to play its role. The insurance industry has carried out some initial explorations in participating in the PPP model. The main cooperation models are[8]: First, establish a PPP fund as a limited partnership (LP), according to the risk-return allocation mechanism, there are two types of investments, "debt under disguise of equity" and equity investment. Second, invest in PPP projects as a financial investor, that is, insurance funds indirectly provide financing for PPP projects through the creditor's rights, equity and combination of equity and debt. The third is to participate in PPP projects as risk managers, such as through the promotion of construction insurance, enterprise property insurance, liability insurance, accident insurance and other types of insurance to reduce the risk of PPP parties, improve project credit rating and reduce financing cost. The fourth is to form a joint venture with various industrial capitals to participate in the PPP project. The insurance agency is responsible for the project financing, the industrial capital is responsible for the design, construction, operation and maintenance, etc. Fifth, act as comprehensive financial consultant of the PPP project in the future. Providing fine financial resources for PPP projects, including investment and investment banking, insurance, asset management and other services. The typical case of insurance funds participating in the PPP project is the Beijing Metro Line No. 16, which adopts the "PPP + insurance equity investment" compound model. Beijing Infrastructure Investment Co., Ltd. ("Beijing Investment Corporation") undertakes the project planning and construction. The total investment is divided into two parts: investment and construction (Part A) and operation management (Part B). China Re Asset Management Co., Ltd. ("China Re Asset") was introduced into Part A through equity financing, and contributed 12 billion yuan in two phases. Beijing-Hongkong Subway Co., Ltd. ("Beijing-Hong Kong Subway") was introduced into Part B and contributed 15 billion yuan for the operation concessions. China Re Asset Management Co., Ltd. entrusted Beijing Investment Company with all of its equity and does not participate in the operation and management of Line 16 Company, and promised not to transfer any equity to a third party. At the end of the period, Beijing Capital Investment Corporation repurchased the equity in China Re Assets at the original value, and China Re Assets obtains an annualized income of 7%.

[8] Yuwen Wang: "Research on the Connection of Insurance Funds to China's Infrastructure PPP Model", "China Insurance Asset Management" No.1, 2016.

3 Interbank Investment: Business Innovation

In this section, we focus on the analysis of the interbank investment in the agreement.

Deposit channel business of insurance and commercial banks, the insurance trust business of insurance and trust company cooperation, and the beneficiary right of margin financing of insurance and securities companies. In the chapter "Bank Wealth Management", we discussed the model of bank-securities-insurance cooperation, that is, commercial banks convert inter-bank deposits into general deposits through the channel services of insurance companies and securities companies, and it will be the same model for the use of insurance funds for insurance-securities cooperation which is to convert inter-bank deposits into general deposits through channels. This is the "regulatory arbitrage" in the "three arbitrages", where the commercial bank invests in an asset management plan established by an insurance company with its own funds, wealth management funds or interbank deposit certificate and hold until maturity. The insurance asset management plan deposit the asset management plan funds into the fund-needing bank, thus forms the insurance agreement deposit business. In this business, the bank that accepts the deposit insurance business is designated by the funding bank, and the funding bank sets the deposit interest rate and duration. It is to convert interbank deposits into general deposits, and the transaction structure is shown in Fig. 13.

One of the main measures that the use of insurance funds to collaborate with securities asset management plans is the beneficiary rights of margin trading. On July 9, 2015, the China Insurance Regulatory Commission issued a notice (the "Notice") on issues concerning the participation of insurance asset management products in the beneficiary rights of margin trading business ("Notice"), stating that "to protect the healthy and stable development of the capital market and prevent the irrational decline of the stock market, effectively protecting the legitimate rights of investors and policyholders, the relevant issues are hereby notified as follows: 'The insurance asset management company raises funds through the issuance of insurance asset management products, and carries out transfer and repurchase of the beneficiary rights of margin trading business with securities companies; the term of repayment can be reasonably determined through negotiation, insurance may not unilaterally

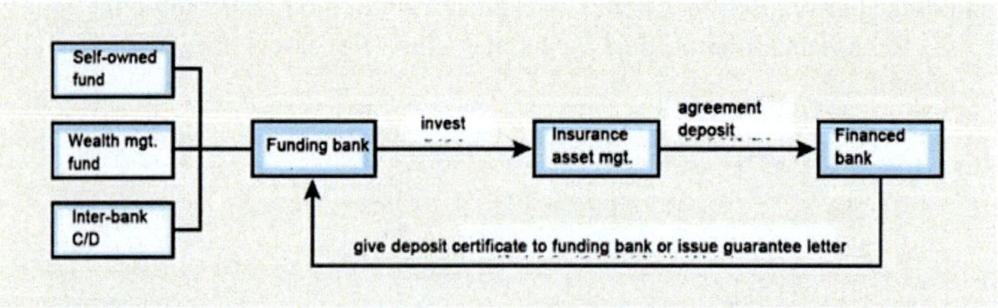

Fig. 13 Agreement deposit transaction structure. *Source* Author's drawing

require the securities company to repay the loan in advance. This notice shall be implemented as of the date of issuance." The notice specifies the method or term for insurance fund investing in the beneficiary rights of marging trading. In practice, an insurance asset management company may directly accept the transfer of the beneficiary rights of margin trading from a securities company. In addition, an insurance company or an insurance asset management company may subscribe for a collective fund trust plan, such as the third phase of the collective fund trust plan of CCB Trust-Youxiang No.1 that CPIC has subscribed for. The trustee of the trust plan is Jianxin Trust, the original equity beneficiary is Haitong Securities, the trust funds is to acquire from Haitong Securities the beneficiary rights of financing business, and Haitong Securities promises to execute the repurchase price at premium as stipulated in the contract. Obviously, the mode of insurance funds participating in the beneficiary rights of marging trading business through the subscription of trust plan can be attributed to project asset plan.

The abovementioned subscription collective fund trust plan is one of the cooperation modes between insurance funds and trust companies. The second type of business for cooperation between insurance companies and trust companies is the corporate annuity model. That is, according to the requirements made by the cooperative annuity legal person for increasing annuity gains, trust companies locate investment targets and set up trust plans. For example, in July 2014, Bridge Trust and China Life Pension Insurance jointly established the "Bridge An Xin No. 1 Single Fund Trust". The trust is connected to the enterprise annuity. Bridge Trust lends the trust principal to the Qinghai Yellow River Upstream Hydropower Development Co., Ltd. in the form of a trust loan. The third type of business is insurance trust business; the insurance benefit based family trust. The traditional family trust structure is that the principal entrust funds or other assets to the trustee and the trustee distributes benefits to the beneficiaries according to the wishes of the principal. The insurance trust has added the benefit of insurance coverage and operats in two ways: one is that the principal entrusts the trustee the insurance benefit under his name to the trustee; the other is that the principal entrusts cash to the trustee, and the trustee pays the premium regularly. After the insurance expires, the insurance benefit will be automatically transferred to the family trust. The transaction structure is shown in Fig. 14.

4 Alternative Investment Development: Legalization

In recent years, with the deepening of the regulatory concept "open the front-end and manage the back-end" of the China Insurance Regulatory Commission, the reform of the marketization of underwriting and investment liberalization with the "reimbursement of the second generation" as the backing of supervision has continued to advance. A series of new policies for the use of insurance funds since 2012 have gradually broadened the use of insurance funds from traditional large category assets such as bonds and stocks to alternative assets such as real estate, unlisted equity, offshore

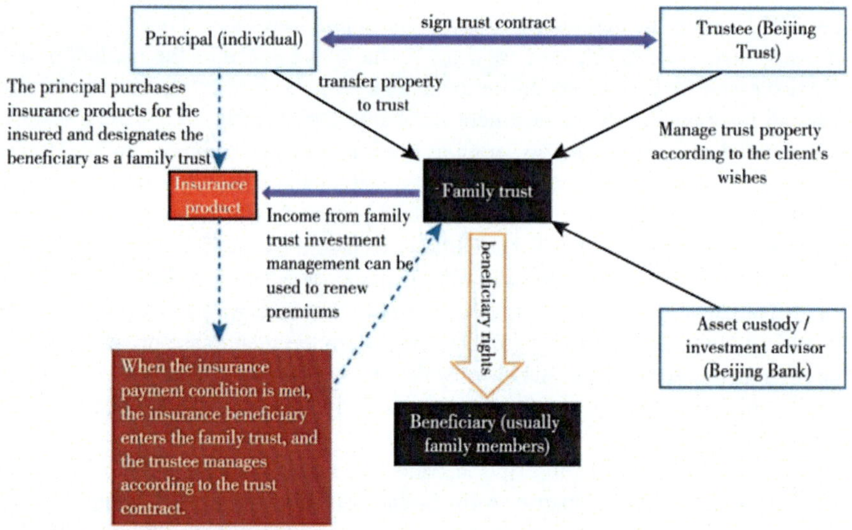

Fig. 14 Schematic diagram of insurance trust transaction structure. *Source* Bank of Beijing, Beijing Trust

investment and asset support plans. With regard to the opening of loan business for insurance funds, even in the "Interim Measures for the Administration of the Use of Insurance Funds" (Exposure Draft) announced in March 2016, investment assets formed by the use of insurance funds are still prohibited from providing guarantees or loans to others, except for insurance pledge loans. This shows that except domestic life insurance policies pledged loans, other insurance guarantees or mortgage loans are banned. Not only can insurance funds not be able to directly carry out loan business, but also it cannot indirectly be involved in individual home mortgage loan business by holding fixed income products such as personal residential mortgage loan securitization (MBS) products.

In the foregoing analysis, we can see that the innovative development of the use of insurance funds in recent years has basically focused on non-standard investments and alternative investments represented by the interbank investment. The credit allocation function of non-standard investment is self-evident, and the innovations in interbank investment include innovations in the credit function, such as "Brige An Xin No.1 Single Fund Trust". In fact, insurance fund engaging in loan business has always been one of the important investment channels in Europe and the United States and other developed countries. For example, the proportion of direct investment of insurance funds in mortgage loans in US, Japan and China Taiwan life insurance industry is 45%, 50% and 35% respectively. It is also an important tool for enhancing the investment income of insurance funds. As for the use of insurance funds in China, there are at least three advantages for engaging in loan business: First, to shoulder the loan pressure of commercial banks; Second, business risks are relatively low, while the income is good; Third, to solve the problem of long-term liability funded by short-term insurance funds, which is conducive to improve asset and liability management. The most important benefits are to "legalize" the controversial non-standard investment and some of the interbank investments. Therefore, for the reform of the regulatory framework, the integration of "one bank and three commissions" or the merger of the China Insurance Regulatory Commission and China Banking Regulatory Commission may be good choices.

Chapter 5
Analysis of Funds Flow and Mechanism of Securities Assets Management

From 2013 to 2016, the participation of securities companies in the entire asset management industry has steadily increased. The scale of asset management of securities companies grew rapidly. As of the end of 2016, it reached 17.31 trillion yuan. The main supporting force for rapid growth came from the directional asset management led by channel products, and the scale of channel services accounted for more than 70% of the total. Most of the funds of the securities company's asset management business come from commercial banks and trust companies. The monotonicity of funding sources determines the passiveness of funds management and the centralization of capital investment. In recent years, securities companies have become important participants in the bank's outsourcing business. Non-standard assets are the major investment targets of securities company asset management plans. In the directional channel business, the vast majority of funds are invested in non-standard assets in the form of trust loans, bank entrusted loans, beneficiary rights of assets, and other investments such as bank wealth management and trust plans. In recent years, mainly due to fluctuations in the capital market, the proportion of bonds in standardized assets has increased significantly. The business cooperation between the securities companies and other asset management institutions such as banks, trusts, funds, insurance, and crossed-products have been further intensified, which is driven by regulatory arbitrage. Innovations in product design mainly focus on margin trading and asset securitization business. For a period of time in the future, the unified supervision of the asset management industry will significantly repress channel services, forcing the transition from channel services to active management services. Giving full play to the license advantages, enhancing the active management capabilities and further exploring the capital market will be the development direction of the securities company's asset management business.

Written by Boying Wang and Yanbing Li.

J. Yin et al., *Whither has the Money Gone*,
https://doi.org/10.1007/978-981-16-4931-8_5

1 Sources and Use of Capital for Brokerage Capital Management

From 2013 to 2016, the asset management scale of securities companies grew rapidly. As of the end of 2016, the asset management size of securities firms reached 17.31 trillion yuan, an increase of 45.6% year-on-year, slightly lower than 2015 (see Fig. 1). In the era of great assets management, the participation of securities companies in the entire asset management industry has steadily increased. The scale ratio has increased from 11.6% in 2013 to 33.4%. From the perspective of business lines, the main supporting force for the rapid growth of brokerage asset management scale comes from the directional asset management business. Although the proportion of directional asset management business has continued to decline in recent years, as of the end of 2016, the proportion still stands at 84.8%, which is a drop of 8 percent from the end of 2014. In the directional asset management business, passive channel services occupy an absolute dominant position. In 2010, after the China Banking Regulatory Commission suspended the bank's use of trust to move and transfer the on-sheet credit assets, the asset management of the securities companies became the main channel for banks to transfer credit assets on-balance sheet to off-balance-sheet. After the brokerage innovation conference in 2012, under the policy guidance of "deregulation and strengthening supervision", the asset management business of the securities companies developed rapidly. Compared with bank wealth management and trust that have been subject to more regulatory constraints, the regulatory environment for such securities company businesses is relatively loose, provided new exports for the channel business in a grey area of supervision. In particular, in recent years, under the background of "asset shortage", some securities companies have become important participants in bank outsourcing operations by

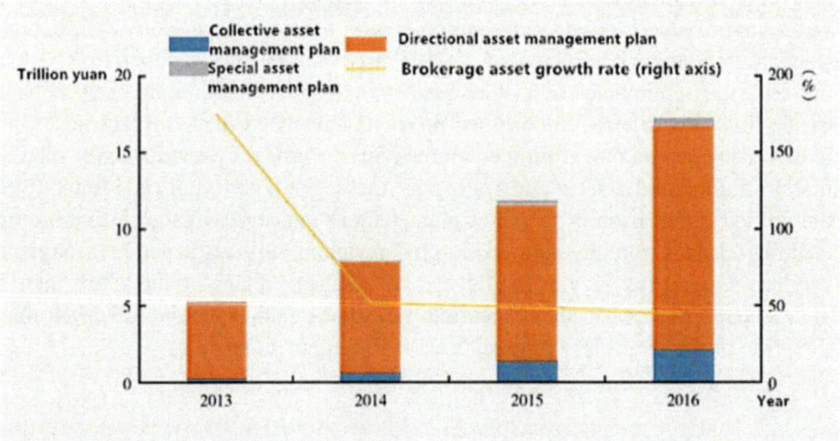

Fig. 1 Asset management business scale of securities companies from 2013 to 2016. *Source* China Securities Investment Fund Industry Association

Table 1 Sources of funds for brokerage asset management business from 2013 to 2016. Unit: trillions yuan

Year	Total scale	Scale	Proportion of individuals (%)	Proportion of institutions (%)	Scale	Proportion of individuals (%)	Proportion of institutions (%)	Corporate or organization scale
2013	5.20	0.36	68.0	32.0	4.83	0.1	99.9	0.01
2014	7.95	0.66	63.9	36.1	7.25	0.2	99.8	0.04
2015	11.89	1.56	48.2	51.8	10.16	0.3	99.7	0.18
2016	17.31	2.19	42.9	57.1	14.69	0.3	99.7	0.43

Source China Securities Investment Fund Industry Association and Authors' finishing

upgrading their active management capabilities, flexible product designs and absolute return on investment.

From the sources of funds, the vast majority of funds of asset management business of securities companies come from commercial banks and trust companies. The investment entities of the directional asset management business and the special asset management business are almost all institutional investors. By the end of 2016, in the directional asset management business, the entrusted scale of commercial banks and trust companies was approximately 12.68 trillion yuan, accounting for 86.3% of the total size, a slight decline in scales compared to the previous two years compared; the proportion of individual investors is less than 1%. In the collective asset management business, the proportion of institutional investors continues to rise. As of the end of 2016, institutional investor entrustment scale exceeded the size of individual investors, accounting for 57.1%, up 25 percentage points over 2013 (see Table 1).

The monotonicity of the source of funds determines the passiveness of funds management and the centralization of capital investment. From the perspective of fund management, passively managed channel products have always occupied an absolute proportion in the asset management of securities companies, mainly in the directional asset management business. Directional asset management services provide services for a single customer. The channel business helps banks adjust their balance sheets, achieve off-sheet asset movement, save capital occupation and grant indirect credit. In 2016, securities companies increased cooperation with banks due to the limited access of fund subsidiaries to channels, and the scale of channel business further grew. As of the end of 2016, the channel business scale of China's securities companies was 12.39 trillion yuan, an increase of 39.9% year-on-year, and accounted for 71.6% of the total capital of securities asset management. Since 2016, the regulator has taken the stand on channel compression and issued multiple documents to increase the barriers for securities companies, funds and fund subsidiaries to carry out channel business. In May 2017, the spokesman of the China Securities Regulatory Commission Zhang Xiaojun clearly stated at the press conference that "the securities fund management organization shall not engage in the 'channel business' of transferring responsibility for the management". The channel business has a high proportion in the asset management business of securities companies. The policy guidance of "abandoning channel and deleveraging" will lead to a short-term contraction of asset management scale, and will force the transformation of channel services to active management.

Although channel-type businesses are large in scale, they have low added value and cannot constitute the core competitiveness of securities companies' asset management. The proportion of directional asset management services based on channel services accounted for more than 70%, but revenue accounted for only 55.4%. Because the channeling party often does not need to be responsible for the project end and capital end, nor does it bear the investment risk, the handling fee is also low. At the same time, due to fierce competition among fund subsidiaries and securities companies, the fee for channel services has been declining. The active management products, such as collective asset and special asset management, put more emphasis on the manager's investment ability and product design capability. The average rate is much higher than the directional asset management. In 2016, the rates for collective asset and special asset management were 0.44% and 0.23%, respectively, which was much higher than 0.09% of the directional asset management.

In recent years, securities companies have continued to seek transformation and development to upgrade their active asset management capabilities. From the perspective of business structure, the proportion of channel-based directional asset management is still relatively large, but the growth rate has begun to slow, and the proportion has continued to decline. The rapid growth of the scale of collective plans and special asset management plans that embody active management capabilities has become a key business for the development of asset management by securities companies. As of the end of 2016, brokers' actively managed business volume was 4.94 trillion yuan, up 62.5% year-on-year, accounting for a ratio of 28.5% from 17.0% at the end of 2014. The scale of the collective plan was 2.19 trillion yuan, an increase of 40.4% year-on-year, which is equivalent to 6 times scale at the end of 2013. 2015 was a year of explosive growth in the collective asset management business. It was closely related to the low-interest-market environment and more relaxed market supervision. The significant increase in the scale of the special asset management business is mainly due to the rapid development of the asset securitization (ABS). In 2014, the "Regulations on the Administration of Asset Securitization of Securities Companies and Subsidiaries of Fund Management Companies (Revised Version)" was promulgated, requiring securities companies (using a special asset management plan as a vehicle) and fund subsidiaries to carry out asset securitization business, and the original examination and approval system was changed to a filing system and a negative list management mechanism. With increasingly relaxed regulation environment and optimization of product structure, the asset securitization business has achieved rapid development, which has led to the fast growing of special asset management businesses. As of the end of 2016, the scale of the special asset management of securities companies reached 431.5 billion yuan, an increase of 140.6% year-on-year, equivalent to 11.8 times scale at the end of 2014.

From the perspective of the use of funds in securities asset management business, non-standard assets are still the major investment, and the proportion of bonds in standardized assets has increased significantly. By the end of 2016, the scale of investment in non-standard assets such as various entrusted loans, trust loans, and beneficiary rights of assets was approximately 11.67 trillion yuan, accounting for 67.4%; the scale of the investment in bond market was approximately 4.90 trillion yuan. Specific to each business line, the collective plans and the actively managed directional asset management plan have similar distribution, while the standardized assets account for an absolute proportion with bonds as the primary allocation product. In 2016, the bond market continued to improve, the supply of bonds raised, and the proportion of bonds in securities company asset increased significantly. As of the end of 2016, 63.5% of collective plans were invested in the bond market, representing an increase of 25.7 percentage points from the end of 2015. Due to the depressed stock market and the frequent occurrence of default in financing projects, the proportion of investment in stocks, funds, agreement deposits and trust plans has dropped remarkably. The asset allocation of active management services in the directional asset management business also shows a similar trend. In 2016, the scale of bond market investment in actively managed directional businesses was 1.56 trillion yuan, accounting for 55.7% of the total, increased by 10.2% compared to the end of 2015. The proportion of investment in trust plans and stock markets has showed overt decline (see Table 2).

The investment distribution of directional channel services is different from those of active management services. The vast majority of funds are invested in non-standard assets such as investment trust loans, bank entrusted loans, beneficiary rights of asset, and other investments based on bank wealth management and trust plans. However, in recent years, the scale and proportion of bond-based securities investment have increased. As of the end of 2016, the scale of bond-based securities investment amounted to 1.96 trillion yuan, accounting for 15.8% of the total, increased by 5.4 percentage points compared to the end of 2014 and was basically the same as at the end of 2015. In addition, the scale of investment in bank-entrusted loans and trust loans has increased rapidly, but the proportion has declined. The right of return on assets and other investments (mainly based on bank wealth management and trust plans) have grown rapidly in scale, with their proportion soaring. The proportion of other investment scales increased from 17.7% at the end of 2015 to 22.3% at the end of 2016, which indicates that the business crossover and product nesting between different asset management agencies are more serious (see Table 2). Looking specifically at the industrial distribution of the financing channel business, the funds are ultimately invested in general industrial and commercial enterprises, real estate, fundamental industries and local financing platforms. In recent years, the debts of local governments have been cleared, and the stock of investment in fundamental industries and local financing platforms has been declining year by year. The scale of funding for general industrial and commercial enterprises has increased significantly (see Fig. 2).

Table 2 Usage of funds for securities asset management business in 2016. Unit: trillion yuan

Business type		Investment direction		Scale
Collective asset management 2.19		Securities investment 1.67	Bond	1.39
			Fund	0.12
			Stock	0.17
		Deposit 0.15	Agreement of time deposit	0.15
		Asset management plan 0.18	Trust plan	0.13
			Spcial asset management plan	0.05
		Other		0.19
Directiona l asset management 15.19	Active managem ent 2.80	Securities investment 1.84	Bond	1.56
			Stock	0.18
			Fund	0.10
		Deposit 0.04	Inter-bank deposit	0.04
		Asset management plan 0.35	Trust plan	0.23
			Broker's collective plan	0.13
		Other 0.57	Bond reverse repo	0.10
			Stock collateral repurchase	0.06
			Asset income right	0.02
			Other	0.39
	Channel business 12.39	Securities investment 1.96		1.96
		Non-standardized asset 6.55	Trust loan	1.48
			Bank entrusted loan	1.75
			Asset income right	1.77
			Bill	1.56
		Deposit 0.58	Inter-bank deposit	0.58
		Other 3.31	Equity collateral repurchase	0.47
			Bond reverse repo	0.07
			Other (mainly bank wealth management and trust plan)	2.77
Special asset management 0.43		ABS mainly		0.43

Source Author compiles

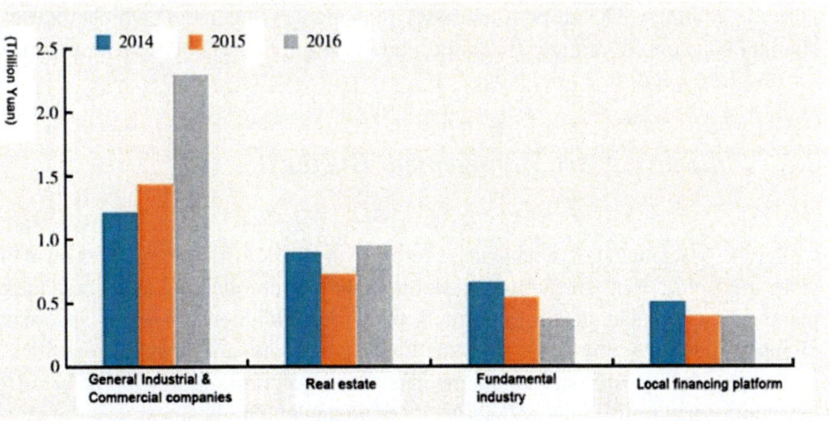

Fig. 2 The ultimate flow of funds of the channel business from 2014 to 2016. *Source* China Securities Investment Fund Industry Association

2 Analysis of Raised Funds and Investment Mechanism

In February 2013, the China Securities Regulatory Commission issued the "Provisional Regulations on the Management of Public Offering Securities Investment Funds by Asset Management Institutions", which allows brokers, private equity and insurance institutions to engage in public offerings, while securities companies are not allowed to initiate collective asset management plan for more than 200 investors (i.e. the "big collection"), the replacement will be the public fund business. Securities companies that meet certain conditions may apply for public funded qualifications. Since then, in addition to public offerings, the securities asset management business has raised funds in three major ways: collective asset management business, directional asset management business and special asset management business. The investment thresholds for all three are one million yuan, of which the collective asset management plan and special asset management plan are issued to multiple clients, but the number of investors cannot exceed 200. The former investors can be natural persons or institutions, the latter only for institutional investors. Directional asset management plans are issued for a single customer. From the perspective of investment scope, the collective asset management plan mainly invests in standardized financial products in exchanges or interbank markets, as well as asset management products such as bank wealth management, collective fund trusts, public funds, and special asset management plans of securities companies. It can also participate in financing activities for margin trading. The investment scope of the directional asset management plan shall be agreed by the securities company and the client through contract and may participate in the margin trading business. The investment scope of the special asset management plan includes equities, creditor's rights and other property rights that have not been transferred through the stock exchanges, and it can also engage in asset securitization businesses through the establishment of special purpose vehicles. The directional asset management business, which focuses on channel business, dominates the asset management business of securities firms.

2.1 Collective Asset Management Business

Collective asset management business refers to those securities companies raise funds from multiple clients through the establishment of a collective asset management plan, sign asset management contracts with multiple clients, operate and manage clients' assets in accordance with the agreed contracts, and provide securities and other financial investment management services. According to different investment directions, the traditional collective asset management business can be divided into: bond-based collective asset management plans, equity-based collective asset management plans and hybrid collective asset management plans.

In recent years, there have been some innovations in collective asset management business, such as innovative fixed-income collective asset management plans and new fund forms such as FOF and FOT. The innovative fixed-income collective asset management plan is generally designed as a graded product. The business process is illustrated by an example of a graded fixed-income collective asset management plan issued by a securities company. A securities company issues a collective asset management plan, and the bank and other capital parties (securities company's owe capital and other investors agreed upon by the bank and the securities company) purchase the plan as the priority and the posterior grade respectively. The securities company commissions the pooled funds raised by the bank and the third-party bank will be the supervisor of the funds. Securities companies purchase fixed-income products such as various types of bonds, funds, government bonds, and trust products from the exchanges and inter-bank bond trading markets in accordance with the law and the agreement with the trustor. When the collective asset management plan expires, the securities company will return the principal and gains to the principal (investor) after deducting the agreed upon fee for asset management of the plan, and the plan ends (see Fig. 3).

FOF (Fund of Funds) is a new type of fund that invests in unaffiliated securities investment funds, that is, funds that invest in other funds. FOT (Fund of Trusts) is a fund that invests in trust plans. Take the FOT as an example, a securities company issues a collective asset management plan, which is divided into a priority level and a posterior level. It will be invested collective trust plans as agreed. The securities company as a manager screens and subscribes for a group of high quality collective trust plans. The trust plan funds are used in the targeted investment projects. The projects generate cash flow and trust plans receive investment income. The trust plan distributes trust income to the collective asset management plan. Collective asset management plans distributes income to investors. Business process is shown in Fig. 4.

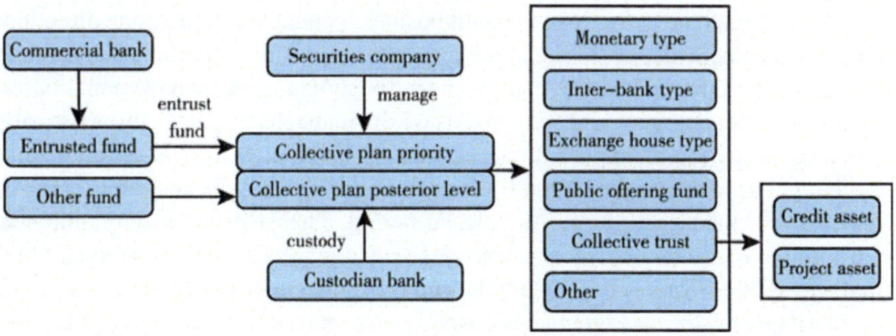

Fig. 3 The transaction structure of fixed-income type collective asset management business

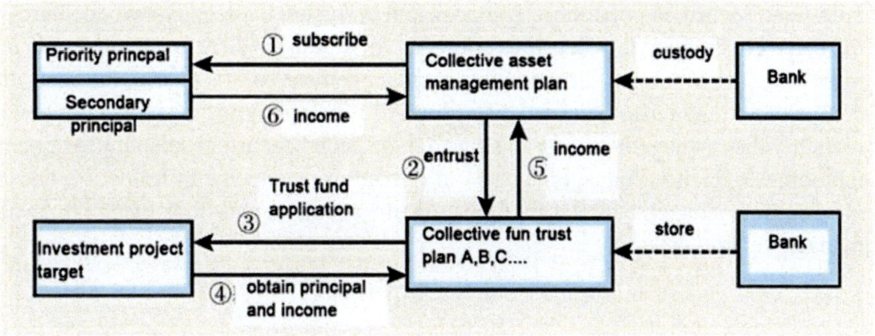

Fig. 4 FOT transaction structure

2.2 Active Directional Asset Management Services

The directional asset management business raises funds from a single client. The investment scope is contracted by both the securities company and the client. It can be categorized as active management and passive management. The actively managed directional asset management business mainly invests in bonds, interbank deposits, trust plans and stocks. It includes active quasi-trust management services, fixed income active management services, and market value management services through directional plans.

The active management business carried out through the directional asset management plan engages mainly in businesses where the project seeks funds or vice versa. The securities company sets up a directional asset management plan and the bank issues guarantees letter, affiliated companies or major shareholders provide guarantees, the directional plan will be invested in the right of returns on certain type of asset of the financing company, or the major shareholder of the listed company pledges his tradable or restricted shares for financing through directional asset management plan.

The fixed income active management business conducted through the directional asset management plan is similar to the fixed income business conducted through the collective fund trust plan. The bank signs a directional asset management contract with a securities company and entrusted its wealth management funds to the securities company, requiring an expected rate of return. The bank will transfer funds to the directional account and be bound by the closed period, and the securities company will actively manage it during the closed period. The investment scope includes, not limited to, interbank deposits, exchange bond market varieties, interbank bond market varieties, bank acceptance bills, and fixed income trust products.

The market value management business is an asset management business in which securities companies provide value-maintaining and value-added services for listed companies that hold banned sales of unbanned shares and has to maintain a certain proportion of shares in accordance with statutory requirements, and for clients who hold fixed securities portfolios. The principal entrusted the legally-owned shares of the listed company to the securities company to establish a directional asset management plan, and signed a "directional asset management contract" with the securities company and the custodian bank. The securities company provides its clients with market value management services through a special securities account for clients, including: reduction management, band operation management, reduction and re-distribution management, margin financing management, and stock pledge financing management.

2.3 Channel-Type Directional Asset Management Business

Passive directional asset management services, that is, broker asset management channel services, mainly invests in trust loans, bank entrusted loans, right of return on assets and bills. Securities companies who carry out such business are mainly meeting bank's demands of moving out the inventory assets out of the balance sheet, granting off-balance sheet loan, adjusting deposit structure and income structure. The main modes include bill investment, letter of credit investment, credit asset investment, bank-securities-insurance transfer business and total return swaps.

The channel business of bill investment refers to the business in which the commercial bank entrusts the management funds to the directional asset management plan to purchase the bank's designated note assets. The securities company entered into an asset transfer contract and an asset service agreement with the bank, the directional plan use the funds to buy the designated note assets only, and entrust the bank with asset management and collection, at the same time the custodian bank allocated funds according to the administrator's order. This business helps the bank to achieve the off-balance-sheet transfer of assets and free up new credit lines. Through bank-insurance cooperation, commercial banks effectively circumvented the regulatory restrictions on the use of wealth management funds, and also make it possible for the transfer of credits from on-balance sheet to off-balance sheet (see Fig. 5).

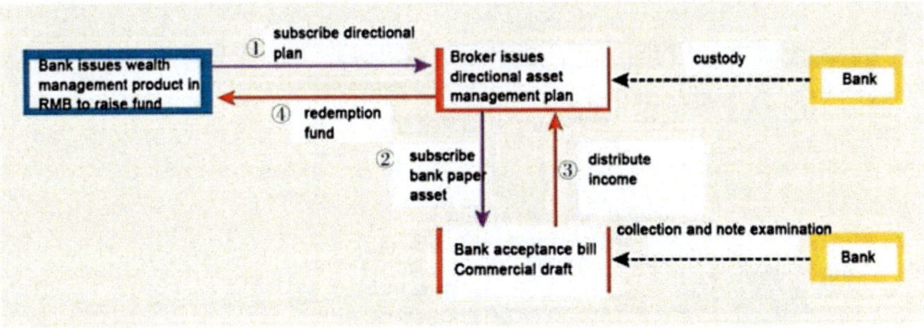

Fig. 5 Business structures of bill investment channels. *Source* Author compiles

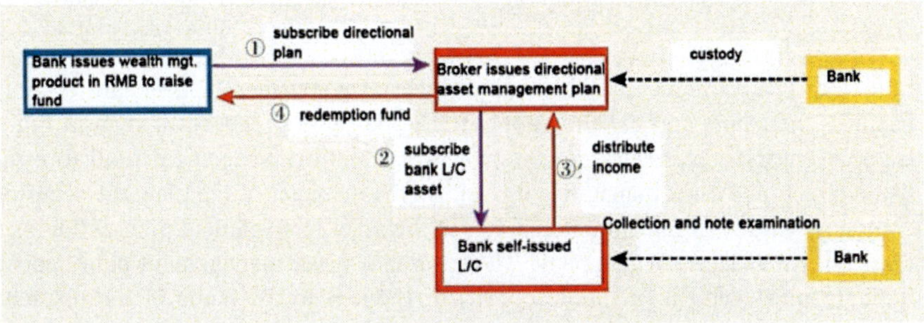

Fig. 6 Structure of letter of credit investment type channel business. *Source* Author compiles

The L/C investment channel business is an inter-bank L/C transfer operation through the securities company's channel of directional asset management plan where the issuance of credit does not squeeze bank credit lines and expand deposits. The essence is for the banks to break through the constrains of loan scale and to expand the off-balance sheet assets. The operation process is shown in Fig. 6.

The channel business of credit assets (trust loans/bank entrusted loans) investment refers to the business that banks grant credit through the channel of broker directional products. It optimizes the structure of bank statements and increases loan income. The commercial bank entrusts the RMB wealth management funds to the directional asset management plan and the plan purchases the designated single trust plan or directly entrusts the bank to grant loans.

The trust plans use trust funds to purchase credit assets from or issue trust loans enterprises that banks have designated. The bought credit assets generate cash flow and trust plans receive investment income (see Fig. 7).

The essence of the bank-securities-insurance transfer business is to convert inter-bank deposits into general deposits, helping banks break through interest rate controls and expand deposits. The policy background of the business is that the deposits of insurance asset management companies do not belong to the interbank deposits of financial institutions, but are general deposits. When calculating the loan-to-deposit

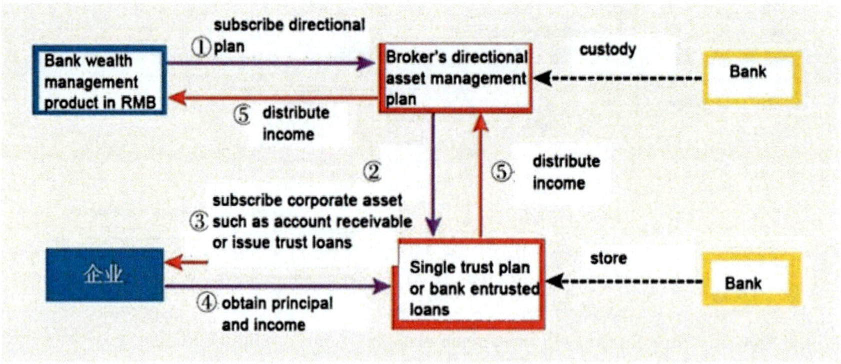

Fig. 7 Structure of credit asset investment type channel business. *Source* Author compiles

ratio, they can be included in the bank deposits. This business helps banks optimize business indicators and expand deposits. The business process is shown in Fig. 8. Bank A entrusts the securities company with wealth management fund to establish a directional asset management plan. As the manager of the plan, the securities company will invest the entrusted assets in the asset management plan of the insurance asset management company. The insurance asset management plan deposits the agreement deposit (general deposit) of Bank B in the name of the insurance company. After the deposit expires, the funds are returned to a bank account through the insurance asset management plan and the broker directional plan.

Total return swaps (TRS) products are one of the innovative forms of channel services. Business process is shown in Fig. 9. The bank issues non-guaranteed floating wealth management products to raise funds. The wealth management funds are invested in the bank's fixed deposits. The funds form margin deposits similar to structured deposits in the margin accounts of wealth management customers. Banks invest their own funds or interbank funds in non-standard assets such as broker directional asset management plans, single trust plans, fund subsidiaries' special plans, and channel financing to customers in the form of entrusted loans through channel agencies such as securities company, trusts and fund subsidiaries. The fixed deposits invested by wealth management products provide pledge guarantees for non-standard assets invested by banks, while wealth management customers sign guarantee contracts with banks. At the same time, asset management plans and

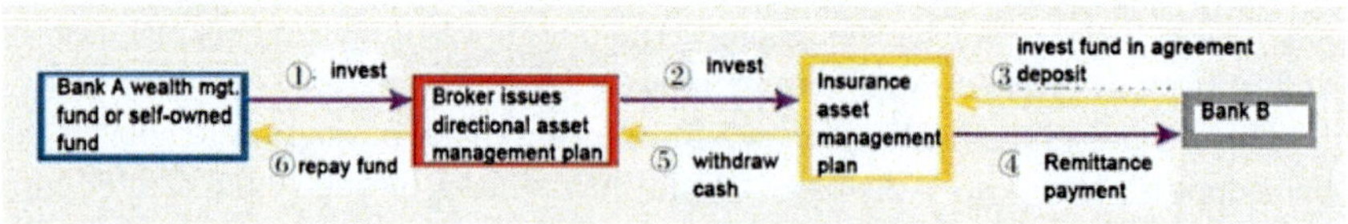

Fig. 8 Structure of bank-securities-insurance transfer deposit channel business. *Source* Author compiles

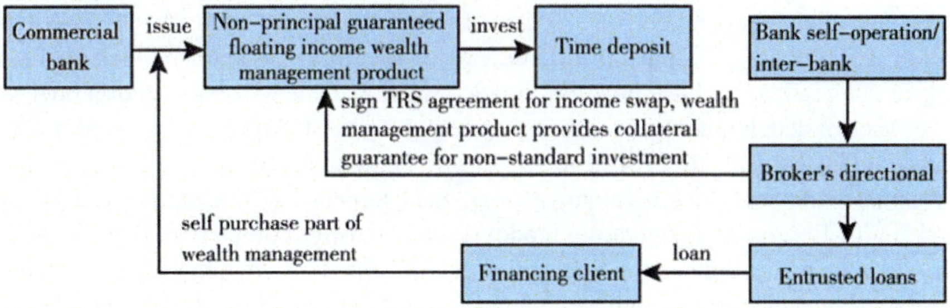

Fig. 9 TRS product operation model. *Source* Author compiles

wealth management products through the TRS agreement, swap the gains on fixed deposit with lower interest rate for floating income of asset management products with higher interest rate.

For commercial banks, the attractiveness of this operating model is threefold. First, realize deposit increase. After the sale of wealth management product is completed, the fund will form a margin deposit similar to a structured deposit in the margin account of the wealth management customer; second, risk-free capital occupation. Entrusted loans and wealth management funds corresponding to asset management plans form exchange incomes, non-standard investments are replaced with full margin investment, and no risk capital is taken up; Third, expansion of wealth management scale and scale of non-standard assets. The nominal investment target of TRS product is margin deposit, which does not belong to the non-standard assets stipulated in "No.8 Document". Therefore, it is not included in the non-standard limit, instead, it expands the total scale of wealth management and enlarges the space for non-standard assets.

There are two major controversies in this type of operation: First, the on-sheet risk now is off-sheet. The credit risk of the non-standard investment on the bank's balance sheet is transferred to the off-balance-sheet wealth management. On the surface, the investment risk is borne by the customer, which is essentially borne by the bank through the implicit guarantees the bank provided. Eventually, non-standard asset investments are achieved but risk capital occupation is circumvented. Second, insufficient information disclosure. The investment direction of the product is stated as "the margin of the bank's investment assets pledged", the retail-end wealth management customers can not see the investment target itself, and the actual credit risk is still borne by the bank.

2.4 Special Asset Management Plan

The "Provisions on the Administration of Securities Securitization Business of Securities Companies" requires securities companies to issue asset-backed securities through the establishment of a special asset management plan. Asset securitization is a process of financing the issuance of securities backed by assets that will generate predictable cash flow. For financing party, the asset securitization business is a type of debt financing; for investors, asset securitization product is a type of fixed income investment. In 2014 filing system was implemented for asset securitization business, the securities company's asset management business showed an explosive growth. The basic operating model is: the securities company initiates a special asset management plan as an SPV for asset securitization. The special asset management plan will issue special beneficiaries certificate of fixed income to qualified investors to raise funds. The funds of the special plan are earmarked for purchasing the specific fundamental assets owned by the original stakeholders. The special plan repays principal and interest to the beneficiary certificate holders based on the cash inflow generated by the underlying assets. Asset securitization business is conducive to optimizing corporate financial statements and reducing financing costs, and at the same time it can bring relatively stable high returns to investors. But in practice, there is no active trading market for such products. Asset management products generally include credit enhancement measures such as balance supplement terms, so the risks of fundamental assets cannot be completely stripped.

a. Creditor's rights of margin trading ABS

In July 2015, the China Securities Regulatory Commission announced that it allowed securities companies to conduct securitization of the creditor's rights assets of margin trading. In August, China's first asset-backed securities (ABS), the "Special Plan of Guojun Huatai Financing Capital Assets Securitization No. 1" was issued, the underlying asset is the claims to the capital financing of margin trading of securities company. It is listed and traded on the Shanghai Stock Exchange and managed by Huatai Assets Management Company, the specific underlying asset is Guotaijunan securities company's claims to the financing party for margin trading and the affiliated guarantee benefit. The initial asset pool involves the assets of creditor's rights in margin trading held by Guojun. The total initial asset pool is 500 million yuan. The plan is divided into priority asset-backed securities and subordinate asset-backed securities. The priority scale is 475 million yuan with AAA rating. The scale of the subordinate asset-backed securities is 25 million yuan, Guojun Securities subscribed all of them and provided balance supplements to securities of various priority levels. It also designs a cyclical purchase structure in the transaction to achieve duration matching between assets end and securities end. The classification of priority and subordinate level is conducive to effective protection for priority securities. The transaction structure is shown in Fig. 10.

Through asset securitization standardized financing tools, securities companies can proactively manage their balance sheets, revitalize existing assets, improve a number of financial and regulatory indicators, and reasonably adjust the term structure of their liabilities to further diversify their financing channels.

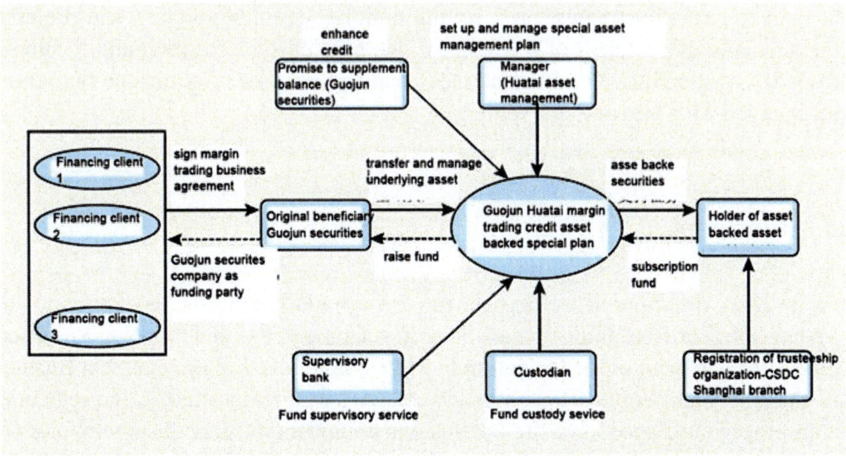

Fig. 10 Operation mode of ABS special asset management plan. *Source* Author compiles

b. Dual SPV REITs

At the end of 2015, the first single-item REITs asset securitization project of the SSE—"Hengtai Haorui—HNA Pufa Building Asset Support Special Project" was completed. The total size of the project is 2.5 billion yuan. The plan manager is Hengtai Securities. The underlying assets are the shares of contractual private equity funds. The private equity fund revenue comes from the rental income and future increased assets value of the office building.

Value-added benefits.

Different from the traditional ABS project, Hengtai-Hui Rui-HNA plan adopts the "Dual-SPV" structure of "Special Plan + Private Equity Fund". During the issuance of the asset support special plan, a contractual fund was introduced to acquire, hold, operate, and manage project companies based on underlying assets. In the specific arrangement, the manager Hengtai Securities initiated the Hengtai Hao Rui-HNA plan, the special plan will be used to acquire and pay for all the fund shares of the "Hengtai Haorui—HNA Pufa Building Private Equity Investment Fund". The manager of the private equity investment fund is Hengtai HNA (Beijing) Investment Management Co., Ltd., which is jointly established by Hengtai Pioneer Investment (a wholly-owned subsidiary of Hengtai Securities) and HNA Investment. The adoption of the dual SPV architecture is for the risk and legal separation between assets and credit-enhancement entities, achieving the indirect holding and ultimate control of the underlying assets, and leaving room for the future exit through public offering of REITs. The plan has a stratified arrangement and is divided into two categories: A and B, the scale of each is 1.531 billion yuan and 969 million yuan respectively, with issuance rates 5.3% and 6.9% respectively. Stratification also realizes an exit mechanism with alternating durations by adding equity-associated arrangement such as coupon rate adjustments, back-selling options, liquidity support, and preferential acquisitions. In terms of risk control, the plan introduced the liquidity support from HNA, the HNA Group guarantees and the prioritized securities liquidation mechanism with a downgrade rating.

3 Summary

From 2016, the supervisory department revised and issued the "Measures for the Management of Risk Indicators of Securities Companies" and "Interim Provisions on the Management of the Operation of Private Equity Asset Management Business of Securities and Futures Institutions", etc., and by February 2017, the regulatory authorities jointly sponsored the drafting of a unified monitoring document for large-scale asset management-"Guidance on Regulating the Asset Management Business of Financial Institutions (Draft for Soliciting Opinions)" A series of policies have shown that a clear trend of unified supervision in the domestic asset management industry. Uniformity and prevention of risks will also become the top priority for the securities and asset management industry in the near future. The channel business and outsourcing business will shrink dramatically, and some illegal operations and grey areas will gradually be eliminated. The channel business will gradually withdraw from the historical stage. The scale contraction will inevitably bring short-term "labor pains", but in the medium- and long-term, it will force the transformation of channel business into active management business. The investment research capability will become an important indicator for evaluating brokerage asset management business.

Looking into the future, the asset management business of securities companies may continue to develop in two directions: improving active management capabilities and exploring deeper the capital market. Under the unified supervision of grand assets management industry, competition and cooperation among different asset management agencies will further intensify. The path of differentiated development is an issue that asset management agencies must ponder. In respect to management approaches, securities companies have natural advantages in active management capabilities, actively managed products will be the focus of future development. The improvement of investment capabilities and product design capabilities is the key. At the same time, it should focus on the integration of resources, cooperation with peers, improving product line and building a comprehensive platform for financial products and services. From the perspective of investment scope, asset management of securities companies has advantages in the capital market. The future investment focus of collective products should shift from non-standard to stock pledges, directional add-issuances, and mergers and acquisitions in the capital market. In addition, the asset securitization business will also become one of the key businesses for securities company, but this needs to strengthen cooperation with commercial banks and make full use of the bank's corporate customer resources.

Chapter 6
Analysis of Capital Flow of Fund Industry and Its Mechanism

In recent years, the asset management of the fund industry has soared. By the end of 2016, it has exceeded 30 trillion yuan, and the industry structure has also undergone significant changes. On the one hand, the proportion of the public fund business continued to decline, while the non-public fund business benefited from the relatively loose monetary policy environment and the institutional dividend of the asset management business. Its scale proportion increased to 73%; on the other hand, it shows a monotonous trend in the source and flow of the fund, and the strange phenomenon that funds circulates within financial institutions has become more frequent. In the special account business of fund subsidiaries, nearly 60% of the funds come from commercial banks, and nearly 40% of the funds have flowed to financial institutions as investments in various asset management plans. In terms of asset allocation, the actively managed public funds and special accounts in fund companies mainly focused on fixed-income investments in bonds, while the special accounts of fund subsidiaries operating channel-based businesses mainly invested in non-standard assets. Structural imbalances accompany the model innovations. The cooperation between fund companies, other institutions, and local governments has been continuously upgraded, such as the "private equity funds + internet finance" model and government guidance funds that reflect the integration of industry and finance. While the business model innovation plays an active role, it also breeds regulatory arbitrage and moral hazard, which leads to accumulation of risks. The combination of private equity funds and internet finance has broken through the regulatory restrictions on qualified investors. Government guidance funds have become the disguised financial tool for local governments through the invisible guarantee backed by local fiscal revenue.

Written by Sijie Chen, Boying Wang and Shen Yang.

J. Yin et al., *Whither has the Money Gone*,
https://doi.org/10.1007/978-981-16-4931-8_6

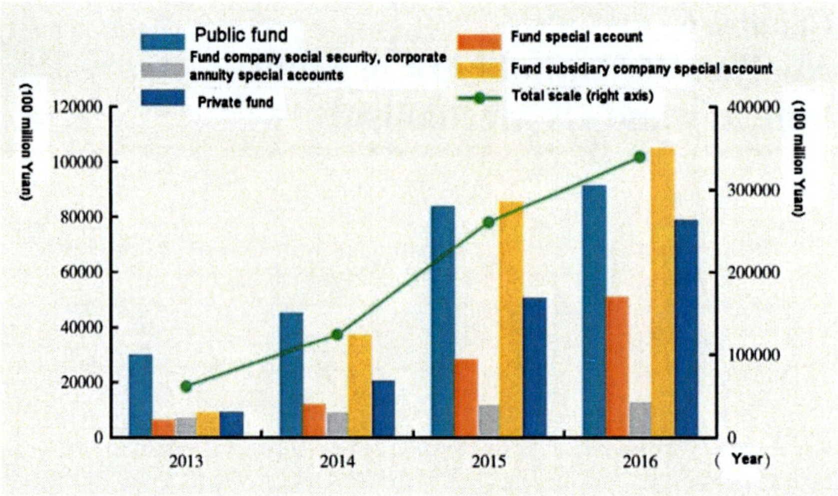

Fig. 1 The size of the fund industry from 2013 to 2016. *Source* China Securities Investment Fund Industry Association

1 Fund Industry Overview from 2013 to 2016

In recent years, China's asset management industry has developed rapidly with several new features and new trends, as well as new challenges. Since 2013, the fund industry has started a new wave of growth. In 2014 and 2015, it was mainly driven by the double bull markets of stocks and bonds and the dividends of the regulatory system. The total asset management scale of the fund industry has doubled. In 2016, due to changes in regulatory policies and the market environment, the growth rate of fund industry's assets scale slowed down. In particular, the scale of the fund subsidiary's business has decreased and the growth rate has declined significantly. As of the end of 2016, the total size of China's fund industry reached 33.94 trillion yuan (see Fig. 1), an increase of 30.2% year-on-year. From 2013 to 2016, the structure of the fund industry changed significantly. The proportion of public offering funds business continued to decline, from 54.6% in 2013 to 27.0% in 2016; the proportion of non-public fund business[1] scale has increased remarkably. At the end of 2016, the total assets of non-public offerings reached 24.78 trillion yuan. Among them, the fund subsidiary account business started only four years before has exceeded the business scale of the public fund. The proportion of special accounts of fund companies and subsidiaries increased from 29.1% in 2013 to 46.0% in 2016, and the proportion of private equity funds increased from 3.7 to 23.3%.

[1] Non-public fund assets management business includes fund company special accounts, social security funds and corporate annuities, fund subsidiary special accounts and private equity funds.

Looking specifically at the sub-sectors, in recent years, the structural changes in the public fund business have been driven mainly by the fluctuations in the macroeconomy and capital markets. As of the end of 2016, the asset size of the public fund business reached 9.16 trillion yuan, a year-on-year increase of 9.1%, which was far below the year-on-year growth rate of 85.2% in 2015. The growth rate decline was mainly affected by fluctuations in the capital market. In terms of product categories, the rapid growth in the size of money market funds and hybrid funds in 2015 drove the public fund assets to a new high. Behind this phenomenon is the repeatedly eased monetary policy, rising yields of capital market investment and increasing investment demand from public. For the third consecutive year, money market funds have become the largest asset class, and hybrid funds have surpassed equity funds in the past two years, ranking second. The official implementation of the "Administrative Measures on the Operation of Publicly-Funded Securities Investment Funds" in August 2015 significantly changed the industry structure of public funds, which increased the minimum stock investment ratio of equity funds from 60 to 80%. As a result, some equity funds have been adjusted to hybrid funds, which have had a significant impact on the market structure of equity funds and hybrid funds. At the beginning of 2016, the performance of the stock market was poor, investors' risk preference declined, resulting in diversion of funds. The net value of partial stock funds turned from positive to negative, while the size of fixed income funds, especially bond funds, increased largely (see Fig. 2).

In recent years, the outbreak of non-public fund business has mainly been driven by institutional dividends. In November 2007, the issuance of the "Trial Measures for the Specific Client Asset Management Business of the Fund Management Company" marked the official start of the fund company's special account wealth management

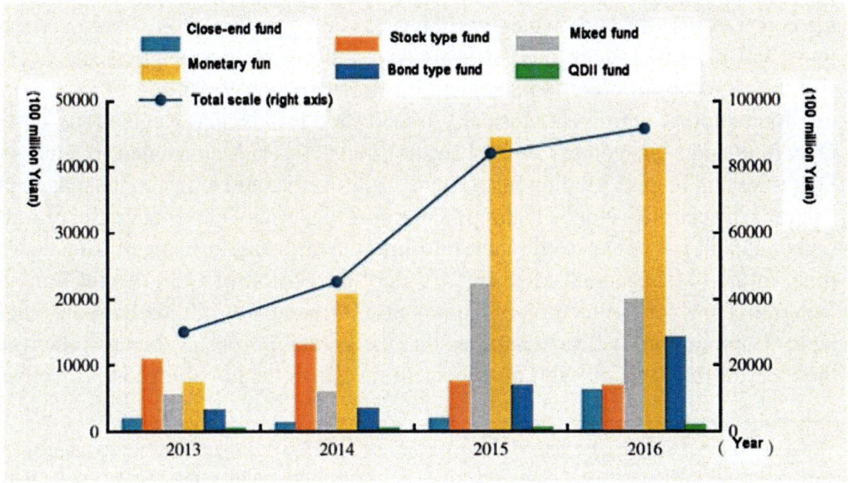

Fig. 2 Scale of public funds and product types from 2013 to 2016. *Source* China Securities Investment Fund Industry Association

business. After the issuance of the above document in September 2012, the investment scope of the fund company has further expanded. It can set up subsidiaries to invest in equity that has not been traded in the stock exchange, creditor's right, other property rights, and other assets accredited by the SFC. In 2014, the China Securities Regulatory Commission successively launched the "Opinions on Further Promoting the Innovation and Development of Securities Institutions" and the "Opinions on Vigorously Promoting the Innovation and Development of the Securities Investment Fund Industry", and clearly stated that "accelerating the construction of modern asset management institutions, supporting product innovation and promoting supervision transformation" are the three major goals. Subsequently, the regulatory agencies issued the "Administrative Measures on Asset Management Business of Securities and Futures Trading Institutions (Draft for Solicitation of Comments)" and "Notice on Regulating the Relevant Matters of Securities Companies, Fund Management Companies and Their Subsidiaries Engaging in the Management of Specific Client Asset Management Business (Draft for Comment))". A series of favorable policies has reconstructed the regulatory framework of the asset management agencies under the jurisdiction of the Securities Regulatory Commission and broadened the business boundaries. Initially, the fund subsidiary was not subject to net capital supervision requirement, this system bonus makes the fee charged for fund subsidiary's channel business far lower than the trust and brokerage asset management agency. As a result, the special account business of fund subsidiary has experienced an explosive growth and has rapidly emerged as the main participant in the outsourcing business of commercial banks. In 2015, the year-on-year growth rates of asset size of the fund company's special account, fund subsidiary account and private equity fund reached 132.9%, 129.2% and 147.4%, respectively.

In 2015, the Chinese stock market experienced the switch from bull to bear. Before and after the outbreak of the stock crisis, the regulatory authorities observed the potential risks of asset management business accumulated from regulatory arbitrage and increased stock market leverages, and began to strengthen the overall risk management of asset management business. In July 2016, the China Securities Regulatory Commission formally issued the "Provisional Regulations on the Operation and Management of the Private Equity Assets Management Business of Securities and Futures Trading Institutions", uniformly regulating asset management business of securities company, funds and futures in terms of leverage ratio, prohibition of capital pools, expected return rate and standardizing investment. At the same time, in the "Management Measures for the Supervision of Commercial Banking Services (Draft for Solicitation of Comments)" issued by the China Banking Regulatory Commission, it clearly requires that the special purpose vehicle[2] (other than the trust) of the bank's wealth management investment is not allowed to directly or

[2] Specific purpose vehicles include, but are not limited to, other commercial bank wealth management products, trust investment plans, securities investment funds other than money market funds and bond funds, asset management plans of securities companies and their subsidiaries, fund management companies and their subsidiaries asset management plans, futures companies and their subsidiaries asset management plans, insurance asset management organization asset management products, etc.

indirectly invest in non-standard debts. This is a huge impact to the channel business of fund and fund subsidiary. At the end of 2016, the China Securities Regulatory Commission officially released "Regulations on the Management of Subsidiaries of Fund Management Companies" and "Provisional Regulations on the Management of Risk Control Indicators for Fund Subsidiaries of Specific Customer Assets Management". It clarified the requirements for fund subsidiaries' net capital supervision, and the fund's subsidiaries formally bid farewell to the channel business dividend.

Due to the tightening of regulatory supervision in the asset management industry and the fluctuations in the capital market, the asset growth rate of non-public funds declined significantly in 2016, particularly, the fund subsidiary's business was affected more by the policy changes. In 2016, the fund company special account sustained a rapid growth in the scale when the stock market went downturn, bond market rose first and declined later, and bank showed strong willing to outsource its fund. As of the end of 2016, the scale of managed assets under fund company special accounts was 5.10 trillion yuan, an increase of 70.4% year-on-year. Under the influence of stricter supervision and capital orientation, the fund subsidiaries reduced the speed of special account business development and the size of special accounts, therefore, the scale of management assets showed a trend of first rising and then falling. At the same time, due to the impact of the macro economy, the development of active management business was also held back. As of the end of 2016, the asset size of the fund subsidiary's management accounted for 10.50 trillion yuan, a year-on-year increase of 22.5%, and the growth rate dropped significantly. The growth rate of private equity management also slowed down obviously, with a year-on-year increase of 55.6%, but its market share increased.

2 Sources of Funds and Their Flow

The overall scale of the fund industry has increased substantially in the past three years. However, the analysis of the industry structure and in particular the sources and flow of funds has revealed that funds have appeared to be circulating among financial institutions. Most of the fund subsidiaries' special account business provides channel services based on the supply of bank funds. Nearly 60% of the fund companies and subsidiaries' special account business come from commercial banks and about 40% of the funds in fund's subsidiary special account flow to financial institutions by investing in bank's wealth management, trust plans, brokers and fund asset management plans.

2.1 Source of Funds

In respect to management, as of the end of 2016, the channel products in the special account business of the fund company and its subsidiaries reached 9.07 trillion yuan, accounting for 58.1% of the total. In terms of the sources of funds, in the special accounts of fund companies and fund subsidiaries, commercial banks directly supplied 9.15 trillion yuan, accounting for 58.6% of the total size of the special account business, and equivalent to 31.5% of the balance of bank wealth management funds. The total funds from banks, brokerages, trusts, insurance companies and fund companies are 1.205 billion yuan, accounting for 77.2%. It can be seen that the special account business of fund companies and subsidiaries has become an important channel for banks.

Specifically, since 2013, the proportion of funds from individual customers in the fund company's special account business has dropped significantly, from 10.0% in 2014 to 4.4% in 2016. As of the end of 2016, 58.1% of the funds came directly from commercial banks, and 20.7% came from trusts, securities, insurance and funds, while this part of funds may indirectly were provided by commercial banks (see Table 1). In terms of management approaches, the scale of active management services showed a growing trend and channel services continued to maintain rapid growth with an increasing proportion. At the end of 2016, the fund company's special account management product scale was 3.51 trillion yuan, an increase of 54% year-on-year, accounting for 68.7%; channel product scale was 1.60 trillion yuan, an increase of 126% year-on-year, accounting for 31.3%, an increase of 7.6 percentage points. Channel products are mainly commissioned by banks, of which the bank-fund cooperation channel is 1.05 trillion yuan.

Table 1 Fund source and application of fund company special account. Unit: 100 million yuan

Source of funds				Application of funds (product type)			
	2014	2015	2016		2014	2015	2016
Bank	6972 57.0%	17,200 61.0%	27,300 58.1%	Bond type product	4967 40.6%	14,000 46.7%	30,500 60.0%
Trust company	1245 10.2%	2249 8.0%	3176 6.8%				
Individual	1228 10.0%	2441 8.7%	2083 4.4%	Mixed type product	3369 27.5%	8560 28.6%	11,300 22.0%
Securities company	361 2.9%	1156 4.1%	2473 5.3%	Stock type product	1738 14.2%	3782 12.7%	4693 9.0%
Financial and Insurance company	715 5.8%	1410 5.0%	2651 5.6%	Cash management type product	1875 15.3%	1933 6.5%	2401 5.0%
Corporate client	606 5.0%	1241 4.4%	2536 5.4%				
Fund management company and its association	259 2.1%	310 1.1%	1395 3.0%	QDII type	262 2.1%	1259 4.2%	1884 4.0%
Other organizations	858 7.0%	2171 7.7%	5394 11.5%	Other	37 0.3%	390 1.3%	222 0.4%
Total	12,244	28,178	47,008		12,248	29,924	51,000

Source China Securities Investment Fund Industry Association

Similar to the investor structure of the fund company's special account business, the bank entrusted funds has the largest proportion in the fund subsidiary's fund source. As of the end of 2016, bank entrusted funds amounted to 6.42 trillion yuan, accounting for 63.1% of the total, the same as 2015. 19% of the funds came from trusts, securities, insurance and funds, totaling 1.93 trillion yuan. The proportion of funds from individual customers decreased from 27.7% in 2013 to 5.5% in 2016 (see Table 2). The management mode of the subsidiary company's special account business is different from that of the fund company's special account business, where the channel products are dominant. As of the end of 2016, the channel product management asset size was 7.47 trillion yuan, accounting for 71.1% of the total, but it was greatly affected by regulatory policies and the growth rate dropped significantly.

In the area of private equity funds, due to the richness in the forms of product issuance, and the overlapping of fund special accounts and specific asset management plans, the proportion of sources of funds cannot be accurately reflected in statistics. However, since 2013, we can still infer from the explosive development of the private equity industry and the frequent appearances of investment structures similar to those of special funds and subsidiary products that the development of private equity is closely related to the flow of funds between financial institutions.

Table 2 Fund sources of fund subsidiary Company. Unit: 100 million yuan

	2013	2014	2015	2016
Bank	4208 44.7%	21,100 56.3%	52,900 63.2%	64,200 63.1%
Individual	2608 27.7%	7225 19.3%	7938 9.5%	5547 5.5%
Enterprise	1120 11.9%	3746 10.0%	7720 9.2%	7157 7.0%
Fund subsidiary company and its association		1260 3.4%	4723 5.6%	10,300 10.1%
Trust company	311 3.3%	1393 3.7%	3737 4.5%	5522 5.4%
Securities company	565 6.0%	1159 3.1%	2490 3.1%	3432 3.4%
Financial and Insurance company		117 0.3%	103 0.1%	56 0.1%
Other organizations		1426 3.9%	4124 4.9%	5459 5.4%
Total	9414	37,426	83,735	101,673

Note 2013 Fund subsidiary company special account holding includes enterprises and other institutions. *Source* China Securities Investment Fund Industry Association

2.2 Flow of Funds

The allocation of major asset classes in the fund industry appears to be obviously more simplistic and centralized due to the structural imbalance of funding sources. On the whole, the actively managed public fund and fund company special account is increasingly focused on fixed-income investments in bonds, while the channel business based fund subsidiaries' special account business is on non-standard assets.

First of all, with regard to the asset allocation of public funds, since 2013, the proportion of bonds and bank deposit assets has risen significantly, while the proportion of equities has decreased largely. At the end of 2015, the proportion of bank deposits and bonds surpassed that of equities for the first time, these two businesses have become the first two deployments directions. This also reflects the decline in the overall risk preference of residents after the financial crisis.

Secondly, from the fund company's special account business, as of the end of 2016, the fund company's special account products had 3.05 trillion yuan in bond products, accounting for 60%; mixed products accounted for 22%, and stock products accounted for 9%. Due to the advantages and convenience of bond investment, the scale of bond investment has grown significantly driven by bank outsourcing funds. From 2014 till now, the proportion of bond products has increased by nearly 20 percentage points; the proportion of mixed products has been almost stable, while the scale of stock products has dropped remarkably. With regard to the ultimate destination of investment, the fund company's special account business is mainly invested in bonds, stocks, funds, and interbank deposits. Among them, the size of bonds investment was 3.86 trillion yuan with allocation ratio as high as 63.7%, and the stock investment stock scale was 682.6 billion yuan, accounted for 11.3% (see Table 1 and Fig. 3).

Finally, at the end of 2016, for the fund subsidiaries businesses, the fund subsidiary's investment in non-standard assets reached 8.87 trillion yuan, accounting for 82.8%. Property income rights and debt financing are its main investment vehicles. The major forms of property income right lie in various types of asset management plans issued by financial institutions such as banks, trusts, funds, and brokers. The investment scale is amounted to 3.99 trillion yuan, accounting for 37.0% of the total. Detailed distributions are shown in Fig. 4. This further proves that various asset management businesses are nested and intersected with each other and funds are circulated among financial institutions. This has led to an elongation in the capital chain and increase of transaction costs, as well as growing risk transmission among financial institutions. The main forms of debt financing are bank entrusted loans, trust loans, income rights and equity rights. The investment scale is 3.95 trillion yuan. The scale of securities investment is 1.38 trillion yuan, accounting for 12.8% of the total, and it has shown a trend of rising first and then decreasing in recent years due to the fluctuation of the capital market. In terms of the industry distributions of the ultimate investment (see Table 3), funds are mainly invested in financial institutions, general industrial and commercial enterprises, and real estate. From 2013 to 2015, the proportion of the fund

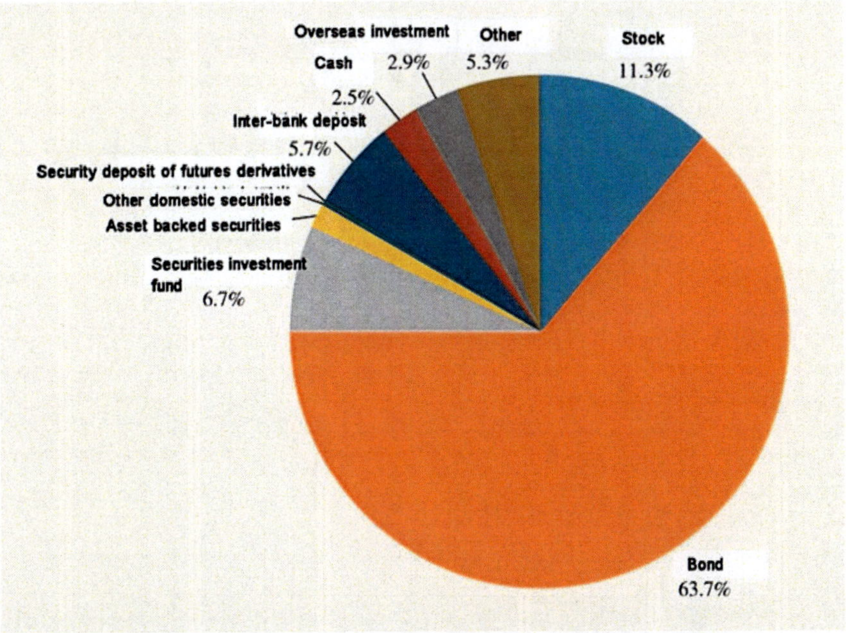

Fig. 3 Distribution of fund company's special account investment at the end of 2016. *Source* China Securities Investment Fund Industry Association

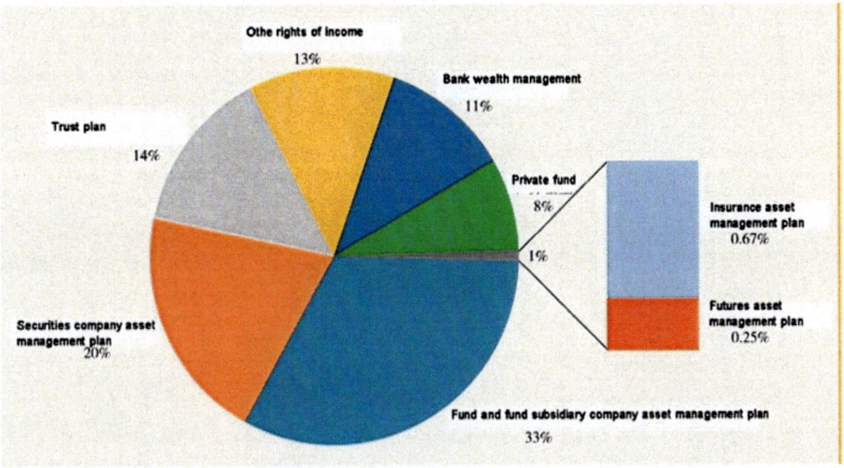

Fig. 4 Distribution of property income rights investment of fund subsidiaries (2016). *Source* China Securities Investment Fund Industry Association

Table 3 Funds utilization of fund subsidiaries

Investment Mode I (million RMB)					Investment mode II (million RMB)				
	2013	2014	2015	2016		2013	2014	2015	2016
Property income rights	3999 41.2%	14,559 38.9%	35,603 41.5%	39,780 37.0%	Financial institution	1553 16.0%	10,128 27.1%	38,061 44.3%	46,667 43.6%
Creditor's right financing	4227 43.5%	15,257 40.8%	27,253 32.8%	39,534 37.0%	General industrial and commercial enterprise	3495 36%	7154 19.1%	14,363 16.8%	19,470 18.2%
Securities investment	436 4.5%	3637 9.7%	13,478 15.7%	13,809 12.8%	Real estate	3009 31.0%	8544 22.9%	12,402 14.5%	12,834 12.0%
Equity investment	710 7.3%	2542 6.8%	5992 7.0%	4030 3.8%	Local financing platform	874 9.0%	3324 8.9%	5278 6.2%	8640 8.1%
Cash scale	228 2.3%	1257 3.4%	2128 2.5%	3105 2.9%	Fundamental industry	776 8.0%	2399 6.4%	4897 5.7%	6249 5.8%
Other	107 1.2%	138 0.4%	1274 1.5%	6777 6.3%	Other	0	5842 15.6%	10,726 12.5%	13,174 12.3%
Total	9707	37,390	85,728	107,034	Total	9707	37,390	85,728	107,034

Note Due to different statistical calibers, the property income rights investment in 2016 Investment Mode I includes commercial bank wealth management plans, trust plans, insurance asset management plans, securities company asset management plans, asset management plans of fund companies and subsidiaries, and futures asset management plans, private equity funds and other asset income rights

Source China Securities Investment Fund Industry Association subsidiary's special account investment in financial institutions increased significantly, and the proportion of investment in general industrial and commercial enterprises dropped sharply, indicating the prominent tendency of "shifting from the real economy to virtual economy" of funds. As regulatory agencies are strengthening risk management and capital constraints of fund subsidiaries, the proportion of funds invested in general industrial and commercial enterprises increased slightly in 2016. In addition, due to market changes and regulatory factors, the proportion of investment in real estate continued to decline, from 31.0% in 2013 to 12.0% in 2016.

3 Analysis of Fund Flow Mechanism

In recent years, the asset management scale of the fund industry has greatly increased, but it does not achieve the purpose for fund industry, which is to serve the real economy with its professional and specialized asset management and create values. In terms of product structure, the pace of overall innovation has slowed down, and regulatory arbitrage has become an important driver for business development. Although the overall development cannot be completely described as benign, many innovative businesses such as the government guidance industry fund with the integration of industry and are realized. In addition, there are some new modes of cooperation between private equity funds and the internet finance sector, but they are generally still channels for each other with the purpose supervision and accompanied by more potential risks.

3.1 Fund Circulation Among Financial Institutions Model—Outsourcing Business

From 2014 to 2016, a typical model of between-agency cash flow was the expansion of outsourcing operations. The overall business of the public offering fund, including special accounts and its subsidiaries, showed explosive growth. Based on the analysis of the sources of funds and the whereabouts of the investments, it was found that up to 60% of the special account funds came from banks, and over 60% of the special account funds were invested in the bond market or non-standard assets. It can be seen that the actual role played by the public fund special account and subsidiary companies at the business level is the "channel" for bank funds, which eventually entered into the bank's targeted market through entrusted investment. In addition, trusts, insurance companies, and various types of sunshine private equity can also play the role of outsourcing investment managers. The most important reason for the rapid growth of asset management in the past three years has been the widespread use of outsourcing services.

a. Basic models of bank outsourcing business

The commissioned investment business, also known as outsourcing business, refers to the investment business model in which the client entrusts the funds to the external agency manager and the external agency manager actively manages according to the agreed scope. Among them, the consigner, i.e. the fund provider, mainly was played by financial institutions such as commercial banks, insurance companies and financial companies. The manager, who actually invests in and manages funds, is the operator, played by securities companies, insurance companies, public fund companies and subsidiaries, as well as sunshine private equity, who have specific asset management capabilities.

At present, the main provider of funds for outsourcing operations is commercial banks, and the attributes of their funds are financial management funds and self-supported funds. The rise of outsourcing business mainly originated from the accelerated growth of various types of commercial banks' wealth management funds and self-operating funds in recent years. On the one hand, commercial banks lack asset management teams that match their funds, so commissioning external investment institutions becomes an important asset allocation method. On the other hand, in 2013, the China Banking Regulatory Commission issued the "Circular on Regulating the Investment and Operation of Commercial Banking Wealth Management Businesses", which imposes restrictions on the targets, terms, trading methods and leverage ratios of wealth management funds. Therefore, some banks can not satisfy the funds income requirement of rigid payments. These banks usually heavily rely on investment strategies such as holding the credit to maturity and their own investment methods. The commercial bank, through the managers of the outsourcing business, satisfies the rationality of its own investments or participates in markets that it cannot directly involve in.

The actual operation form of outsourcing business is generally through a specific asset management plan issued by a fund company, brokerage firm, insurance company or sunshine private equity. A private equity investment fund also includes the operation of certain public offering securities investment funds' products at a specific point in time. In respect to business models, outsourcing investment business mainly has two product modes: product and investment advisory. The outsourcing business models were generally accepted by banking financial institutions. It began with city commercial banks, later, joint-stock banks and state-owned banks also joined in. They were being able to utilize the management of external agencies and their investment channels to allocate assets. In terms of the nature of funds, large banks and joint-stock banks mainly focus on wealth management funds, and the mode of operation is basically a product investment cooperation model. The self-operated and wealth management funds of the city commercial bank and agriculture commercial bank participates in the outsourcing investment mainly in product investment cooperation mode, supplemented by commissioned investment advisory mode. The entrusted funds are managed by external financial institutions, the management is assumed by securities companies, fund companies, insurance companies and sunshine private funds, some banks also appear in the outsourcing market as managers.

b. The flow of funds between financial institutions stems from regulatory arbitrage

In recent years, the outsourcing business has seen operated through various forms of financial instruments such as packaged and channelized business represented by fund sector. The typical forms include the one-to-one special account of the fund, the specific asset management plan of fund subsidiaries for institution investors, and the private equity fund products issued by the various private equity fund managers through contractual fund.

We use a simple analysis of the core model of funds circulation between financial institutions for description. Basically it is the transfer of funds stocked in a particular financial institution or financial sector through investment channels established through funds issuance or similar forms, while the funds and related institutions with similar functions act as managers. The party that acts as the manager collects the relevant management fee and transfers or holds the funds and completes the capital investment according to instructions from the capital provider. The fund supplier completed the corresponding risk transfer on the balance sheet, but it can still act as the actual controller of the funds. At the same time, the fund supplier can make agreement with funds' manager on sharing gains based on the transfer of funds and other acts, in order to obtain considerable income.

The supplier of funds pursues returns and remunerations, while the managers of funds pursue the scale of management, the interests of the two are the same, and the overall scale is also accelerating. In this type of cooperation, the separation of capital and investment will indeed result in a better governance structure. However, whether the actual investment efficiency and profit return are better than the original capital investment methods still need to be proved by time. This model emerged mainly for regulatory arbitrage. The "Circular of the China Banking Regulatory Commission on Regulating the Investment and Operation of Wealth Management Business Banks" issued by the China Banking Regulatory Commission in March 2013 ("Document No. 8") was considered as one of symbolic documents that shows the CBRC's continuously increasing supervision over the use of funds in the existing banking system. The notice classifies the assets of the bank's outside investment as standard and non-standard assets, and the definition of non-standardized debt assets has greatly reduced the banks' free choices of investment. More importantly, the total scale of investment in non-standard assets by wealth management funds is controlled. Subsequent introduction of more detailed rules has also strengthened the supervision of the use of bank funds, making the original business model difficult to sustain. As a result, banking financial institutions are faced with increasing operating pressures, and superposition of supervision has continued to increase. The result of the game play is to appeal to external institutions to reduce the impact of regulation on traditional business models (see Fig. 5). Among them, the best partners are the various types of financial institutions in the fund industry. There are three main reasons: First, as financial institutions, the fund industry can easily meet the screening criteria of bank internal control for partners; second, the fund satisfies relevant funds

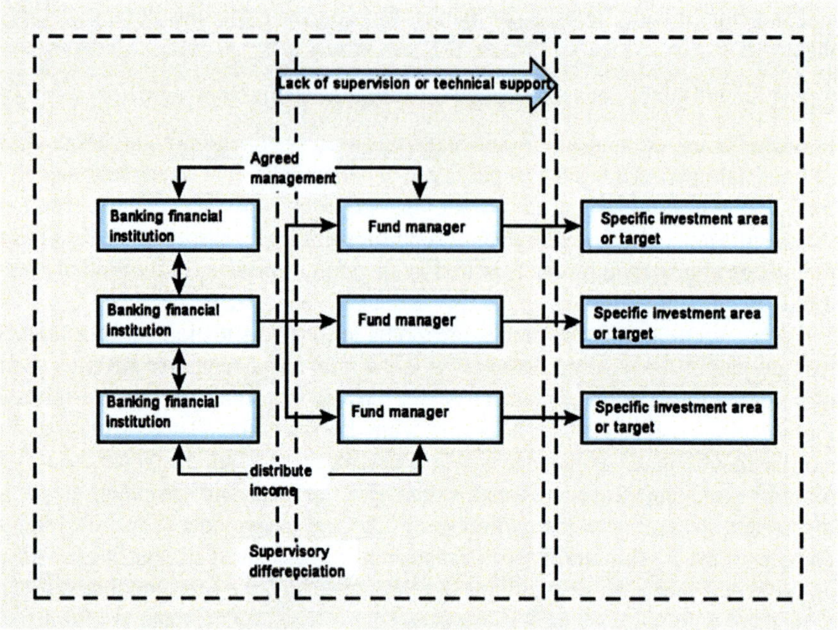

Fig. 5 Cross-supervision system arbitrage. *Source* Author finishing

management conditions; finally, the fund industry and banking financial institutions belong to different regulatory systems, and it is capable to include more businesses than the bank's existing regulatory system.

In summary, the reason why capital flows between various financial institutions in the fund industry is that, banking financial institutions who are the dominant players in the domestic capital market are facing the dual pressures of operation and supervision, and therefore are in urgent need to seek cooperation with external agencies. The possible regulatory arbitrage in the fund industry appeals to banking institutions, thus has led to a proliferation of a large number of channel and outsourcing businesses, which has interfered with the effectiveness of supervision and has also exacerbated risks in certain specific areas.

c. Models of fund companies participating in bank outsourcing

The development of outsourcing business has exacerbated the circulation of funds among financial institutions, the scale of asset management has continued to rise. However, investment area has become increasingly narrow. Taking the fund subsidiary special account business as an example, more than 40% of funds flow to financial institutions (inter deposits, bank notes etc. as investment targets), and the proportion of investment in general industrial and commercial enterprises continues to decline. This shows that a large proportion of funds are circulated within financial institutions with no obvious promoting effect in the real economy. The situation of "shifting from the real economy to virtual economy" has been intensified. Changes in the investments of fund subsidiaries are a microcosm of the overall fund industry.

Public funds are also one of the important vehicles for banks outsourcing. In 2016, a total of 1,151 public funds were established, of which 587 were customized products. A customized product can be generally interpreted as a general type of product that interfaces with a bank's outsourcing business. In terms of asset classes, fund mainly flowed to pure debt in 2016. Customized funds in 2015 were mainly focused on mixed "stagging", while in 2016 they were mainly concentrated on bond funds (especially pure bond funds) and mixed "stagging" funds. Among them, a total of 407 bond funds were issued, raising a total amount of 449.2 billion yuan and the proportion of number and size of institutions (mainly commercial banks) accounted for a 74% and 79% respectively. A total of 569 hybrid funds were issued, raising a total amount of 455.5 billion yuan, the proportion of number and size of institutions accounted for 42% and 22% respectively.

It can thus be seen that the vast majority of funds are centralized on specific types of bond-based objects based, and the transfer of funds to the most important general industrial and commercial enterprises in the real economy is negligible. Such a high proportion of capital flows is concentrated on bond investment is due to two reasons: On the one hand, in recent years, the capital is relatively loose, and the supply of quality assets is insufficient. In order to meet the demand for return on investment and to create a higher level of income, investment in fixed income assets based on bonds is an ideal choice; on the other hand, banking supervision system has many restrictions on bond repurchases and other transaction models that can easily amplify investment leverage, resulting in banks to focus on other financial institutions that have convenient trading conditions. Fund companies have management capabilities and sound trading channels, and have a natural advantage in the regulatory mode in certain investment areas, thus have become the main investment channels to undertake bank funds.

The legal structure commonly adopted by domestic public offering funds is a contractual fund structure. In the private equity fund field, the "Securities Investment Funds Act", which was revised in June 2013, gave legal status to contractual private equity funds for the first time. Therefore, at present, both domestic public and private equity funds use the same product kernel. The main difference between the two is in the way the fund is raised and qualified investors. There are also some differences in fee rate design. However, in the overall legal relationship, the structure of public and private equity funds is basically the same, as shown in Fig. 6 that is, investors sign a fund contract with a qualified fund company, and entrust the fund manager to manage the collected funds. At the same time, the fund custodian is commissioned to supervise the funds. Through this structure, the fund has realized the fund pooling and established a path for investing in specific areas. The constraints are general supervision requirements and the corresponding investment agreement between fund managers and fund investors in the regulatory framework. Therefore, the fund has a relatively superior governance structure and legal basis for overall capital flow, providing a basic business platform for outsourcing operations.

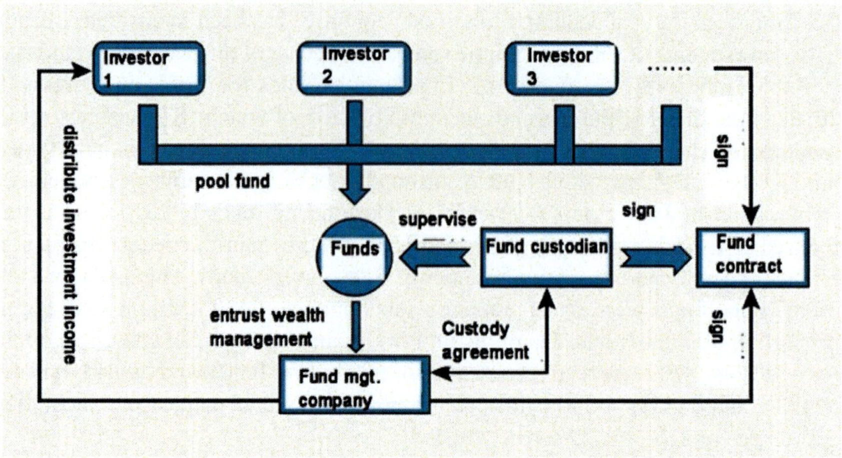

Fig. 6 Product structures of generalized contract funds. *Source* Author finishing

Next, taking a customized public fund product, "ICBC Ruixin Taixiang Three-year Wealth Management Bond Investment Fund" as an example, we will analyze the model on the fund companies' participation in the banking business. Look at the product elements (see Table 4), we can see that the fund is an ordinary open-end fund, and the fund has the same rate setting as the common bond fund, with a management fee of 0.25% and a custodian fee of 0.05%. The fund has a closed period. The author did not obtain clear closed period information after consulting public information. However, "three years" has appeared in the name of the fund, we can thus infer that there is a corresponding time limit for the operation of the fund, which is in contrast to the general open-end fund. With regard to investment scope, the fund mainly invests in fixed-income financial instruments based on bonds, and promises not to actively buy equity assets such as stocks, it also promises to invest only in the pure bonds part of separable convertible bonds in the area of convertible bonds. In the face, the fund appears to be a typical pure debt fund. What merits attention is the investment strategy of the fund, which is "purchase and hold" for the overall fund, and the type and structure of bonds held will not change during the closed period. This shows that the fund has locked the corresponding investment target before the issuance, and the three years in the fund's naming may also be connected to the locked three-year bond.

In addition, as for the general strategy adopted by the bond fund investment, financial institutions with banks as the main body of investment tend to adopt the "purchase and hold" approach in order to ensure the certainty of expected returns. This is different from the investment strategy of a general fund company. Common bond funds usually do not abandon the transaction-type gains brought about by the conversion of positions within a certain period of time in order to enhance returns. This further shows that the fund's management strategy is set according to the specific needs of the funding party. At the same time, the fund has a description of its leverage strategy. Increased leverage is a mode of investment operation that cannot be achieved by banking financial institutions within their own systems. This is a major reason for the growth of bank outsourcing operations. Meanwhile, the author reviewed the asset allocation of the fund as of December 31, 2016. The fund has already completed the rapid opening of position within the closed period and the proportion of bonds is as high as 97%, which is consistent with the product description of the fund.

This product is a typical outsourcing business formed by banks investing in products through the channels of public funds. Others outsourced businesses through private equity funds, brokerage asset management and insurance asset management, the transaction structures and models are similar. Outsourcing business is created under the background of "asset shortage" and catalyzed by regulatory differentiations under the separate business supervision frame. Assuming that the asset management industry has the unified supervision, from 2014 to 2016, bonds may remain as the capital pool for investment fund like before, but it is highly probable that

Table 4 ICBC Credit Suisse Taixiang 3 year wealth management bond-type securities investment fund product elements

Fund abbreviation	ICBC Taixiang 3 year wealth management bonds	Fund code	002,750
Full name of the fund	ICBCCS Taixiang 3 year wealth management bond type securities investment fund		
Fund type	Bonds	Date of establishment	5/5/2016
Fund status	Closed period	Trading status	Subscription closed, redemption closed, add-on investment closed
Fund Company	ICBCCS	Fund manager	Chen Guidu and Lu Xin
Management fee	0.25%	Custodian fee	0.05%
Initial offering	30 billion	Custodian Bank	Bank of Ninbo Co., Ltd.
Scope of investment	The fund's investment scope includes fixed-income financial instruments such as treasury bonds, central bank bills, local government bonds, financial bonds, corporate bonds, corporate bonds, short- term financing bonds, ultra-short-term financing bonds, medium-term notes, subordinated bonds, short-term corporate bonds of securities companies, and pure debt of detachable transactions, asset- backed securities, bank deposits, interbank deposit certificates, and bond repurchases, as well as other financial instruments allowed by laws and regulations or the China Securities Regulatory Commission for fund. The Fund does not actively buy equity assets such as stocks and warrants, and does not participate in new share subscriptions and new share issuances and only invest in the pure debt portion of detachable convertible bonds		

(continued)

Table 4 (continued)

Fund abbreviation	ICBC Taixiang 3 year wealth management bonds	Fund code	002,750
Investment strategy	The Fund operates in a closed period. During the closed period, the Fund uses a purchase-and-hold strategy to build a portfolio, matching the remaining maturity of the fixed-income variety invested with the remaining maturity of the fund, and investing in fixed-income instruments with the remaining maturity (or resale period) does not exceed the remaining closed period of the fund. Under normal circumstances, the types and structure of bonds held by the Fund will not change during the closed period 1. Generic configuration strategy The generic configuration mainly includes asset category selection, appropriate combination of various assets and management of asset portfolios 2. Credit bond investment strategy Due to the adoption of the purchase-and-hold strategy, the Fund holds a bond with a remaining maturity (or resale period) that does not exceed the remaining closed period of the fund. The Fund invests in credit bonds, and its debt rating should be AA (inclusive) or above. The bond issuer should have a net asset of more than RMB 1 billion at the end of the previous year 3. Leverage investment strategy The Fund will consider the risk and return on bond investment and the cost of repurchase, and within the scope of risk control and laws and regulations, through the bond repurchase, enlarge the leverage for investment operations		

Source ICBCCS Fund Management Company

most of the management scale will be kept within the banking system, rather than being replaced by other non-banking financial institutions replaced it. Although the outsourcing business does promote a substantial increase in the overall size of the industry, the expansion of the scale does not equate to the improvement of management capabilities. The characteristics currently exhibited by the outsourcing business more closely resemble the instructed investment that the manager has very limited autonomy, which runs counter to the original intention of the fund industry to create value through management capabilities.

3.2 Private Equity Funds and Internet Financial Cooperation Model

In recent years, the market acceptance of private equity funds has gradually increased and the management scale has also steadily grown. There are also some new modes of cooperation in the private equity fund and internet financial sectors. The strength of private equity funds lies in investment, and the strength of internet finance based on P2P services lies in financing. Especially in the context of the lack of quality assets since 2015, the two achieved perfect integration. In October 2016, the State Council issued the "Implementation Plan for Special Internet Finance Risk Remediation Work," which clearly stipulates that without approval, internet financial companies may not sell privately issued various financial products through packaged or split-up forms to the public, therefore the "private equity fund + P2P" model attracted much attention. According to the regulations of the China Securities Regulatory Commission, since private equity funds usually have the characteristic of high-risk income, private equity investors must invest more than 1 million yuan, and also must meet the criteria that their financial assets could not be less than 3 million yuan or three consecutive years of average annual income is not less than 500,000 yuan. Therefore, the "marriage" between private equity funds and internet finance is essentially to circumvent the legal restrictions on qualified investors. Here are some controversial typical models in the market sorted by the author.

a. Share pledge financing model

The general trading process of this model is similar to that of ordinary P2P. All financing entities publish financing request on the pertaining internet financial platform, and investment users of the platform invest in their debt. However, the mortgage and pledge collaterals are private equity fund shares or shares of other financial products (such as trust plans, asset management plans, etc.). The amount of investment and promised return stipulated in their product contracts are the source of repayment, and the issuer of such financial products assumes credit enhancement. The corresponding share is held by a third-party service provider of the internet financial platform or a proxy holder to ensure that the assets are under control (see Fig. 7).

This financing mode in essence is to cash out the issued assets through the secondary packaging on the internet financial platform. At the same time, the share will be split to achieve the secondary circulation of financial assets. Currently, since most of the financial assets are registered with third-party registration platforms that do not have credibility and the secondary issue is in essentially different from the original financial product design, which lowers the investment threshold. Therefore, if the product itself is subject to bank run, it will affect the general public investor groups and have a negative social impact.

Similar to this model, some internet financial institutions will cooperate with other asset exchanges in order to make the split of financial assets appear more compliant. They will split financial assets through listings into beneficiary certificates with the financial asset as the underlying assets. The beneficiary certificate of the asset is put on the platform for secondary sell. The transaction structure of this model is similar to the aforementioned one, except that the other service organizations of the internet financial platform play the role of "holding" financial assets or "listing" financial assets.

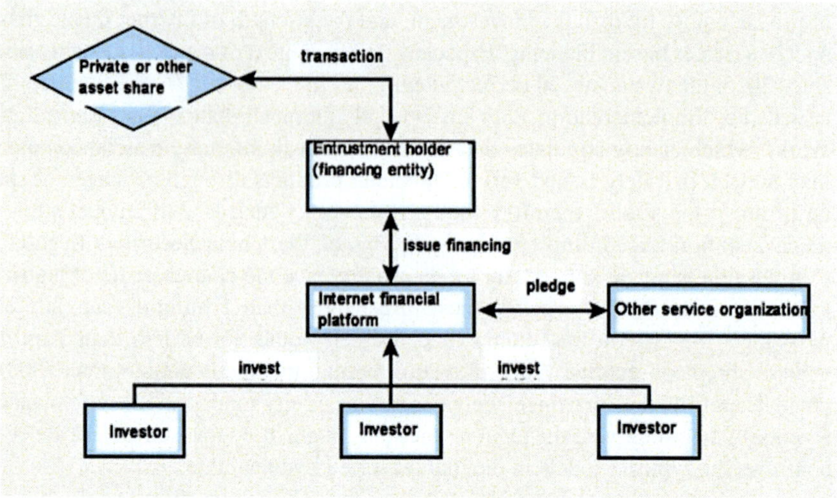

Fig. 7 Share pledge financing structure. *Source* Author finishing

b. Directional investment model

This model is similar to group purchase, in which a platform initiates a specific financing plan and pools funds to specific financing entities, and the entity meets the regulatory body's relevant requirements for qualified investors in form. The financing entity represents the above-mentioned internet financial platform investors, and purchases corresponding products from private equity funds or other financial institutions. In the end, the platform will carry out the liquidation of the funds and shares to complete the share split of financial products. The essence of this model is to raise funds in the form of group purchases. Financial assets are held by a qualified person on behalf of the investor, and are finally dismantled (see Fig. 8).

Under this model, the platform itself or the proxy holder has a high moral hazard. The threshold for private equity fund shares or financial products is relatively high. After fund raising, product registration and confirmation are carried out entirely in the name of the entity itself. If there is a corresponding risk, it is difficult for the participants in the fund raising to claim their own rights. In addition, this model can easily breed false investment targets, that is, platform fabricates and promote targeted investment products, the security of funds and assets cannot be guaranteed therefore.

c. False stock and false debt model.

The origination of this model is that the regulatory agencies placed segmented restriction on the private equity investment, that is, private equity funds are not encouraged to invest in debt or "debt under the disguise of equity", and the debt investment issued by the internet financial platform should meet the principle of dispersed mall denominations. The purpose of the organization that uses this model is to circumvent regulation.

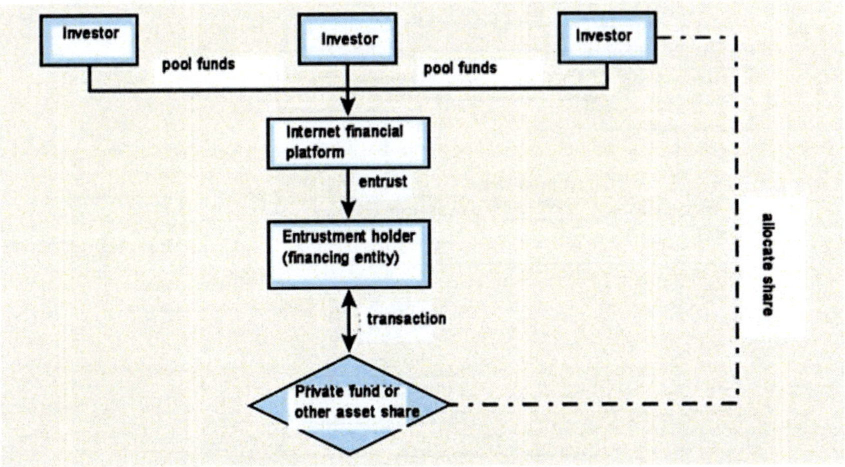

Fig. 8 Diagram of Directional Entrustment Investment Agency. *Source* Author finishing

This mode of financing consists of two parts. On the one hand, private equity funds first initiate a fund product, and increase the capital and shares by means of equity investment in institutions such as factoring company or financial leasing company, completing the compliance filing of private equity funds. Later, the factoring company will invest in creditor's rights of the targeted company, carry out risk control measures such as mortgage and pledges of related assets, and complete the capital injection. On the other hand, the factoring company launches refinancing request to internet financial platform. After platform investor completes investment, the factoring firm will repurchase its own equity held by the private equity fund. Investors of the private equity fund or the bridged capital will recover the funds and interest. At the same time, the factoring companies recoup the principal and interest of the borrowed funds, repay the platform investors and complete the entire transaction process (see Fig. 9).

This model is relatively hidden, if we dismantle it, we can see that the private equity did indeed invest in equity, and also fully meet the current regulatory requirements. The factoring companies lend to target companies, or carry out refactoring financing through the internet financial platforms, these are all relatively common businesses. However, in this model, the equity investment by the private equity fund is not a true equity investment. They are different stocks. This process deviates from the original intention of the equity investment. The factoring company itself only serves as a channel, helping the private equity funds to complete the issuance of loans, so their claims are not risk control tools based on factoring company's own debt assets. The entities carry channel services for each other. It seems there is the convergence of interest, but actually it is "false equity and false debt."

In summary, although the cooperation between private equity funds and internet finance has satisfied the interest appeals of all participating parties, the huge information "black box" can easily breed all kinds of risks. The author believes that such

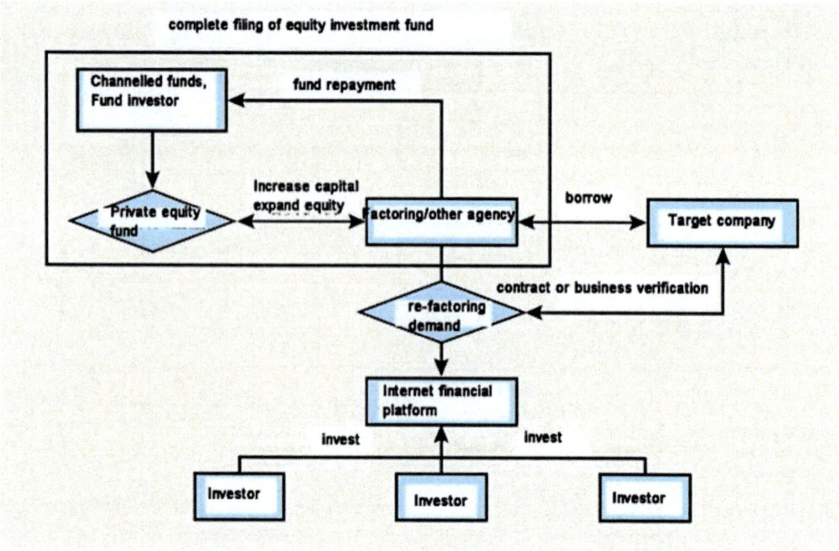

Fig. 9 Structure of "false equity false debt". *Source of data* Authors organize

exchanges of interests should be strictly insulated and such transaction structures should be eliminated, so that private equity funds can focus on professionalism, and internet finance can return to general benefits.

3.3 Government Guidance Fund Model

Government guidance funds refer to a special fund that are partially funded by the government and jointly initiated with financial institutions, professional investment institutions, and social capital. The funds are invested in the equity or debt of emerging industries, state-owned enterprise reforms, urban development and construction to support regional economic development. Government guidance funds are not only funds that are market-oriented but also bear policy guidance function. Therefore, they cannot be considered as private-equity funds issued by general institutions. Government guidance funds generally operate in a private-equity fashion. According to different set goals and investment strategies, they have multiple attributes such as entrepreneurial guidance, equity investment, industry guidance, and urban development and construction funds. In addition, the government guidance fund also has the feature of the parent fund of FOF, which enhances the leverage of fiscal funds and has unique advantages in supporting local industries and serving regional economic development characteristics.

a. Government guidance fund trading structure

Since 2014, the explosive growth of government guidance funds is mainly due to the full play of its role as a new type of financing tool for local governments. At the end of 2014, the State Council successively issued the "Opinions on Strengthening the Management of Local Government Debts" ("No. 43 Document") and the "Notice on Clearing and Regulating Taxes and Other Preferential Policies" ("No. 62 Document"), to standardize the local government debts raising. It is clearly stated that local governments are not allowed to directly support enterprises through subsidies and tax incentives. Since then, local governments have changed the original government subsidies into government guidance funds that aim to increase the efficiency of the use of fiscal funds through market-based operations.

Taking the industry guidance fund as an example, it involves in the company in the form of equity, which is an off-balance-sheet financing and does not increase the debt of local governments. However, in actual operation, local governments generally provide invisible guarantees to other LPs (limited partners, mainly asset management products represented by bank off-balance sheet wealth management), with land, real estate and equity as mortgage and pledge collaterals. Nominally its ownership rights, but it is actually claims. In addition to investing in entity enterprises, some government guidance funds have invested large sums of money in infrastructure construction, such as urbanization construction funds, infrastructure industry investment funds, and PPP funds. It has become new financing platform for local governments. What is more, the demand for certain industrial fund projects is not true, and the guided funds have become a tool for disguised financing by local governments. In order to guard against the implicit debt risk of local governments, the central government issued a series of tightening policies[3] from the beginning of 4Q16, prohibiting local governments from providing invisible guarantees for guided funds, and explicitly requiring local governments not to borrowed funds to set up various types of investment funds. It was also stated in these policies that local governments participating in PPP projects or setting up various types of government-funded investment funds shall not commit to repurchase, guarantees or minimum returns for social capitals, and shall not impose additional provisions on the equity investment such as limited partnership funds to disguise borrowings.

Government guidance funds generally adopt the form of limited partnership in the legal structure, and the overall existence of the fund is generally more than 5 years. In terms of capital structure, flat-level and structured modes are generally adopted. The government forms a funding platform in conjunction with external cooperation agencies, and then employs an external management agency to conduct overall management of the fund's investment, banks usually play the role of independent

[3] In November 2016, the General Office of the State Council promulgated the "Preliminary Plan for Emergency Management of Local Government-based Debt Risks" ("No. 88 Document"); in December 2016, the Ministry of Finance promulgated "Guidelines for Disposal of Local Government-based Debt Risks" ("No. 152" In May 2017, six ministries and commissions such as the Ministry of Finance issued the "Notice on Further Regulating Local Government Debt Financing Behavior" ("No. 50").

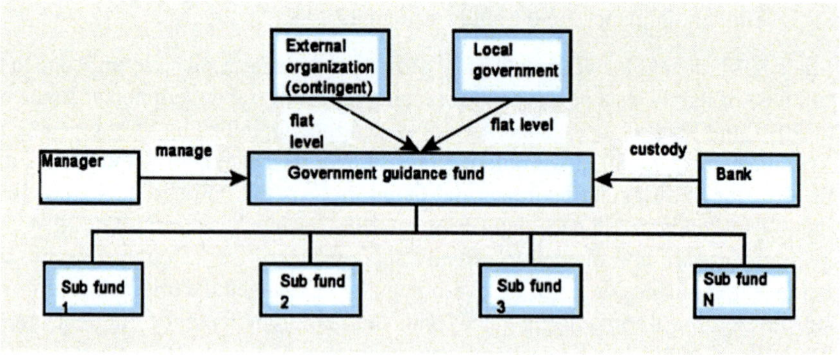

Fig. 10 Schematic representation of the level structure of government guidance funds. *Source* Author finishing

third-party trustee to ensure the safety of funds. Since government guidance funds tend to invest in multiple industry sectors, it is common to set up a platform based on the whole government guidance funds, multiple sub-funds are established under it to invest in different fields. On the sub-funds level, they operate in a more market-oriented manner and independently with consideration of the characteristics of the invested fields. The government guidance funds themselves can be investors of the sub-funds, provide additional credit to the sub-funds and enhance the market-based financing capabilities of the funds (see Fig. 10).

Due to the relatively large scale of government guidance funds, it will place too much pressure on local finance if the funds are solely raised with fiscal revenue and external institutional funds in a flat-layer manner. Therefore, in actual operation, government guidance funds tend to use structured forms for fund establishment. Under this structure, banks and other financial institutions were introduced to participate in the establishment of government guidance funds as priority funds. The posterior contributors and priority funds shall agree on corresponding revenues and terms. Under this kind of structure, the role of special fiscal funds will be amplified by leveraging funds, which is conducive to forming a larger scale of management for more extensive investment (see Fig. 11).

b. Typical cases of government guidance funds

(i) Chongqing Shuangqiao Urban Development Fund

In 2016, Chongqing Shuangqiao Economic Development Zone initiated the Shuangqiao Urban Development Fund. The fund adopts the legal structure of a limited partnership. China Merchants Bank's wealth management funds are the priority capital and contributed funds in the form of an asset management plan. The Shuangfa Fund and Shuangqiao Urban Development and Investment Co., Ltd., which were established in Chongqing Shuangqiao Economic Development Zone, were posterior investors. The external fund manager is hired. The guidance fund for the local urban development and construction is established. The fund structure

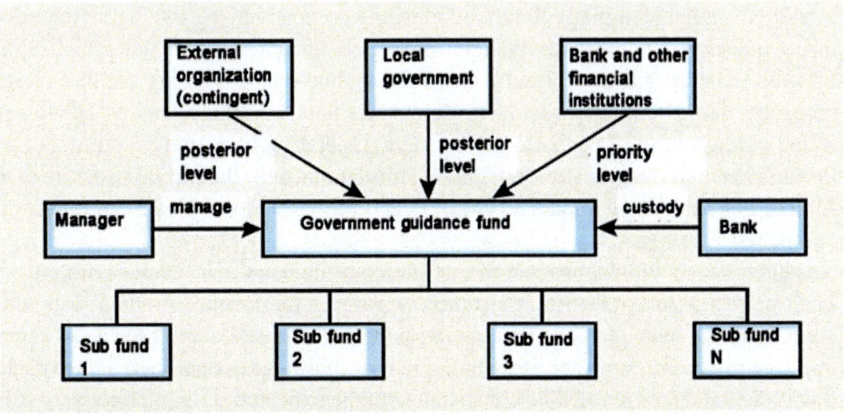

Fig. 11 Schematic structures of government guidance funds. *Source* Author finishing

is a typical government guidance fund that leverages bank funds to optimize the effectiveness of local fiscal funds (see Fig. 12).

(ii) Nanning Mingjiang Smart Manufacture Industry Investment Fund

The Nanninging Mingjiang Smart Manufacturing Industry Investment Fund has duration of 4 + 2 years. It is mainly invests in intelligent manufacturing service companies in the Industry 4.0 area. The fund management is commissioned to Zhujiang Xijiang Industrial Investment Fund. Shanghai Tongchuan Investment Management Co., Ltd. serves as the fund investment advisor. The distribution order is priority, intermediate level and posterior level, and the partner of the priority class expects annualized return rate to be 6.35%. The fund is a typical "government guidance + industry support"

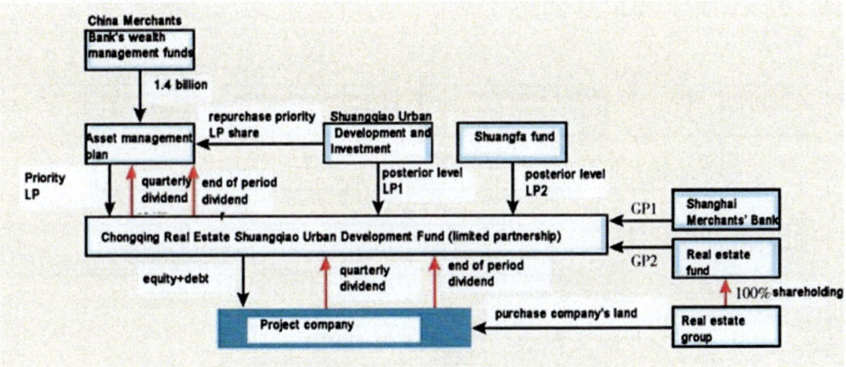

Fig. 12 Schematic structures Chongqing Shuangqiao Urban Development Fund. *Source* Author finishing

model. Shanghai Mingjiang Smart, as a leading company in the intelligent manufacturing industry, in addition to financial support, contributed more intellectual capital into the industry guidance fund to help the technology upgrading of the invested company. The Nanning Investment Guidance Fund, introduced policy advantages as the guiding fund of the local government. Operating in a fund-based model and through structured market fundraising will further optimize the capital structure of the fund to free up limited financial resources and promote more investment in relevant companies (see Fig. 13).

This fund is a typical product of integration of industry and finance with government guidance and industrial assistance. Assuming the form of funds, it can better coordinate the resources of participating parties and create a complementary operating environment. At present, the fund is in its initial stage of operation. It is expected that its actual operation will be consistent with the expected setting, effectively solve the major pain points of system integration, improve the company's cash flow, and show positive demonstrating effect.

In summary, the emergence of government guidance funds has provided a good platform for the allocation of market resources and implementation of policies, and solved the problem of policy deployment and market resource complementation. The development of this type of fund in recent years has indeed helped the regional economic construction with local characteristics and a sound situation has emerged. However, it is undeniable that there are certain flaws in the supervision of government guidance funds. As government guidance funds release government credits to market-based funds, some funds or sub-fund modules may take the advantages of government credit for arbitrage, causing unnecessary moral hazard. The government lacks talents for specialized fund management and can only rely on the support of external agencies. Therefore, the pre-risk management and supervision of the funds in the middle are subject to certain restrictions. Although local government guidance funds are supervised by higher-level regulatory agencies, under the current situation of rapid expansion of fund size, the implementation effectiveness may be

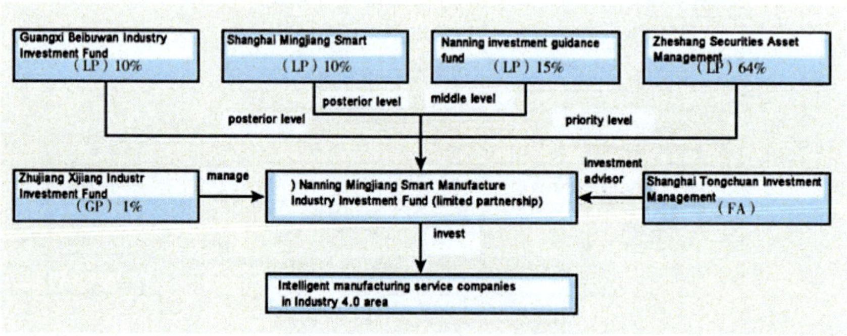

Fig. 13 Structure of Nanning Mingchan Smart Manufacturing Industry Investment Fund. *Source* Author finishing

greatly reduced. It is necessary to introduce third-party auditing agencies to actually supervise the entire environment in which funds operate.

4 Industry Outlook and Policy Suggestions

China's fund industry took its initial shape of policies and systems in 2006, it has 10 years history until 2016. The industry as a whole has gradually evolved from the securities investment and has developed various types of fund products with investment targets such as equity, real estate, and overseas assets, infiltrating all aspects of the market economy. In terms of management scale, the overall scale of the industry at the initial stage is less than 100 billion yuan, and it is now more than 30 trillion yuan in market size. However, in the general environment of pan-asset management, the fund industry seems to have a game of being bigger or being stronger. Some institutions focused on scale-based, ignoring the enhancement of management capabilities that are core strengths of asset management. Considering the macro-environment, this is more likely a forced behavior. After all, the rule of thumb of market-oriented operations is to survive and continue the business. The author believes that the vast majority of organizations understand that the development of the industry is driven by the improvement of management capabilities. Without continuous upgrading of management level, "Achilles heel" will occur with the huge management scale.

In order to promote a more healthy development of fund industry in the future, the author proposes the following suggestions in terms of supporting system construction, institutional service capability enhancement and regulatory system.

First, to further improve the overall supporting environment for the fund industry. On the one hand, it is necessary to improve the multi-dimensional construction of the capital market, and a multi-level advanced capital market with depth and breadth is an indispensable foundation for fund development. The fund industry is in need of the full support of the capital market. At present, the vast majority of the industry's overall capital operation is concentrated in the secondary market. Although there has developed a considerable market capacity so far in the secondary market for the investment and trading of securities investment funds, the trading strategies have continued to escalate, and products with unlisted company equity, property rents, and cultural property rights as investment targets have emerged. These are in urgent need for capital market support. The multi-dimensional capital market itself is a prerequisite for improving the overall development of the fund industry. Only with this market, investment strategies could be implemented, such as the formation of the linkage between the primary market and the secondary market, and the cross-market strategy with the combination of the new Third Board trading and property rights. On the other hand, it is necessary to increase participants in various fields of the fund industry. At present, the participants in the fund industry are mainly managers and other traditional financial institutions as service providers. However, in other supporting areas such as administrative management, fund rating, fund clearing, etc., there are no professional third-party service organizations. With reference to the development of the overseas fund industry, third-party professional service organizations are the indispensable entities for market participation and can help the industry operate more efficiently. At the same time, they help managers focus on strategic R&D and management capabilities, and reduce the administrative cost of fund managers.

Management costs.

Second, to improve service capabilities and form an internal echelon system in the overall fund industry. On the one hand, there is a need to increase investment in product innovation and R&D. The fund industry is still dominated by securities investment as a whole, which has caused the fund industry, especially the public fund, to fall into a fierce homogenous competition. The fund industry itself should be diversified, and investment targets should not be restricted to a specific area. Instead, it should form differentiated competitions through the allocation of major assets. At present, many public fund companies have already set up asset management subsidiaries. It is worth the attention of the manager to consider cooperation between subsidiaries and the parent company of public funds in asset management and set up platforms for the R&D of innovative product development. On the other hand, it is necessary to establish the cooperation and linkages between public and private funds. Public funds and private equity funds currently are in competition for excellent fund managers and capitals. However, the author believes they shall take on more benign interactions, with the echelon team playing their respective advantages. For example, the public fund has a more sound trading platform and research system, which could be used for an incubation platform of managers. Through the fund's special account, it is able to select talented fund managers and verify strategies. Therefore, it is possible to form a private fund who seeks absolute returns in the public offering system. The private equity system is more flexible and efficient, and it is easier for private fund to capture the trading opportunities in a specific period. This is different from the general risk-return characteristics of public offering funds and each type appeals to different suitable investors. All in all, public and private systems have their own specific differences. If there is better linkage and a differentiated competition, they can serve each other and benefit the overall development of the industry.

Finally, with regard to the supervision of the fund industry, the author believes that the regulatory objectives should be clearly defined first, and the ideology of "regulation means prohibition" should be changed to "regulation or encouragement". One of the reasons for the large-scale growth of asset management in the fund industry in recent years is that the set of regulatory objectives by different regulators is not uniform. At present, the fund industry as an important part of the asset management industry, it has presented an obvious cross-domain feature in the business. However, the current segmented supervision system for separate industries makes it difficult to regulate and coordinate, and it is easy to cause inconsistency in the supervision of similar businesses. Therefore, the author believes that before the implementation of the supervisory policy, the supervisory objective should be set uniformly, and supervisors in different areas should design supervisory rules according to their own industry characteristics. At the same time, directional guidance should be set in the regulatory objectives, such as encouragement of the direction of industry development and discouragement of the type of business engaged in by regulations, which will help the participants in the fund industry to better understand the regulatory objectives and achieve healthy development based on their own advantages. Furthermore, supervision should focus on the real-time monitoring of the overall development of the industry, rather than implementing certain regulatory rules after the size of a specific asset exceeds a certain range or a business model becomes an industry trend. In terms of technology, it is currently possible to collect data on fund operations (data on fund size, operating performance, funding sources, and whereabouts of investments) through relevant industry self-regulatory organizations, and use big data technology for real-time monitoring. When there occurs certain specific trend in the industry and it is not in line with the regulatory objectives, we can use window guidance and other methods to remind the specific managers, leaving time for the introduction or amendment of specific regulatory rules, and enriching the diversity of regulatory enforcement methods.

To sum up, the sound development of the fund industry needs the basic support of the market system, and the constant pursuit of the self-value in the fund industry, as well as the reform and improvement of the regulatory system, supervision methods. The increase in scale in recent years does not represent a real increase in the overall strength of the industry itself, but each step is a necessary accumulation for the industry's continued forward momentum. The fund industry is the "pioneer" of the capital market and pathbreaker in the integration of industry and finance. The author believes that with the growing development, the fund industry as the basic supporting industry will surely influence all aspects of the market economy and become the core platform assisting in financial, economic and social development.

Chapter 7
Review and Prospect of Assets Management Market Supervision Policy

Since the China Banking Regulatory Commission issued the "Interim Measures for the Administration of Personal Banking Business of Commercial Banks" and the "Guidelines for the Risk Management of Commercial Banks' Personal Wealth Management Services" in 2005, China's asset management market has gradually entered the stages of exploration, development and standardization. On the one hand, the asset management business model transitions from bank wealth management, bank off-balance sheet and off of off-balance-sheet operations to "great asset management". It shows characteristics such as multi-agent and whole life cycle, and the industry scale has soared; on the other hand, the asset management market also presents a series of chaos such as rigid payment, multi-level nesting and leverage superposition. This is a necessary step in the process of innovation and development of asset management business. However, it is also closely related to the regulatory mechanism. In order to guide asset management to return to its origin, the regulatory agency did not "give up eating for fear of choking", but actively explore and introduce new products in order to realize the balance between regulation and financial innovation in the market.

1 Management of Chaos and Regulatory Process

Since 2008, China's bank wealth management business has begun the explosive growth. At the same time, other forms of asset management businesses have also expanded rapidly. After the China Securities Regulatory Commission and the China Insurance Regulatory Commission launched a series of new "deregulation" policies in 2012, commercial banks, securities firms, funds, trusts, and insurance institutions can all carry out asset management operations. China has gradually entered an era

Written by Songwei Chen.

J. Yin et al., *Whither has the Money Gone*,
https://doi.org/10.1007/978-981-16-4931-8_7

of diversified, multi-leveled "great asset management." In terms of business entities, commercial banks have a strong position in risk management and control. Securities companies are strong in business chains, asset management and investment research. Trusts and insurance companies have outstanding advantages in terms of investment scope, integrated risk protection and tax incentives. The differentiated needs of investors can therefore be satisfied. From the perspective of business characteristics, "grand asset management" breaks the boundaries of the business and opens the door to mixed operations, providing investors with a full range of financial or non-financial services. However, at the same time, a large number of asset management funds "idling" in the financial system. This is the result of the profit-driven behavior of market players and the regulatory environment in which they are located.

1.1 Chaos in the Asset Management Market: Capital "Shifting from Real Economy to Virtual Economy"

In 2016, when the new shares were placed offline, some asset management plans, such as brokerage collective wealth management, fund subsidiaries, fund accounts, etc., were allegedly in violation of regulations, and the amount of purchase application far exceeded the scale of their own assets. In the secondary market, a large number of bank financing funds through securities, futures and other asset management plans have entered the stock market, pushing up the leverage ratio significantly; some banks have used asset management plans to move non-performing loans "off-balance sheet" to mask real bad debts. Similar chaos in asset management emerges in an endless stream, and it can be summarized as follows: channel business, leverage superposition, rigid cash payment, capital pool business, multi-level nesting, illegal investment in non-standard assets, etc.

For asset management agencies in the exploratory stage, these phenomena are unavoidable. After all, obtaining high-yield assets is the basis for their survival. However, this also makes the asset management business to associate with the shadow banking system at the beginning of its establishment. According to the definition by academic circles, all kinds of businesses that are outside the banking supervision system and may cause regulatory arbitrage and systemic risks can be incorporated into the shadow banking system, including bank wealth management, interbank business, broker directional asset management plans, and insurance asset management business. Under the shadow banking model, cross-sector business is widespread. As different types of asset management agencies are subject to different regulatory policies, strictly regulated asset management agencies will "channel" through loose-regulated agencies with multi-nested products for disguise to break business restrictions. It has greatly increased the risk relevance and infectivity between asset management products and institutions, and has also made the asset management business an important part of the credit system expansion.

Although various supervisory departments have repeatedly regulated the investment of asset management, through multi-layered nesting and capital pool business models and leverage superimposition, asset management organizations can still effectively avoid business restrictions. Therefore, with the rapid development of asset management business, there is a large amount of money flowing into the stock market, real estate industry, industries with overcapacity, local government financing platforms and bulk commodities, etc. Even the niche products such as garlic are showing capital rotation and industry surge under speculation. With respect to the influences, asset management funds flow into the real estate market in the form of trust loans and entrusted loans, which objectively limited the effectiveness of the government's macroeconomic regulation and control; funds enters into industries with overcapacities and therefore impacted structural transformation and upgrading of the economy and the supply-side structural reform process; capital flows to the local government financing platform, causing rapid growth of local government debt and pushing up local fiscal risks; funds flows to the stock market for "staging" new stocks, margin financing, directional addition and share allotment, which has spawned a "leveraged bull" from 2014 to 2015 "and subsequent stock price fluctuations.

The rapid development of the asset management business and the shadow banking system led to excessive expansion of the financial industry in China. Since 2005, the proportion of added value of China's financial industry in GDP has continued to rise, reaching 8.5% in 2015, far exceeding the 7% in the United States and 4.9% in Japan in the same period; the scale of internal financing within the financial sector exceeded more than 90 trillion yuan in 2016, the proportion is up to 1/3 of total social credit (debt financing scale), while in the real economy debt financing in the same period, the proportion of bank credit was less than 60%.[1]

The boom in the asset management market has also increased the degree of financialization of non-financial corporate profitability tools. With the characteristics of high-yield and rigid payment of bank wealth management products, some listed companies place funds in bank wealth management and directional asset management plans. According to the statistics of the Banking Industry Association, about 25% of the funds for bank wealth management products subscription in 2012 came from non-financial industry companies. If the return on real estate investment is also classified as such, the trend of non-financial companies profiting through financial channels will become more apparent. According to annual report data, about 151 non-real estate listed companies had real estate investment records in 2012, and many of them invested their funds in financial instruments due to the decline in profits from their main operations. For example, *ST Ningtong B, through the open transfer of two apartments in school districts in Beijing in 2016, achieved a profit of 21,429,900 yuan, which basically offset the main business loss of approximately 21.109 million yuan in the first half of the year.

The phenomenon of "shifting from real economy to virtual economy" of asset management funds is manifested as a serious differentiation between monetary aggregates and credit aggregates, in which the monetary aggregates constitute the main

[1] Jianfeng Yin, "The Over-inflated Financial Industry", Wealth Management, Issue 6, 2016.

part of the bank's liabilities. In 2016, the deposits of residents and enterprises in the broad money M2 only accounted for 60% of banks liabilities, even with the inclusion of "liabilities to other financial companies" in broad money, it is still less than 70% of bank liabilities; the credit aggregates are assets of the entire financial sector (including banks and non-banking financial sectors) in non-financial sectors, including domestic and foreign credit, non-bank financial institutions provided credit, non-financial bonds, net credit of interbank business, etc. With the rise of non-financial sectors and the development of non-traditional banking services within banks, the credit aggregates in 2009 obviously exceeded the broad money M2, and the current credit aggregates (debt financing scale) of the non-financial sector has reached 1.2 times[2] of the broad money M2. Compared with potential inflation, the increase in overall leverage caused by the expansion of credit aggregates is more likely to lead to systemic risks. The indicator of loan/capital in China already reached 70% in 2009, ignoring the possible errors, and then only 30%[3] of investments made in that year were funded by self-owned capital of the economy.

In short, the innovation and development of the asset management market has brought stable customers, funds and intermediary businesses revenues to financial institutions such as banks. It has also provided investors with various value-preserving and value-adding tools, as well supported the real economy to some extent. However, under the constraint of a series of chaos, a large amount of funds have entered the financial system and become "idling". Although it has increased the degree of financialization of China's economy, it also exposes asset management agencies to greater credit risk, market and liquidity risks, and legal compliance risks, etc., increasing the pressure of strictly observing the bottom line of systemic financial risks.

1.2 History of Asset Management Market Regulation: Progressive Development

With the gradual emergence of issues in the asset management market, the regulatory authorities have continued to supplement and perfect the systematic framework. This regulatory process basically corresponds to the asset management development in stages. Overall, it followed the path of the regulatory start-up (2005–2006), guided development (2007–2009), standardization and governance (2010–2011), and regulatory transitions (from 2012 to the present), the regulatory content has also been improved from the initial refinement of specific business regulations to strengthening business compliance and regulatory compliance, and to the promotion of back-to-basics of asset management business.

---

[2] Jianfeng Yin: "The rise of non-bank financial sector", "China Finance", Issue 7, 2017.

[3] Jianfeng Yin: "Currency, Credit, and Analysis of China's M2/GDP", Journal of the Communist Party School of China, No. 4, 2013.

From 2005 to 2006, the China Banking Regulatory Commission formally incorporated the wealth management business into the scope of supervision. The relevant systems focused on four aspects: the definition and classification of bank wealth management, business management system, risk management system, and supervision and management. For example, the "Interim Measures for Personal Wealth Management Business of Commercial Banks" ([2005] No.2 Document) and the "Guidelines for the Risk Management of Commercial Banks for Personal Wealth Management Business" ([2005] No. 23 Document) implement regulations on the definition, management systems and risk management systems of wealth management business. In the "Interim Measures for Commercial Banks to Administer the Valuation of Overseas Wealth Management Services by Valuators" ([2006] No. 121 Document), it further regulates the behavior of bank wealth management funds for investing in overseas markets.

With the extensive development of wealth management services, some problems with relatively high risks and relatively big social repercussions have emerged, such as unregulated business operations and misleading sales. In response to this, the China Banking Regulatory Commission has further standardized certain specific links under the original systematic framework. For example, according to "Notice on Adjusting the Provisions on the Management of Commercial Banks' Personal Wealth Management Business" ([2007] No. 241 Document) and "Notice on Further Regulating the Issues Related to the Reporting Management of Personal Wealth Management Business of Commercial Banks" ([2009] No.172 Document), the original examination and approval system of financial products was changed to a reporting system. The "Notice on Further Regulating the Issues Concerning the Investment Management of Commercial Banks' Personal Wealth Management Business" ([2009] No.65 Document) unified the customer stratification and starting point of sales of wealth management products, and for the first time specified the investment targets of wealth management funds, including fixed income products, credit assets, trust loans, asset portfolios for open or closed market transactions, financial derivatives, collective fund trust plans, overseas financial markets, etc. For the stock market, wealth management funds can not invest in publicly traded stocks in the domestic secondary market or associated securities investment funds, unlisted corporate stocks, and shares that are not publicly placed or traded by listed companies.

Since 2010, innovations such as bank-trust, bank-securities and bank-insurance cooperation have emerged in an endless stream. Banks have been increasingly circumventing the credit scale restriction through "channels". The supervision ideology of the CBRC has shifted from guided development to standardized governance. The "Notice on Regulating the Related Matters of the Cooperation between Bank and Trust on Wealth Management Business" ([2010] No.72 Document) and "Management Measures on the Sale of Wealth Management Products of Commercial Banks" ([2011] No. 5 Document), "Notice on Further Regulating the Bank's Wealth Management Cooperation Business" ([2011] No.7 Document) and "Notice on Further Strengthening the Risk Management of Commercial Banking Wealth

Management Business" ([2011] No.91 Document), have been successively promulgated, to rectify non-compliance behaviors and risks in areas such as the differentiation of private banks clients / high net worth customers, sales management, prohibition of wealth management funds from directly purchasing credit assets, etc.

In 2012, the potential risks of rigid redemption, capital pool model and leverage superposition gradually emerged. The China Banking Regulatory Commission began to promote the essential transformation of wealth management services to asset management. The scope of supervision at this stage involved the source of funds and investment usage of rural cooperative financial institutions, and standardized the way of wealth management fund investing in non-standard debt assets, shadow banking supervision, behavioral regulation of wealth management business, classification management of wealth management product sales, etc. In July 2014, the China Banking Regulatory Commission promulgated the "Notice on Concerning the Improvement of the Organizational Management System of Bank Wealth Management Businesses" ([2014] No.35 Document), and officially launched the reform of the banking wealth management division. Later, in 2016, the "Measures for the Supervision and Management of Commercial Bank's Wealth Management Business (Draft for soliciting comments)" abolished more than 10 documents such as [2005] No.2, [2009] No.65, [2013] No. 8, etc.

Since 2012, the China Securities Regulatory Commission and the China Insurance Regulatory Commission have started to relax and standardize the asset management business of the regulated parties. The People's Bank of China also first incorporated the growth rate of bank's off-balance sheet wealth management in the broad credit growth assessment in the first quarter of 2017 as an important part of the macro prudential management assessment system (MPA), in order to achieve the goal of "deleveraging, squeezing bubbles and mitigating the risk of off-balance sheet wealth management", and gradually enriching the "one bank and three commissions" regulatory system for grand asset management.

1.3 Supervision of Asset Management Market: Coexistence of "Concentration" and "Imbalance"

From 2012 to 2016, the China Banking Regulatory Commission, the China Securities Regulatory Commission, and the China Insurance Regulatory Commission successively issued more than 20 supervisory documents related to asset management to standardize matters such as investment targets for asset management funds. However, compared with the ever-changing financial innovation, there is still a certain degree of lag in the asset management market supervision, and there is still a contradiction between the segmented financial supervision system and the mixed operation. Objectively, although the asset management business relies on market-based mechanisms for innovation and development, it still needs reasonable guidance from the regulatory authorities. If the boundary between supervision and the market is ambiguous, or if supervision is too weak, it will be impossible to stop the frequent occurrence of regulatory arbitrage, idling arbitrage and some others. This is indeed the case. Many current chaoses in the asset management market are closely related to the segmented industry supervision system, which is reflected in the following four aspects.

First, the regulation is uneven. In the era of grand asset management, the business types that banks, brokerages, insurance companies, trusts, funds, and other asset management agencies can carry out are clearly homogenized, and customer objects, investable financial products, etc. become gradually convergent, resulting in the competition of different types of asset management institutions. However, due to different starting points and different levels of business development, various types of asset management services are subject to significantly differentiated supervision. They are manifested in two aspects: first, the same regulatory agency is inconsistent with the regulation of financial services of the same nature; second, different supervisory institutions are inconsistent with regulations of similar financial services. In the context of business convergence, unbalanced supervision will inevitably lead to regulatory arbitrage. Asset management agencies that are subject to strict supervision have the incentive to lengthen the business chain through product nesting and evade regulatory requirements for funds and investment ends, while the loosely regulated agencies have become the business "channels." In the first case, the CBRC stipulates different scopes for the investment objectives of bank wealth management and trust plans. Wealth management funds can dock collective trust plans to extend investment targets from fixed income assets, structured products and financial derivatives to standard products such as bonds and stocks, it may also participate in margin financing, futures trading, equity investment, nonfinancial corporate debt financing instruments and central bank bills through a single fund trust. In the second case, the supervisory standards for asset management between the "three commissions" are not uniform. The asset management of securities companies can invest in non-standard assets such as unlisted equity, property rights and bank credits through collective fund trusts, and can even issue entrusted loans.

Second, supervision lags behind. The asset management business has broken down the separation of business operations among different types of financial institutions such as banks, brokers, and insurance companies, and present new business forms such as cross-sector competition, mutual intersection and innovative cooperation in the industry. With the intensification of competition in the asset management market, technological innovations, product innovations, and institutional innovations of asset management have emerged in an endless stream. In particular, investment targets have undergone frequent and multiple conversions, and institutional-based financial supervisory agencies cannot timely pay attention to new issues and situations, resulting in the continuous accumulation of risks in intersected areas. From the perspective of the regulatory level, one of the reasons is that the regulatory technology is lagging behind innovation. For example, under multi-agency supervision the statistics system for information management of asset management products is fragmented and dispersed and it is difficult to form unified shared business data, which seriously limits the availability and integrity of regulatory information, and leads to a delayed regulatory response; the second is the backwardness of the institutional supply. The introduction of each asset management policy is almost always passive in following the process of financial innovation, the system is in lack of flexibility and forward-looking; and the third is the lag in regulatory reforms. Despite there is a financial joint meeting system between the "three commissions", the coordination mechanism is not mature. In the case of different regulatory objectives and poor communication of information, there is a lack of synergy between the asset management market supervision and the macro-prudential policy framework. For example, the trend in information technology and digital development has strengthened the linkage between asset management and financial markets, thus the asset management supervision reform require the cooperation of the exchange rate system reforms and capital account liberalization. However, coordination and cooperation in these areas are not sufficient.

Third, the lack of supervision. With rapid changes in the asset management business, the regulatory authorities should keep pace with the times, but under a number of constraints, there is long-term lack of supervision of some asset management businesses, therefore cannot support the stable development of the asset management market. Firstly, the legal vacancy, the legal relationship applicable to asset management business is not clear, nor unified, there are existences of trusts, agents as well as limited partnerships, etc., resulting ambiguous boundaries of responsibilities and liabilities between the asset management business entities. It is difficult to effectively balance the interests of all parties. At the same time, the "Securities Law" lacks a definition of the function of "securities", resulting in a lack of clear legal definition of asset management innovations that are homogeneous in the legal "securities" function[4]; secondly, the regulatory concept is not clear, and the current regulatory system still upholds supervision of institutions and industries. However, asset management innovation products are usually between direct financing and indirect financing, and often fall into a vague regulatory area under the segmented supervision system; thirdly, the long-term absence of macro-prudential supervision and the lack of effectiveness of micro-prudential supervision, which exacerbate speculation in the financial markets and limit the transparency, predictability and independence of the asset management market. In practice, there are still a lot of regulatory vacuums in the shadow banking system, asset management and innovation business. In particular, business innovations in the channel model and capital pool-asset pool model obscure the potential risks of the asset management business. For example, the lack of supervision of private equity funds has resulted in violation of regulations on design, sale and operation, including illegal principal and interest guarantees, repeated financing and illegal sales.

Fourth, regulatory evasion. Under the segmented supervision system, not only is there supervision fragmentation and supervision competition, but passive supervision and negative supervision. There are two situations, first, for the segmentally regulated objective, the supervisory organization is eager to become bigger and stronger.

[4] Shusong Ba: "2016 China Asset Management Industry Development Report", Renmin University of China Press, 2016.

Despite the understanding of business risks, it is not willing to break the pattern; second, for cross-domain businesses and business of other areas, regulators do not want to intervene, but it also does not allow other regulatory agencies to enter into its own regulatory areas. At present, asset management products issued by brokers, futures, public funds and private equity companies are supervised by the China Securities Regulatory Commission. Products of banks and trusts are supervised by the China Banking Regulatory Commission. Insurance asset management products are regulated by the China Insurance Regulatory Commission. They are often in contradictory situations with each other while promoting the rapid development of the industry and prudent supervision of the industry. At the same time, various types of regulatory agencies are often in conflict with one another, making regulatory actions appear to be somewhat distorted. In practice, the "three commissions" hope to enlarge their industry scale, strengthen their institutions and market strength, and actually act as the protectors of the industry. Therefore, they tend to relax their supervision or even evade supervision; it also tends to form "site awareness" in segmented supervision. The "three commissions" do not want to interfere with each other's regulatory objectives, which makes cross-industry regulatory coordination more difficult. Obviously, the reasons for supervision to evade the regulatory system are also inseparable from the regulatory agencies' lack of professionalism and service awareness.

In short, the supervision of the asset management market cannot be either "vacant" or "imbalanced". If there is a regulatory vacuum, it is bound to cover up the real situation of the entire asset management industry and misleads the market entities in the analysis of business risks; if the regulatory rules or standards are not uniformed, asset management organizations will choose regulatory arbitrage or arbitrage idling arbitrage and undermine the fairness and competition in the market. The chaos in the current asset management market is rooted in the "vacancy" and "imbalance" of supervision. To rectify the misconduct of asset management, the reform of the supervision system must be implemented by "two-pronged approach" and joint efforts.

2 Segmented Supervision of Current Asset Management Market

In order to become bigger and stronger, banks have gradually transformed into asset management businesses. Financial institutions such as securities firms and insurance companies have also vigorously promoted asset management innovation. However, when all types of financial institutions are influx, asset management products are multi-nested and leverage superimposed, a large amount of funds are stranded in the financial system for "idling". The Braess's Paradox[5] of asset management innovation has occurred. There are two main points of view on this paradox. One is to ban financial innovations, for example, the "Volcker Rule" prohibits bank's self-operation business; the second is to abandon the unreasonable control in existing financial business and promote the market-oriented reforms of mechanisms of financial supervision and regulation.[6] In the practice in China, the "three commissions" formed a distinctive policy system. Among them, the China Banking Regulatory Commission actively implemented penetration supervision. The China Securities Regulatory Commission upholds the principle of legality, strictness and comprehensiveness, while the Insurance Regulatory Commission has established a "pigeon" regulatory prototype.

2.1 The CBRC Policy System: The Principle of Penetration

If 2004 is the "first year" of financial management for banks, then 2013 is the "first year of transition". Since 2013, the China Banking Regulatory Commission has successively promulgated various rules and regulations such as the "Notice on Regulating Investment Operations of Commercial Bank's Wealth Management Business Related Issues" ([2013] No.8 Document), guiding the wealth management business gradually into standardized and rational development, and return to its basics. Among these regulatory systems, the penetrating supervision of bank wealth management focuses on two aspects: one is the investment management of wealth management funds, and the other is the sales management of wealth management products.

The No. 8 Document of the China Banking Regulatory Commission regulates the investment of non-standardized credit assets by wealth management funds. The main contents are as follows: First, the source of wealth management funds is required to be in line with the investment subject matter, and the fund pool-asset pool model is cleared; second, all assets that are not traded between banks and in exchanges are all classified as non-standardized debt assets, such as equity financing with repurchase terms, and basically incorporated trusts, securities companies, funds and property exchange listed products; third, set up separate account for non-standardized debts for management and accounting to avoid confusion between self-owned funds and wealth management funds, and also to prevent risks arising from misalignment of wealth management funds; fourth, disclose non-standardized debt investments of wealth management products to specific investors, in order to prevent bank from blurring the investment direction through duration and risk premium mismatches;

[5] The "Braess's paradox" means that adding an expressway to the existing transportation network will result in an even greater congestion of the entire transportation network. The reason is that the original transportation network has high commuting costs and the new expressway is faster. As a result, all vehicles choose new high-speed roads, disrupting the commuter traffic of the original transportation network, and greatly increasing the cost of the entire commuter service.

[6] Jianfeng Yin: "The rise of non-bank financial sector", "China Finance", Issue 7, 2017.

fifth, conduct due diligence study, compliance review and post-lending management of wealth management products just like the self-operated funds, in order to increase the cost of non-standard investment of banks; sixth, put forward the principle of limit management, set 35% of the balance of wealth management products and 4% of the total assets of the previous year as the "red line", whichever is lower shall be used as the limit, this is to control the total amount of non-standardized wealth management products; seventh, the restricted wealth management products must be approved by the Central Bank; eighth, no direct or indirect, explicit or implicit guarantees or commitment of repurchase shall be provided, in order to cut off the disguised credit enhancing business and the channel business for banks; ninth, retrospectively review the failed requirements, accrue capital reserves and risk reserves in line with the self-operated loans; tenth, build a more stringent responsibility mechanism and time limit for implementation.

After "No. 8 Document", the CBRC launched direct wealth management financing tools and plans, which stipulated that banks can only subscribe for the shares of wealth management direct financing tool through the bank's wealth management plan, after registration, they can quote and transfer through the integrated financing platform of wealth management direct financing tools; wealth management direct financing tools must be in one-to-one correspondence with corporate debt financing, and the share of any wealth management direct financing tool of wealth management plans held by a single bank must not exceed 80% of the total share. The wealth management plan makes the financial risk explicit and transparent, which can reduce the risk of shadow banking and help clarify the legal status and direction of bank financial management.

In December 2014, the China Banking Regulatory Commission issued the "Measures for the Supervision and Administration of Commercial Banking Wealth Management Services (Draft for comments)" to promote the conversion of the expected return-rate products to net-value products, but was later put on hold until July 2016 when it was restarted. The new "Draft for Soliciting Opinions" abolished more than 10 documents such as "No. 8 Document". The main contents are as follows: First, improve the risk isolation mechanism for wealth management business, and establish the bankruptcy isolation mechanism for wealth management assets for the first time; second, implement classification management for banks wealth management, divide it into basic and comprehensive financial services based on the scope of investment. Basic financial products can invest in bank deposits, large deposit certificate, government bonds, local government bonds, treasury bills, government agencies bonds, financial bonds, corporate credit Bonds, credit asset-backed securities, monetary market funds, bond-based funds. Comprehensive basic wealth management products can also invested in non-standardized debt assets, equity assets, and other assets recognized by the China Banking Regulatory Commission in addition to the basic business scope; third, prohibit the bank from issuing graded wealth management products. Wealth management funds shall not directly or indirectly invest in the bank's own credit assets and the corresponding beneficiary/income rights, and shall not directly or indirectly invest in wealth management products issued by the bank itself, or in securities investment funds other than monetary market funds and bonds, and may not invest directly or indirectly in domestic listed company's publicly or privately issued or tradable shares or the related beneficiary/income rights, except for those wealth management products that are issued to experienced investors, private bank clients who have higher risk tolerance, high net-worth customers and institutional customers; fourth, require banks to make provision for risk reserves, and the total assets of each wealth management product must not exceed 140% of the net assets of this wealth management product; fifth, the information registration time of the financial product is uniformed, that is, "the head office submitted an electronic report to the China Banking Regulatory Commission through the national banking wealth management information registration system 10 days before the sale of the wealth management product, and complete the termination registration within 5 days after the wealth management product expires".

The supervision of interbank wealth management started in 2014. In order to standardize non-standard investment by banks through their interbank business, five ministries jointly promulgated the "Notice on Regulating the Interbank Business of Financial Institutions" ([2014] No. 127 Document), which stipulates "the balance of a single commercial ban's financed funds through interbank businesses shall not exceed 1/3 of the bank's total liabilities"; the CBRC use the "Circular on Regulating Commercial Banks' Interbank Business Governance "([2014] No.140 Document) as the supporting policy for the "No. 127 Document", specified the applicable institution scope, business scope, bank corporate headquarters legal person duties, specific requirements of the franchised department, penalties for non-compliance, etc., and standardized the interbank non-standard business. For example, financial institutions may not accept or provide any direct or indirect, explicit or implicit third-party financial institutions credit guarantee (unless otherwise provided by the state) when engaging in reverse purchase/repurchase business or interbank investment businesses.

In April 2017, the China Banking Regulatory Commission issued the "Guiding Opinions on Risk Prevention and Control of the Banking Industry" ([2017] No.6 Document), which clarified ten key areas of risk prevention and control in the banking industry, including traditional risks such credit risk, liquidity risk, real estate risk, local government debt default risk, etc., as well as non-traditional risks such as bond fluctuation risk, cross-financial product risk, internet financial risk, and external shock risk, etc., and put forward a series of risk prevention and control requirements, such as prohibiting multi-layered interbank investment nesting for arbitrage. Afterwards, the China Banking Regulatory Commission issued the "Notice on Conducting Specialized Governance of Regulatory Arbitrage, Idling Arbitrage and Associated Arbitrage of the Banking Industry" ([2017] No. 46 Document) and "Notice on Conducting Specialized Governance on Improper innovations, Improper transactions, Improper incentives, and Improper Charges for the Banking Industry" ([2017] No. 53 Document,) requires banks to self-examine "three arbitrages" and "four improper". In May 2017, the Banking Wealth Management Registration and Trusteeship Center issued the "Notice on Further Regulating the Banks' Wealth Management Products Penetration Registration", requires the bank to register its contractual outsourcing and the status of underlying assets of asset management plans by last Sunday on each Fridays every week, in order to promote the net-value management of asset management plan and the transparency of information disclosure, and forcing asset management organizations to cut off capital pool.

In summary, the CBRC's has incorporated banking businesses such as channel business, interbank business, cross-finance business, etc. into comprehensive risk management in accordance with the principle of "substance is more important than form", and penetration supervision has been continuously strengthened. With the increasingly stringent regulation of channel services and wealth management services, commissioned investment, another form of banking asset management, may grow rapidly. As banks and non-banking financial institutions are involved, the China Banking Regulatory Commission must take precautions to guide banks to improve relevant business risk control system as soon as possible.

2.2 Policy Framework of the Securities Regulatory Commission: Lawful, Strict and Comprehensive

In 2012, the China Securities Regulatory Commission successively promulgated the "Pilot Measures for Asset Management Business of Futures Companies", "Administrative Measures for Clients Asset Management Business of Securities Companies", "Detailed Rules for the Implementation of Collective Asset Management Business of Securities Companies," "Rules for the Implementation of Directional Asset Management Business for Securities Companies," "Pilot Measures of Customer Asset Management Business of Fund Management Companies " and other rules to regulate the development of futures, brokerage, and fund asset management businesses.

According to the pilot scheme of futures asset management, futures companies can provide capital management services through special account wealth management approaches. The scope of investment includes stocks, funds, bonds, bills, collective asset management plans and asset-backed securities in addition to commodity futures, financial futures and options; Customers of futures asset management products should be well funded and have strong risk tolerance, and the single client's initial entrusted assets must not be less than one million yuan.

The "Measures for the Management of Clients' Asset Management Business of Securities Companies" relaxed the restrictions on the asset management business of brokerage firms from six aspects: First, the administrative examination and approval of collective plans was cancelled, industry association filing system was applied; Second, the collection, orientation, and specialization were adopted. Asset management treats the scope of investment and the way assets are used differently, for example, adopt differentiated treatment according to different investment scopes and ways of capital usage of collective, directional and specialized asset management respectively, allowing collective and directional asset management plans to participate in margin trading, and allowing collective plan to carry out positive repurchase, etc.; Third, cancel double 10% restrictions on collective and directional asset management plans, the double 10% restriction and its associated transaction restrictions are exempt for indexed collective plans; fourth, allow grading of shares of collective management plans based on based on risk-return features as well as conditional transfer between investors; fifth, cancel restrictions on the asset scale for securities company carrying out collective asset management business; Sixth, securities companies are allowed to handle registration and settlement business, and brokers recognized by the CSRC can also provide asset custody services. The investment scope of the directional asset management plans is stipulated in the contract between the securities firm and the client. They may participate in margin trading financing, but it must not violate laws and regulations; the collective asset management plan can be invested in domestically-issued financial products and overseas financial products approved by the China Securities Regulatory Commission, but may not be used in violation for loans, capital lending, mortgage financing or external guarantees, etc., and may not be used for investments that may be subject to unlimited liabilities. From the perspective of the client, the net asset value of a single client of the directional asset management plan should not be less than one million yuan. The entrusted assets should be legally held cash, stocks, bonds, funds, collective asset management plan shares, and other financial assets permitted by the CSRC; the collective asset management plan is for compliant investors only, with a cumulative total of no more than 200 people, the amount contributed by participating individual customer shall not be less than one million yuan, and the total amount of funds raised shall be less than 5 billion yuan, but not less than 30 million yuan.

The revised "Trial Measures for Fund Management Company-Specific Customer Asset Management Business" allows the fund company to set up a special asset management plan to invest in "equity, creditor and other property rights that have not been transferred through the stock exchange", and implement a qualified specific customer system and record system. The fund company can provide specific asset management business for single customer and multi customers, of which the former requires the customer's initial assets to be more than 30 million yuan; the number of customers of the latter must not exceed 200, however, this limit is not applicable to customers with the single commissioned amount over 3 million. Also for the multi customer business, the total initial assets shall be over 5 billion yuan, but not less than 30 million yuan (except as otherwise provided by the CSRC). Specific asset management plans can invest in cash, bank deposits, stocks, bonds, funds, central bank bills, non-financial corporate debt financing instruments, ABS, futures and other financial derivatives, "equity shares, claims and other property rights not transferred through stock exchanges" and other assets recognized by the CSRC, of which the specific assets to be invested in the latter two categories are called special asset management plans and require fund companies to set up specialized subsidiaries.

With the development of asset management of brokers, futures and funds, some agencies carry out " credit, investment banking or brokerage services" in the name of "asset management," such as providing capital-protected arrangements for priority investors through structured products, or internally graft capital allocation or add leverages to internal products. In response to these issues, the China Securities Regulatory Commission issued the "Detailed Rules for the Prohibited Conducts of the Eight Base Lines of Implementing Asset Management Business by Securities and Futures Business Institutions" in March 2015, and promulgated the" Provisional Regulations on the Operation and Management of the Private Equity Asset Management Business of Securities and Futures Institutions" in 2016, ("New eight bottom line"), eventually formed the regulatory documents of the Securities Regulatory Commission, improving legal effectiveness and strengthening institutional binding force. The "new eight bottom line" incorporates managers of private equity investment funds into the regulatory system, emphasizing penetration verification principles, reducing leverage, encouraging active management, and standardizing sales management; "New eight bottom lines" strictly control the leverage ratio up to 2 times in structured asset management plans, and set up constraints by type; reiterates the prohibition of capital pool business, do not allow mixed management of different asset management plans; if the same asset manager establishes a number of asset management plan of similar type and similar investment target, the penetration verification shall be implemented and the number of investors shall be counted; prohibit asset management plans from illegally engaging in securities and futures business based on the account real-name system, account control rights, add-in transaction system and establishment of umbrella-type asset management products, etc.; strictly control investment advisory model; in order to align the old and new rules, the "new eight-bottom line" make transitional arrangement for structured products in accordance with the principle of "delimitation of new and old". The surviving product shall not increase the leverage ratio before the expiration of the contract, and may not increase the scale of the net subscription for new shares with priority, and shall be liquidated and may not be renewed after the expiration date. On May 19, 2017, the CSRC first mentioned the complete ban on channel services at the press conference, and did not allow the management responsibility to be exempted. It covered the channels of brokerage asset management, fund companies, and fund subsidiaries, and promoted the "de-channeling" of asset management agencies and the enhancement of their active management capabilities.

In response to the problems in the development of fund subsidiaries, the China Securities Regulatory Commission revised the "Management Regulations for Subsidiary Companies of Fund Management Companies" in November 2016 and issued the "Provisional Regulations on the Management of Risk Management Indicators for Specific Customers' Asset Management Subsidiaries of Fund Management Companies", which has systematically regulated the subsidiary's organizational structure and conflicts of interest, strengthened the position of subsidiaries and parent company's management and control responsibilities, and at the same time built a risk control index system with net capital as the core indicator to increase risk resilience; the regulation also classifies the existing business of the fund's subsidiaries, guiding the industry to return to the basics of asset management business and supporting subsidiary companies to conduct professionalization, specialization, and differentiated operations according to laws and regulations, and cultivate core competitiveness.

In short, the regulation of the relevant asset management business by CSRC started relatively late, but its response was quite acute. In response to new issues and new situations in the industry, it can promptly provide policy guidance. In particular, the introduction of the "new eight-bottom line" has unified restrictions on the securities companies, funds, and futures systems from the aspects of leverage, prohibition of capital pools, expected rate of return, and regulated investment, however, "While the priest climbs a post, the devil climbs ten," the supervision of the China Securities Regulatory Commission on asset management is still a long way to go.

2.3 Policy System of Insurance Regulatory Commission: "Dove Cage" Prototype

The start of insurance asset management supervision was relatively late, but its introduction of policies was more intensive. In July 2012, the China Insurance Regulatory Commission issued four new policies: "Interim Measures on Insurance Funds Investment Bonds", "Interim Measures for the Administration of Entrusted Investment of Insurance Funds", "Notice on Relevant Issues concerning Investments in Equity and Immovable Properties of Insurance Funds", and "Interim Measures for the Administration of the Configuration of Insurance Assets". In October, the "Notice on Matters Related to Insurance Asset Management Companies", "Notice on Insurance Funds Investment Related Financial Products", "Interim Provisions on Management of Infrastructure Debt Investment Plans", "Detailed Rules for the Implementation of Interim Measures for the Administration of Overseas Investment Insurance Funds", "Interim Measures for the Participation of Insurance Funds in the Transactions of Financial Derivatives", and the "Regulations on the Participation of Insurance Funds in Stock Index Futures Trading", total of six policies were issued. These policies clarified the market position of insurance assets, insurance assets has entered into the era of great assets management.

In accordance with the "Notice on Relevant Matters of Insurance Asset Management Companies", insurance assets management may be entrusted with the management of funds other than insurance funds, such as funds from pensions, corporate annuities, housing accumulation funds, and qualified investors who can identify and bear risks; Insurance assets management can be entrusted by clients to carry out asset management business in the name of the trustor, it can also set up products for the benefit of beneficiaries or for specific purposes; eligible insurance asset management can apply for public asset management business; insurance assets management can set up subsidiaries to engage in special asset management business in accordance with regulations. The "Notice on Insurance Funds Investment in Financial Products" stipulates that insurance funds can be invested in domestically issued bank wealth management products, credit asset-backed securities, collective fund trust plans, brokerage special asset management plans, insurance asset management company infrastructure investment plans, real estate investments and project asset-backed plans. The

"Regulations on the Implementation of the Interim Measures for the Administration of Overseas Investment Insurance Funds" has not limited overseas investment regions to Hong Kong and China, but has extended to 25 developed countries and 20 emerging market countries. Investment products have been extended with immovable assets, unlisted company equity, securities investment funds, equity investment funds, etc. in addition to stocks and bonds. "Interim Measures for the Participation of Insurance Capital in Financial Derivative Products Trading" and "Regulations on Insurance Funds Participating in Stock Index Futures Trading" enable insurance asset management to apply financial derivatives.

In order to strengthen asset-liability coordination management and prevent risks of mismatch and liquidity risks, the CIRC issued the "Circular on Strengthening the Supervision over the Prudential Regulation of Asset Allocation of Insurance Companies" at the end of 2015. The main contents are as follows: First, setting standards, demarcating the scope of the companies that needs to submit the stress test report; Second, the asset allocation stress test, assessing the impact on the return on assets, cash flow and solvency; Third, the prudence assessment of the company's asset liability management and stress testing, and impose regulatory measures accordingly. The establishment of insurance asset allocation risk investigation and early warning mechanisms will help guide the stable operation of insurance companies.

In June 2016, the China Insurance Regulatory Commission promulgated the "Notification on Strengthening the Supervision and Administration of Portfolio Insurance Asset Management Products" ([2016] No. 104 Document), classified the pilot qualification of insurance asset management and pension insurance company's product business, the scope of basic product assets, and registration and issuance, as well as prohibited actions, etc. When non-standard investments are connected to insurance asset management products such as collective ones or insurance funds related ones, China Insurance Regulatory Commission requires that non-standard investment docked with insurance asset management can only be its own infrastructure investment plan, equity investment plan, asset-backed plan, etc.; Asset management shall not issue products with the nature of "capital pools" to prevent the liquidity risks of insurance asset management products caused by duration mismatches; it is forbidden to issue products with a nested structure including products that mainly invests in single non-open market investment objectives, or products that invests in directional alternative asset management products, or the product that is directionally invested in targets set up by the same manager, etc.; it is forbidden to issue graded products to non-institutional investors; it is forbidden to issue graded products to institutional investors for situations that the graded equity or mixed products have over 1 time leverage ratio, or other types of graded products that has over 3 times leverage ratio; it is forbidden to operate through setting up sub-account under the product; it bans investment without clear underlying asset type and ratio; it bans the transfer of products in the form of external investment consultants; the custodian bank branch cannot serves as the product custodian (except that the branch is authorized by the custodian bank's head office). "No. 104 Document" helps to form a product business management model combining external constraints and internal supervision, and improve the supervision and monitoring system of product business.

In April 2017, the China Insurance Regulatory Commission issued the "Notice on Further Strengthening Insurance Supervision and Safeguarding the Steady and Healthy Development of the Insurance Industry" ("No. 34 Document") with reference to the relevant documents of the China Banking Regulatory Commission, in order to regulate the market through strengthening supervision, filling up regulatory oversight, adhering to the bottom line thinking, and innovating institutional mechanisms. It was later refined through the "Notice on Further Strengthening the Risk Prevention and Control of the Insurance Industry" ("No. 35 Document").

In a word, the CIRC gradually formed the supervision idea of "opening investment authority and building the bottom line of risk control", taking the "dove cage" style supervision model into shape. However, it should be clarified that the investment behavior of the insurance asset management market is involved in multiple areas. Apart from the CIRC, it must also meet the regulatory requirements of the China Banking Regulatory Commission, the China Securities Regulatory Commission, the People's Bank of China, and other departments. The CIRC should actively establish and improve insurance asset management coordinated supervision mechanism.

3 Supervision Trend of Asset Management Market

Regulatory arbitrage, idling arbitrage and other chaos continue to force the reform of the regulatory system. In February 2017, a document was leaked, the "Guidelines on Regulating the Asset Management Business of Financial Institutions (Draft for Soliciting Opinions)" (hereinafter referred to as the "Guiding Opinions") allegedly initiated by the People's Bank of China in collaboration with the "Three Commissions", triggering the industry's deep concerned. Although the official documents have not yet been issued, the "Guidance Opinion" reflects the trend and direction of China's asset management market supervision to some extent, according to the demand for innovation in the asset management market, the continuity of regulatory policies, and the official response of the "Three Commissions."

3.1 Unified Supervision

The "Guidance Opinions" unifies the standards of asset management products, including qualified investors, registration and filing systems, investment scope, distinguishing between public offerings and private placements, custody and information disclosure; unifies the caliber of non-standard assets and classifies investors as the public and qualified investors, and further classifies qualified investors as institutional investors and qualified individual investors; implements unified leverages for all asset management products, of which leverage ratio for equity and hybrid, fixed income, and other structured asset management plans shall not exceed 1x, 3x and

2x respectively; sets a uniform debt ratio (total assets/net assets) cap for similar asset management products, in which the total assets of public offerings shall not exceed 140% of the net assets, and the total assets of private equity products must not exceed 200% of net assets, and calculates the aggregated total assets of a single product in accordance with the penetration principle; implements unified risk reserve and capital constraint, setting the provision of risk reserve according to 10% of the management fee and up to 1% of the balance of the asset management product; the data is submitted to the central bank for unified monitoring and unified supervision—the People's Bank of China will implement macro-prudential management, while the "Three Commissions" as well as other departments are responsible for micro-prudential supervision.

3.2 Continuous Supervision

Part of the "Guiding Opinion" is a continuation of existing regulatory policies. First, the capital pool model is forbidden. Asset management organizations must not engage in or participate in roll-outs offering, pooled operations, maturity mismatches, and separate pricing fund pool operations to ensure that the duration of asset management products matches the duration of investment in production. For each product, separate management, separate account shall be set up and they shall be accounted for separately either; second, limit the leverage ratio, leverage ratio of structured asset management products investment in fixed income or bond funds not less than 80% shall not exceed 3 times, and leverage ratio of investment in stock assets not less than 20% shall not exceed 1 times, the leverage ratio of other classes shall not exceed 2 times, and the debt ratio of public offerings shall be limited to 140%, while the debt ratio of private placement products shall be limited to 200%; third, double 10% concentration limit, the market value of a single asset or fund invested by a single asset management product must not exceed 10% of the net assets of the asset management product (except for private equity products). The market value of a single security or fund invested by all asset management products must not exceed 10% of the market value of the security or fund, in order to prevent the risk of high positions of single assets; fourth, to break the rigid payment, the People's Bank of China has included off-balance-sheet financing in broad credit as an assessment factor, in the future, the principal-guaranteed management will gradually shrink; fifth, to de-channelize, financial institutions may entrust other financial institutions with professional investment capabilities and qualifications to invest overseas, but cannot add another channel, and a white list system will be applied for the outsourcing; Sixth, the "Guiding Opinions" implement "new and old delimitation", and gradually standardize products that do not meet the requirements, they will no longer be renewed after expiration, and new products will be applied of new regulations accordingly.

3.3 Tighter Regulation

The "Guidance Opinion" takes the overall situation into consideration and further strengthens the management of investment behaviors and sales behavior of asset management products. First, financial institutions, especially banks' wealth management must not carry out the on-balance sheet asset management business, and must not promise for principal-guaranteed gains, despite the difficulty of implementation, the government is determination to break the rigid reform. Second, public offerings must not invest in unlisted stocks and financial derivatives. Asset management products are prohibit from directly or indirectly investing in non-standard credits and their income rights, as well as in asset management products or managed financial assets issued by non-financial institutions, in particular issued by local financial asset exchanges or trading centers. Asset management products investment in non-standardized debt assets, shall meet the regulations on limit management, prohibition of term mismatches and etc., and shall gradually reduce the scale of non-standard assets; third, off-balance-sheet wealth management services will be returned to on-balance or converted to net-value products. The capital constraint shall be matched with the actual business risk it bears, and the asset management agency shall provide a risk reserve according to 10% of the management fee up to 1% of the product balance, in order to make up for losses to the property of the asset management product and clients caused by the violation of laws and regulations by financial institutions, violation of asset management product agreements, operational errors, or technical issues; fourth, eliminate multiple nesting of products. In addition to FOF and MOM products, asset management products cannot invest in other asset management products, nor can they provide channel services to expand investment scope and avoid regulatory requirements.

In short, the "Guidance Opinion" has set up a great deal of reform and is relatively difficult to implement. However, no matter whether it can be successfully introduced, there will be no change of the trend toward a unified, continuous, and stricter regulation, nor the transition from institutional supervision to functional supervision. Under the segmented supervision system, the chaos of regulatory arbitrage, idling arbitrage and others keep occurring. In the future, in order to guide asset management operations to return to basics, it is essential to improve regulatory coordination mechanism, and the supervisory policy shall promote asset management fund to serve the real economy.

4 Conclusion: What Kind of Regulation is Needed in the Market?

Regulation and innovation have always been a contradiction. Since 2016, the "Three Commissions" have demonstrated their understanding and attitude towards the asset management market in their actions. Continued enhancement of regulation has become irreversible and has become the main feature in the coming period of time. The effect of this policy is immediately obvious. Some irregularities such as improper innovation and regulatory arbitrage in the asset management market have been eliminated. At the same time, some new asset management innovations have emerged, such as Robot-advisor and fixed-income securities., currency and commodities (FICC), internet finance, etc., while promoting the transformation of the asset management organizations, it also brings greater challenges to the current regulatory framework. In view of this, "vacant" or "imbalanced" regulation is certainly not feasible, but excessive supervision is not a panacea either. Moderation is the key to maintaining the balance between the two. After all, the responsibility of "One Band and Three Commissions" is to "clear mines" rather than "detonate them".

4.1 Regulatory Framework: Focus on Coordination Mechanisms

Under the trend of mixed operation, the reform of the supervision system for separate industries has become the basic consensus of the academic community and the market. However, there are still many controversies about how to reform. Some people think that the "super-central bank" will become the direction of evolution. Under the central bank set up the Monetary Authority and the comprehensive regulation committee, which not only meets the requirements of the macro-prudential policy framework, but also meets the "three overall plans", popular in international society; Some people proposed a "double-peak" model of supervision. The central bank is responsible for maintaining financial stability. The Financial Regulation and Management Committee are responsible for micro-monitoring of market access and market behavior. There is also a calling for the preservation of "One Bank and Three Commissions" framework, but with certain changes to it. Whether the "super-central bank" or the merged "Three Commissions" is adopted, it is more practical to establish an efficient coordination mechanism for asset management regulation.

In August 2013, the People's Bank of China took the lead in establishing an inter-ministerial joint meeting of financial regulation and coordination reconciling the financial supervision under the current regulatory system, especially for the supervision of cross-finance products and cross-market financial innovation. However, in the real operation, it is more of a platform for information sharing and daily communication, lacking a clear implementation mechanism. The current constitution of "Guidance Opinion" in 2017 is a new round of experimentation of collaborative supervision of the asset management business by "One Bank and Three Commissions". The policy is quite intensive and its implementation will be difficult. Whether it can break the conflict of interests and prejudices between the departments and form a joint cooperation remains to be further observed.

At present, the "Three Commissions" have strengthened supervision of asset management within each own jurisdiction, however, the mixed-industry characteristic of the above business impose higher requirements on regulatory coordination. The first is to set up unified standard of asset management regulation, including asset management standards, investor appropriateness, leverage, concentration degree, risk reserves and capital constraints. This has already been incorporated in the "Guidance Opinions"; the second is the efficient information sharing mechanism, it will set product information that the asset management organization shall disclose, the organizations submit the information according to standard format to be included in the information sharing platform; third, the decision-making mechanism of inter-ministerial joint meeting, rules of procedure and decision-making authority shall be clear. Set unified rules, standards and procedures for "One Bank and Three Commissions" and gradually form the regulatory framework where the inter-ministerial joint meeting make decisions and various regulatory agencies are responsible for execution; Fourth, the willingness and awareness of "One Bank and Three Commissions" for collaborative cooperation are strong, therefor, various regulatory agencies can be guided to form synergy through appropriate incentive and restraint mechanism.

4.2 Regulatory Concept: Focusing on Functional Supervision

Institutional supervision is an important source of a series of chaos. It is necessary to adjust the concept of supervision from the focus of institutional supervision to functional supervision for effectively governance. No matter how the regulatory framework is set, supervision and coordination should be based on functional supervisory basis. The theory of functional supervision was put forward by Merton in 1993. It mainly focused on the regulatory deficiencies under the separate industry supervision system and believed that the basic functions of the financial system would not change with financial innovation. Therefore, based on the financial function or the nature of the business, it could classify regulatory bodies and rules to all cross-market and cross-industry financial products, and uniformed supervision standards could be applied to similar businesses of different types of asset management agencies to avoid regulatory arbitrage caused by overlapping supervision and regulatory vacuum.

Functional supervision should be supplemented by institutional supervision, behavioral supervision, etc. This is not only an embodiment of changes of the regulatory concept, but also an inevitable choice for "taking each owns advantages" under the current national conditions. As the trend of mixed-industry operations becomes more pronounced, the scope of supervision is gradually expanding from institutional targets, and the mere reliance on institutional supervision has become increasingly unsuited to the new challenges under the new situation. However, it still has its advantages due to the division of responsibilities based on "who has issued licenses and supervises". The China Banking Regulatory Commission has begun to explore effective coordination mechanisms between functional supervision and institutional supervision, such as the adjustment of internal institutions and integration of regulatory functions. Functional supervision is also inseparable from the behavioral regulation, that is, the supervision of opportunistic behavior of financial institutions and to protect the legitimate rights and interests of consumers by regulating the nature of financial institutions' behaviors.

It is also necessary for the functional supervision to give full play to the role of penetration supervision methods, especially for asset management services with multiple channels or nesting. It shall penetrate through the surface morphology of asset management products, and connect the source, intermediate links and final investment direction of the asset management products in order to distinguish the nature of business and behavior according to the principle of "substantiality over form", and define the supervision subject and applicable rules according to the nature of business and its legal attributes, and implement the whole process supervision over the business and behavior of the asset management organization. The "Three Commissions" have reached a consensus on this point. However, due to the decentralized financial infrastructure and the lack of control system over the financial holding companies, it is difficult to implement penetration supervision system. Therefore, it is imperative to improve conditions to facilitate penetration, such as unified supervisory standards, construction of statistical monitoring frameworks for asset management products, detailing penetration systems, etc.

4.3 Regulatory Tools: Introducing Regulatory Sandboxes

For balancing financial innovation and regulatory systems, regulatory sandboxes have unique advantages and can be introduced into the innovative regulation of asset management. In November 2015, the UK Financial Conduct Authority (FCA) issued a regulatory sandbox report, proposing to establish a security space and appropriately relax regulatory constraints so that financial companies can test innovative products, services, business models, etc. without immediate consequences of normal supervision, it is currently used mainly for testing the intelligent investment advisors, risk management of FICC complex derivatives and online wealth management product portfolios. The introduction of a regulatory sandbox can protect the rights and interests of financial consumers and prevent risk spillovers, while achieve a win–win situation between business innovation and risk prevention through rational relaxation of the regulatory standards and encouraging more realization of innovative projects for asset management businesses.

Regulatory sandboxes can also be used to change passive supervision to active supervision. For a long time, financial supervision always lags behind financial innovation, making "Three Commissions" unable to cope with their risks. By regulatory sandboxes, the "Three Commissions" can actively follow the progress of asset management business innovation, saving both the compliance costs of asset management agencies and also solving the problem of information asymmetry. Prior to any placement of financial innovations, the "Three Commissions" can discuss with the asset management agency and set specific requirements of the sandbox, provide interpretation and regulatory guidance for those agencies, and offer customized guidance for their innovative products and services; During and after the innovation being processed, the asset management agency shall submit a report to the "Three Commissions" in order for them to better understand the business innovation and its risk, so they can formulate targeted and forward-looking policies. The regulatory sandbox helps the "Three Commissions" recognize the potential risks before the innovative products enter the market, and coordinates the corresponding mechanisms in advance to reduce the regulatory collaboration costs afterwards. It will also help promote the healthy development of the asset management business. In terms of the operational mechanism, the main body of regulatory sandboxes can still be determined according to the principle of "who has issued the license and supervises", and the regulatory sandbox can be categorized into general sandbox innovations, virtual sandbox innovation and sandbox protection umbrella three modes according to the degree of innovation risk and the risk control capabilities of the asset management agencies. As innovative regulatory tools, its specific regulatory system is still in continuous improvement, where it will be applied to the regulation of asset management operations may only remain in theoretical discussions. However, after all, it provides an example of moderate regulation, with the continuous growth of implementation conditions, it will surely help form a long-term mechanism for asset management regulation.

In short, it is imperative to strengthen the regulation for risk preventions. But it is also not preferable to "give up eating for fear of choking and to restrict the normal innovation of asset management business, regulation and innovation should be dynamically balanced. Therefore, some of the current regulatory reforms are well supported, such as unified regulation, penetration supervision and strict control of channel operations, etc. However, at the same time, the "Three Commissions" also need to pay attention to the balance of regulation. By setting up a regulatory framework, changing supervision concepts, and innovating regulatory tools, the "degree" of supervision will be set. This will further help force the asset management organizations back to the basics of business and direct the rational flow of funds.